Cambridge Studies in Chinese History, Literature and Institutions
General Editors
Patrick Hanan and Denis Twitchett

YÜAN HUNG-TAO AND THE KUNG-AN SCHOOL

Professor Chou here offers a new perspective on the rise and fall of the Kung-an school as a key to understanding the development of Chinese literary criticism in the late sixteenth and early seventeenth centuries. His book focuses upon the literary theories of Yüan Hung-tao (1568–1610) – the leader of the Kung-an school – and his two brothers. Its core is a detailed study of the poetry and prose of Yüan Hung-tao, comparing his theories with his writings and analysing systematically the merits and flaws of his work. The book concludes with a discussion of the legacy of the Kung-an school, treating the school not only as the major force behind the expressive trend in the late Ming period, but also as one of the precursors of the modern Chinese literary movement.

Other books in the series

STEPHEN FITZGERALD: China and the Overseas Chinese: A Study of Peking's Changing Policy 1949–70

DAVID R. KNECHTGES: The Han Rhapsody: A Study of the *Fu* of Yang Hsiung (53 B.C.–A.D. 18)

J.Y. WONG: Yeh Ming-ch'en: Viceroy of Liang Kuang (1852–8)

LI-LI CH'EN: Master Tung's Western Chamber Romance (*Tung hsi-hsiang chu-kung-tiao*): a Chinese *Chantefable*

DONALD HOLZMAN: Poetry and Politics: The Life and Works of Juan Chi (A.D. 210–63)

C.A. CURWEN: Taiping Rebel: The Deposition of Li Hsiu-cheng

P.B. EBREY: The Aristocratic Families of Early Imperial China: A Case Study of the Po-Ling Ts'ui Family

HILARY J. BEATTIE: Land and Lineage in China: A Study of T'ung-Ch'eng County, Anhwei, in the Ming and Ch'ing Dynasties

WILLIAM T. GRAHAM: The Lament for the South: Yü Hsin's 'Ai Chiang-nan fu'

HANS BIELENSTEIN: The Bureaucracy of Han Times

MICHAEL R. GODLEY: The Mandarin-Capitalists from Nanyang: Overseas Chinese Enterprise in the Modernization of China 1893–1911

CHARLES BACKUS: The Nan-chao Kingdom and T'ang China's Southwestern Frontier

VICTOR H. MAIR: Tun-huang Popular Narratives

IRA E. KASOFF: The Thought of Chang Tsai (1020–1077)

A. R. DAVIS: T'ao Yüan-Ming

RONALD C. EGAN: The Literary Works of Ou-yang Hsui (1007–72)

TIM WRIGHT: Coal Mining in China's Economy and Society 1895–1937

JOHN W. CHAFFEE: The Thorny Gates of Learning in Sung China: A Social History of Examinations

Yüan Hung-tao and the Kung-an School

CHIH-P'ING CHOU

Associate Professor of Chinese, Princeton University

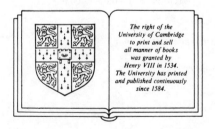

The right of the
University of Cambridge
to print and sell
all manner of books
was granted by
Henry VIII in 1534.
The University has printed
and published continuously
since 1584.

CAMBRIDGE UNIVERSITY PRESS

CAMBRIDGE

NEW YORK   NEW ROCHELLE

MELBOURNE   SYDNEY

Published by the Press Syndicate of the University of Cambridge
The Pitt Building, Trumpington Street, Cambridge CB2 1RP
32 East 57th Street, New York, NY 10022, USA
10 Stamford Road, Oakleigh, Melbourne 3166, Australia

First published 1988

Printed in Great Britain at the University Press, Cambridge

British Library cataloguing in publication data
Chou, Chih-p'ing
Yüan Hung-tao and the Kung-an school.
(Cambridge studies in Chinese history, literature and institutions).
1. Chinese literature – Ming dynasty, 1368–1644 – History and criticism
I. Title
895.1'09   PL2296

Library of Congress cataloguing in publication data
Chou, Chih-p'ing 1947–
Yüan Hung-tao and the Kung-an school.
(Cambridge studies in Chinese history, literature, and institutions)
Rev. and expanded version of the author's thesis (doctoral) – Indiana University.
Bibliography.
Includes index.
1. Yüan, Hung-tao (1568–1610) – Criticism and interpretation.
I. Title.   II. Series.
PL2698.Y85Z64 1987   895.1'8409   87-6357

ISBN 0 521 34207 4

To Shan-chen

CONTENTS

PREFACE

Modern studies on the literature of Ming China have concentrated on several renowned novels written between the fifteenth and the seventeenth centuries, in particular *The Water Margin, Journey to the West* and *Chin P'ing Mei*. The development of the literary criticism, poetry and prose of the Ming dynasty has attracted little attention from Western scholars. Since the early twentieth century, many scholars have treated these novels as the most prominent and innovative works of Ming literature; the novel, however, was hardly at the center of the literary scene in Ming times. For the majority of the Ming intellectuals, poetry and prose were still the only two literary forms worth their time and effort, and literary criticism, a popular and important subject, often appeared in their writings.

Offering a new interpretation of the rise and decline of the Kung-an school, this book studies the development of Chinese literary criticism from the early sixteenth to the early seventeenth centuries, and emphasizes the continuity of interest in the expressive quality of literature found in the theories of the Archaist and Individualist schools. This study focuses on the literary theories of Yüan Hung-tao (1568–1610), the leader of the Kung-an school, and his two brothers, giving special attention to the theoretical differences that developed among these three critics. Through a critical analysis of his poetry and prose, Yüan Hung-tao is portrayed not only as a distinctive poet and prose writer, but also as a man of considerable wit and humor. The conclusion evaluates both the influence that the Kung-an school exercised on late Ming literature, and its impact on the rise of the Ching-ling school.

This book is a revised and extended version of my doctoral dissertation written at Indiana University under the supervision of Professor Irving Lo. I wish to express my sincere gratitude to Professor Lo for his scholarly guidance in the preparation of my dissertation and his support throughout my graduate years.

I am also deeply indebted to Professor Ta-tuan Ch'en of Princeton

University, who has been my mentor during my career as a teacher. His unfailing support and encouragement helped me through some very difficult times. My heartfelt appreciation goes also to Professor Frederick W. Mote for his invaluable instruction, his critical comments, and his painstaking reviews of various drafts of my manuscript. I have greatly benefited from several seminars on Chinese literature conducted by Professor Yu-kung Kao of Princeton University; his profound knowledge led me to explore late Ming literature from a new perspective. He has constantly offered me his critical insights and provided me with much-needed advice on various occasions. Professor Andrew Plaks has also carefully reviewed the entire manuscript. I appreciate very much his well-considered advice and suggestions.

The publication of this book would not have been possible without the strong support and encouragement of Professor Denis C. Twitchett of Princeton University, to whom I am very grateful.

Professors Leo Ou-fan Lee of the University of Chicago and Friedrich Bischoff of Hamburg University have always been considerate and encouraging in the process of writing this book. I owe a great deal to their intellectual instruction and kindness. Professors James T. C. Liu and Willard Peterson of Princeton University have also read the manuscript and offered valuable suggestions.

My friend Dr James Geiss helped me edit the entire final revision of the manuscript. He has taken pains to polish the language and has corrected numerous mistakes. His patience and time have greatly improved the readability of this book. I am most grateful for his help. My sincere thanks also go to my friends James Hargett, Susan McFadden and Thomas Bartlett, whose assistance in many translations has been very helpful.

I gratefully acknowledge the support provided from the Pacific Cultural Foundation in Taipei, Taiwan, and grants from the Princeton University Committee on Research in the Humanities and Social Sciences for the production of the typescript.

1

THE LITERARY SCENE BEFORE THE RISE OF THE KUNG-AN SCHOOL

Literary criticism in the late Ming

Literary criticism flourished during the late Ming as never before. Never in the history of Chinese literature had so many educated men dedicated themselves to the study of literary theories. During the last century of the Ming dynasty literary theory no longer remained the exclusive preserve of theorists; it became a popular subject among many men of letters. As one of the major channels through which writers expressed themselves, literary criticism became almost inseparable from philosophy and was more closely related to common sentiment and feeling than had ever before been the case.

Late Ming poets and essayists consciously tried to put their theories into practice. Although applications of theory were not always consistent in their works, their enthusiasm and sincerity about practicing what they believed cannot be questioned. It was this enthusiasm that turned late Ming literary criticism into a highly polemical subject, so much so that a skeptical and adversarial tone colored almost all discussions of literature. As soon as one critic established a theoretical basis for criticism, it was immediately subjected to revision by another critic. Late Ming literary criticism is consequently characterized by a wide range of distinctive attitudes toward literature and a variety of literary movements.

The development of literary criticism during the Ming dynasty coincided with the decline of classical poetry and prose. This decline was most often attributed to the adoption of the eight-legged essay (*pa-ku wen*) in the civil examination system.[1] Huang Tsung-hsi (1610–95) stated in his preface to the *Ming-wen an* that during the three centuries of Ming rule, intellectuals had exhausted themselves writing nothing but eight-legged essays and had paid no attention to the classical prose (*ku-wen*).[2] Under such circumstances, the decline of classical prose was only natural.

Wu Ch'iao, a seventeenth-century critic, offered a similar interpretation of the decline of poetry during the Ming dynasty:

> People are willing to concentrate on things that are related to their honor and wealth. During the T'ang period, honor and wealth lay in poetry, therefore people gave their full attention to poetry and created new styles . . . During the Ming dynasty, honor and wealth lay in *shih-wen* [i.e. the eight-legged essay], people exhausted themselves on *shih-wen*, and poetry was only composed with their spare energy.[3]

While the precise reasons for this decline may be debatable, scholars are in general agreement that the quality of Ming poetry and prose is not on a par with that of the T'ang and Sung dynasties.[4] Literary discussion and argument among Ming critics therefore focused for the most part on the revival of classical poetry and prose. No matter how different these critics' approaches might seem to be, they shared a similar goal: to breathe new life into poetry and prose. During the sixteenth and seventeenth centuries, members of various literary schools all believed that their theories would not only prolong the life of classical poetry and prose, but would also instill new spirit into these two ancient genres. Literary criticism for Ming critics was not merely a special study, but rather a life-long commitment. Their sense of mission and their desire to resuscitate the life of literature in general, and of poetry and prose in particular, are clearly reflected in their writings.

Even though the major portion of Ming literary criticism centered on poetry and prose, the evolution and flowering of fiction and drama was not altogether ignored by Ming critics. This was especially true during the late sixteenth and early seventeenth centuries, when a considerable number of intellectuals devoted themselves to writing novels and dramas. In a very short period of time various theories regarding these new genres appeared.[5] In respect of the traditional concept of literature, which excludes fiction and drama, late Ming literary criticism comprised an unusually diverse body of critical writings.

The general intellectual climate of the last century of the Ming dynasty was characterized by the synthesis of Confucianism, Taoism and Buddhism; every intellectual of this period was more or less influenced by these three teachings. The traditional Confucian ethics faced serious challenges from Taoism and Buddhism. Intellectuals were eager to explore new directions not only for their scholarly interests, but also for the guidance of their daily lives. Long-established Neo-Confucian doctrines were no longer accepted as the ultimate authority; such basic philosophical concepts as 'mind' (*hsin*), 'nature' (*hsing*), 'reason' (*li*) and 'emotion' (*ch'ing*) all came under careful scrutiny and were redefined in more human terms. Human emotions, especially the love between men and women, were no longer regarded as an evil instinct, but were recognized as a part of human nature which should be treated with respect. Sensualism became a shared aesthetic among men of letters during the late sixteenth and early seventeenth centuries. In this diverse intellectual climate, literary critics passionately argued as never before that the function of literature was nothing but the exhibition of human emotions. The word emotion, or *ch'ing*, became a central theme in literary criticism.[6] The concept of literature as a vehicle for moralistic and utilitarian purposes was no longer dominant during this period. Thus the major trend in the literary criticism of the late Ming was expressive and not pragmatic.

The Archaist school

The development of late Ming literary criticism has often been represented as a confrontation between the Archaist and Individualist schools. The Archaist school was represented by the 'Former and Latter Seven Masters' (*Ch'ien-hou ch'i-tzu*),[7] and the Individualist school by the three Yüan brothers (*San Yüan*)[8] from Kung-an, Hupeh; this school consequently also came to be known as the Kung-an school.

Historical evaluations of the Archaist and the Kung-an schools have differed greatly over the course of time. During the Ch'ing dynasty (1644–1911) the three Yüan brothers were criticized as radicals and were said to have been responsible for the decline of Ming literature in general and of poetry in particular. Their expressive theories of literature were seen by many Ch'ing critics as a formula for vulgarity and shallowness.[9] Only with the rise of the modern literary reform movement in the early twentieth century was the reputation of the Kung-an school restored. After having been criticized and then ignored for three centuries, the Yüan brothers became literary heroes in the 1930s and 1940s. What had been defects for the Ch'ing critics became for twentieth-century scholars laudable features of their works.[10] In a similar reversal of opinion, the Former and Latter Seven Masters, once the dominant figures of Ming literature, were in turn criticized as uncompromising conservatives and mindless imitators.

Such changes in the reputations of historical literary figures strongly reflect the biases and preconceptions of both Ch'ing dynasty and twentieth-century critics. With few exceptions, critics have exploited the ideas of the Archaist Masters as well as those of the Yüan brothers and have molded them to serve various contemporary needs. This is especially true of scholars writing during the 1930s. Whether they condemned or acclaimed their ideas, critics of the 1930s constantly sought to use Ming literary figures to serve the modern purpose of opposing classical Chinese and supporting the vernacular literature movement. In addition to these literary goals, Lin Yutang (1895–1976) was interested in promoting a leisurely lifestyle which he believed was best illustrated through *hsiao-p'in wen*, a short and informal essay of the late Ming.

In 1932 Chou Tso-jen (1885–1968) directly linked the Kung-an school with the modern literary movement and designated it as 'the origin of modern Chinese literature' (*Chung-kuo hsin wen-hsüeh ti yüan-liu*).[11] In so doing, he made explicit his purpose for praising the Kung-an school; however, he failed to provide a dispassionate verdict on the school. In other words, the history of late Ming literature has to a great extent been treated by modern scholars as a tool to support or to denigrate modern literary theories. Modern critics have not really tried to understand Ming writers in their historical context.

On the surface, scholarly opinions of the 1930s seem to be completely at odds with the Ch'ing critical stance. In reality, both Ch'ing and twentieth-century critics shared a similar approach to late Ming litera-ture. In both periods the Archaist and Kung-an schools were considered mutually exclusive, and the three Yüan brothers were seen as radical reformers who found fault with whatever the Archaist Masters ex-pounded. In order to make this dichotomy work and to widen further the gap between these two schools, both Ch'ing critics and modern scholars either overlooked or purposely neglected the expressive elements of Archaist theories and the conservative side of the Kung-an school. It is this dichotomy that has led people to believe that the Former and Latter Seven Masters and the three Yüan brothers were as different as black and white and that there was no continuity in the development of the trend toward self-expression from the sixteenth to the seventeenth century. Once freed from the preconceptions of such traditional interpretations of late Ming literature, one finds that the points of theoretical difference between the two schools are fewer than might be expected. Furthermore, some theoretical points were actually shared by both sides. With this in mind, a different picture of the rise of the Kung-an school emerges. The trend toward self-expression was not initiated by the Yüan brothers, but was instead part of a long tradition in the literary criticism of the Ming period which the Yüan brothers inherited and enhanced.

This introductory chapter will investigate some arguments favoring expressive qualities found in the writings of the three major Archaist Masters, Li Meng-yang (1473–1529), Hsieh Chen (1495–1575) and Wang Shih-chen (1526–90), and will give them the long overdue critical atten-tion they deserve.

The literary theories of the Archaist school can be summarized by two statements which have been attributed to Li Meng-yang. First, the prose of the Ch'in (221–207 BC) and Han (206 BC to AD 220) dynasties, and the poetry of the High T'ang (*Sheng T'ang*) period comprised the only acceptable models for students of literature.[12] Second, imitation of ancient works was the only and necessary way to achieve literary excellence.[13] In view of their limited regard for the literature of the past and their imitative approach to literary creation, theories of the Archaists have often been described by modern scholars as anti-individual, anti-natural and anti-creative. Some of their works indeed contain many archaic expressions, sometimes to the point of plagiarism.[14] However, it is not fair to state that the Archaist Masters actually advocated plagiarism. While it may have resulted as a consequence of their theories, plagiarism was hardly what they had originally advocated. In fact, the Archaist Masters actually despised writers who pilfered from ancient works. In a preface to the collected works of Chu-ko Liang (181–234), Li Meng-yang wrote: 'Those who truly know how to speak do not plagiarize in order to gain fame, and those who have true command of language do not follow old ideas in order to make their opinions known.'[15] To say that the works of the Archaist Masters are marred by slavish imitation is quite different from saying that they advocated plagiarism. It is my opinion that the literary criticism of the Archaist Masters was more far-reaching and inventive than their literary works, and that their achievements in theory should not be overshadowed by the defects of their *works*.

'Imitation' (*mo-ni*) is certainly not a prominent term in the modern vocabulary of literary criticism. It is often equated with lack of creativity and is even associated with plagiarism. However, when Li Meng-yang spoke of imitation in his arguments, he meant adhering to certain basic rules of writing exemplified in ancient works.

Ho Ching-ming (1483–1521), another leading member of the Former Seven Masters, once criticized Li Meng-yang by saying that 'the best of your works are but shadows of the ancients, and the lesser ones have already lapsed into contemporary idiom.'[16] Ho also pointed out the lack of creativity in Li's works and sarcastically said: 'I have never seen you build a hall or open up a door or window by yourself. How can you seek [literary] immortality so eagerly?'[17]

Li Meng-yang defended himself by arguing that in following ancient works 'foot by foot and inch by inch' (*ch'ih-ch'ih erh ts'un-ts'un*), he was like a carpenter who used a compass and ruler to make a circle and a square. No matter what the carpenter had to build, the basic tools – compass and ruler – were always the same. With this analogy, Li Meng-yang expressed his belief in the existence of universal rules governing excellence in literary writing. He held that if such rules could be ascertained and then closely followed, the qualities of the ancient works could be attained once again.[18] The problems with such an analogy are threefold. Do universal rules exist for writing? If they do, are they as tangible as a carpenter's compass and ruler? Is writing poetry and prose the same kind of activity as building a house? The answers to these three questions are highly debatable. Li Meng-yang's theory is based on an unproven premise, and this defect in his argument later became a target of criticism. However, as Li Meng-yang defined it, imitation was by no means a synonym for plagiarism; it was the means whereby one rediscovered the rules of ancient writers.

There is no doubt that Li Meng-yang emphasized the importance of models and rules for literature, but this does not imply that he was anti-expressive. According to Li Meng-yang's theory of literature, adherence to poetic rules and expression of emotion were not mutually exclusive; they were in fact compatible and complementary. Thus, for Li Meng-yang, a good poet was one who could blend these two qualities into a single work, and a good poem was a harmonious amalgamation of rules and emotions. In fact, his writings do not lack individualistic and expressive elements. He never denied that poetry was a reflection of one's emotion. In his preface to the poetry collection of a certain Master Chang ('Chang-sheng shih-hsü'), he quoted a famous line from the major preface to the *Book of Poetry* ('Shih ta-hsü'): 'Poetry expresses intent' (*shih yen-chih*),[19] a statement that has been widely recognized as the origin of expressionism in the history of Chinese literature.[20] In another preface to the poetry of a certain Master Lin ('Lin-kung shih-hsü'), Li Meng-yang wrote: 'Poetry is a reflection of one's personality' (*Shih che, jen chih chien che yeh*).[21] On the basis of this realization, he praised folk songs and called them 'true poetry' (*chen-shih*).[22] In a short postscript to a folk song entitled 'Kuo-kung yao,' he stated:

> People say that there was no poetry after Confucius edited the *Book of Poetry*. This only refers to official and political poetry (*ya*); as for folk poetry (*feng*), it was derived from folk songs, so how can one say that there was no poetry? Now, I have recorded this folk song in the hope that people will realize that true poetry is indeed to be found among the people.[23]

In Li Meng-yang's complete works, *K'ung-t'ung hsien-sheng chi*, there are two *chüan* of *yüeh-fu* containing seventy-two very colloquial poems,[24] which show that his high opinion of folk songs manifested itself both in theory and in practice.

A more comprehensive statement of Li's views on the nature of literature appears in a preface to one of his own poetry collections. In this preface he expressed his opinions in a conversation with a certain Wang Shu-wu:

> Poetry is the natural sound of heaven and earth. The chants and rhymes in the streets and lanes, the groans of the ill, and the cheers of the healthy, all that which is sung by one person and harmonized by a group is true poetry and is called *feng*. Confucius said: 'When the ritual is lost, it can be found in the countryside' (*Li shih erh ch'iu chu yeh*).[25] Nowadays, true poetry is among people, yet the literati and scholars usually regard rhymed words as poetry . . . Genuineness is the beginning of sound and the source of emotion; it is not a matter of elegance versus vulgarity.[26]

These ideas were put forth through the mouth of Wang Shu-wu, and Li Meng-yang expressed great admiration for him, saying at the end of the preface:

> I was both frightened and ashamed and said: 'My poetry is not true poetry. It is merely what Master Wang calls the rhymed words of literati and scholars. Such poems are devoid of emotion and filled with refined diction.' Since these poems were written during the period of Hung-chih [1489–1505] and Cheng-te [1506–21], I therefore entitled it the *Hung-te Collection* (*Hung-te chi*). I also wanted to revise [the poetry in this collection] and seek genuineness, but I am too old [to do that] now![27]

Li Meng-yang, the first to lay the theoretical foundation for the Archaist school, does not seem to have been an unreasonable conservative. He was quite able to point out the shortcomings of his own poetry. According to Shen Te-fu's (1578–1642) *Wan-li yeh-huo pien* (*Anecdotes Collected during the Wan-li Reign*), Li Meng-yang was extremely fond of such current folk songs as 'So-nan chih,' 'Pang-chuang t'ai' and 'Shan-p'o yang.' He even considered these songs the continuation of the *Kuo-feng* tradition from the *Book of Poetry*.[28] The above remarks illustrate that pristine human emotion was highly valued in Li Meng-yang's theory of literature and that he believed the function of poetry was simply to exhibit this emotion. Here Li Meng-yang seems quite unlike his stereotypical image – not at all a die-hard classical and orthodox critic who was interested only in poetic formalism and who ignored the expressive function of poetry. Some of the concepts discussed above were

shared by the members of the Kung-an school and further developed into more fully articulated theories about a century later.

Some differences, nonetheless, were real and important, one of the fundamental differences between the theories of the Archaist and Individualist schools being found in their respective approaches to Sung poetry. Li Meng-yang held that Sung poetry was not worth studying, whereas the Yüan brothers argued that the corpus of Sung poetry contained works of great value that could not be ignored. This disagreement later became the focus of a dispute between these two schools. Modern scholars are usually very critical of Li Meng-yang's rigid dictum that only High T'ang poetry was worth emulating. However, Li's exclusion of Sung poetry was based on an expressionistic rather than an archaist criterion. In the preface to *Fou-yin chi* (*A Collection of Earthy Poetry*), he offered his criticism of Sung poetry:

> Sung poets advocated writing poetry with reason (*li*); therefore, [personal feelings toward] wind, clouds, the moon and dew were all abandoned. Later they wrote *shih-hua* [talks on poetry] to teach people [how to write poetry], and people no longer knew what poetry was. It is not that we cannot discuss reason in a poem, but if [a poet] only writes about reason in poetry, why does he not write prose? . . . I have observed that country people often know what poetry is. They do not write in pedantic words; they only write earthy poetry.[29]

Li Meng-yang held that the functions and styles of poetry and prose were quite different; Sung poetry was in his opinion too prosaic, too rational and not expressive enough.

Another mistaken notion associated with the Archaist Masters has been that the idea of reviving classical literary standards by 'restoring antiquity' (*fu-ku*) was conservative. As Chu Tung-jun, one of the leading modern Chinese literary historians, has pointed out in an article on Ho Ching-ming's literary criticism, 'restoring antiquity' was quite different from 'holding onto the old' (*shou-chiu*), that is being adamantly conservative. 'Holding on to the old' connoted refusing to abandon an old idea or resisting what seemed to be inevitable change, while 'restoring antiquity' connoted dissatisfaction with the present situation and an eagerness to search for a change.[30] In the context of late fifteenth- and early sixteenth-century Chinese thought, one could say that the idea of 'restoring antiquity' advocated by the Former Seven Masters was more revolutionary than conservative. Frederick Mote has offered a similar interpretation of the concept of *fu-ku* as it relates to Chinese art in his article 'The Arts and the "Theorizing Mode" of the Civilization,' and his explanation can also be applied to literary theory. '*Fu-ku*, or recovering the past,' Mote wrote, 'could be a self-deceiving slavishness in many minds, but in other minds it could be a revolutionary archaism that spawned competing repudiations of the present, and that bolstered creative approaches to all of man's activities . . . It was a way of linking the universality of human experience with the personal uniqueness of each man's inner experience.'[31] This was very likely what Li Meng-yang had in mind when he promoted ideas on 'restoring antiquity.'

During the first century of the Ming dynasty, the world of literature was led by highly ranked scholar–officials. Among them the three grand secretaries, Yang Shih-ch'i (1365–1444), Yang Jung (1371–1440) and Yang P'u (1372–1446), were the most influential. They came to be known as the 'Three Yangs' (*San Yang*), and their writings were often referred to as the 'grand secretary style' (*t'ai-ko t'i*). This style was viewed by the eighteenth-century editors of the *Ssu-k'u ch'üan-shu tsung-mu t'i-yao* as 'graceful and majestic' (*yung-jung*), yet 'monotonous and lacking vitality' (*ch'an-huan jung-t'a*). It was precisely this spiritlessness that inspired Li Meng-yang to launch his campaign to revive classical literary standards.[32] His introduction of the 'restoring antiquity' approach was by no means intended to prolong a deteriorating poetic style, but rather to direct the course of literary development so that prose and poetry would become healthier and more substantial than was then the case. Although the results of this movement proved that 'restoring antiquity' was not the right prescription for the 'illness' of Ming poetry and prose, Li Meng-yang's motivation in initiating a literary reform should not be misinterpreted.

Hsieh Chen (1495–1575) was the key figure in the transition from the era of the Former Seven Masters to the era of the Latter Seven Masters. A distinguished poet and literary critic, he was the oldest member of the Latter Seven Masters and the leader of that literary group in its formative stage. His *Ssu-ming shih-hua*, a book of comments on poetry and poets, laid a theoretical foundation for the second phase in the development of the Archaist movement.[33] Although Hsieh Chen's approach to poetry was essentially imitative, he was far more flexible in his approach to imitation than was Li-Meng-yang. Li believed that the act of writing poetry was like practicing calligraphy and that poets, like calligraphers, ought to imitate their models as closely as possible. Li Meng-yang held that a poet had achieved something if his work was similar to that of the ancients.[34] Hsieh agreed that although such imitation was important, it could only be regarded as a preliminary attainment in poetic composition.

The final goal for a poet was to 'achieve enlightenment' (*ju-wu*).[35] Once a poet achieved enlightenment, imitation was no longer necessary. Although Hsieh Chen did not precisely define what 'achieving enlightenment' meant, in order to achieve 'enlightenment,' a poet had to explore within himself, and imitation was only the preparation for enlightenment.

Hsieh Chen drew upon two analogies to illustrate what he thought the process of writing poetry was. He said in one of his comparisons: 'Writing poetry is similar to making liquor. In the several areas of Chiang-nan, the basic materials [for making liquors] are rice and yeast, yet the tastes of the liquors are different.'[36] Hsieh used 'rice and yeast' as a metaphor for scenes and events that a poet encounters in his life, and the different tastes as a metaphor for the different personalities and experiences of each individual poet. Hsieh Chen also compared writing poetry to the process by which bees made honey. He said that while honey was made from the nectar of various flowers, one could not distinguish the flavor of each flower in the honey. He thereby implied that a poet should learn from ancient poets but that the 'flavor' – the characteristics – of each ancient poet should be blended in one's own work.[37] In both cases Hsieh Chen emphasized the process of internalizing what one learned from the ancients. The process of making liquors and honey demonstrated by analogy how this internalization might take place. Of course, these two analogies oversimplify a very complex intellectual process by comparing activities which are essentially different in nature, and the inadequacy of the analogy is quite obvious. However, Hsieh Chen's purpose was not to draw literal-minded analogies but rather to indicate the importance of creating one's own style in poetry and of not being overwhelmed by the ancients.

The essential character of poetry, as far as Hsieh Chen was concerned, resided in the spirit of each individual poet: 'Writing poetry lacking spirit,' he said, 'is similar to drawing the sun and the moon without light.'[38] Hsieh Chen further indicated that in writing poetry a poet needed a 'heroic state of mind' (*ying-hsiung ch'i-hsiang*); he had to be able to 'say something that others dare not say and to do something that others dare not do.'[39] Such an attitude was actually quite individualistic and certainly cannot be characterized as slavish imitation of the ancient poets.

Hsieh Chen strongly opposed rigid imitation because it reflected neither social reality nor the personality of the poet. He poignantly criticized the imitation of Tu Fu practiced by his contemporaries:

> Nowadays, those who imitate Tu Fu are living in wealth and yet talk about poverty and sorrow, living in a time of peace and yet

imagining wars. They talk about old age while they are still young and about illness while they are healthy. This kind of imitation to excess does not reflect genuine personality.[40]

We may deduce from this quotation, without exaggerating its implications, that Hsieh Chen's poetic theory emphasized the importance of the individual poet's personality and of genuine descriptions of real circumstances. The act of writing poetry was for him not an imitation of ancient poets but rather a reflection of one's own experience and of one's own society.

With regard to refining artistic expression, Hsieh Chen on the one hand emphasized the importance of revising a poem (*shih pu yen kai*);[41] on the other hand, he also realized the value of spontaneity and casual writing. He spoke against contemplation before writing. 'Inspiration,' according to him, 'comes while one is writing and does not need prearrangement.' He used 'The Nineteen Ancient Poems' ('Ku-shih shih-chiu shou') as examples of poetry that were 'like a scholar (*hsiu-ts'ai*) carrying on an ordinary conversation in which nothing is affected.'[42] On the basis of such remarks Kuo Shao-yü held that Hsieh Chen's literary theory combined formal structure (*ko-tiao*) and innate sensibility (*hsing-ling*).[43] This combination not only foreshadowed the future development of the Archaist movement in the sixteenth century, but also anticipated the more coherent amalgamation of formalism and expressionism in Wang Shih-chen's (1526–90) literary theory.

Wang Shih-chen, an eminent member of the Latter Seven Masters, mixed archaism and expressionism in his literary theory even more than Li Meng-yang and Hsieh Chen did. Wang Shih-chen's concept of 'rules for writing' (*fa*) was more intuitive and flexible than Li Meng-yang's. 'Rules for writing,' as Wang Shih-chen interpreted the concept, was not something imposed from the outside that restricted one's freedom in writing. Instead, 'rules for writing' came from within and were, he believed, a natural outgrowth of one's inspiration. In the preface to the *Wu-yüeh shan-fang wen-kao*, he pointed out the relationship between inspiration and rules:

My poetry is derived from inspiration and moves toward rules; when inspiration comes, rules come with it. Inspiration is formless, but rules bring a framework. Inspiration comes with great difficulty, but when it comes it seems to be easy. Rules are achieved very easily but seem difficult. This is what is meant by the phrase 'mutual enhancement' [of inspiration and rules].[44]

In his famous work on literary criticism, *I-yüan chih-yen*, Wang Shih-chen summarized his idea about 'rules for writing' in one line: 'The supreme rules leave no traces' (*fa-chi wu-chi*).[45] Like a carpenter's square and compass, Li Meng-yang's *fa* was still an objective reality, whereas for Wang Shih-chen, *fa* became subjective. 'Rules for writing' (*fa*) existed within a writer's mind: it was the writer who dictated the rules for his writing, the rules did not govern the writer.

In his later years Wang Shih-chen came to regret that he had over-emphasized the importance of imitation and the significance of ancient works. He was reported to have said on one occasion that *I-yüan chih-yen*, his major work of literary criticism, was written before he was forty and that his ideas were not yet mature. He wished to correct some of his mistakes so that this book would not lead later generations astray.[46]

Even though Wang Shih-chen was one of the leaders of the Latter Seven Masters, he never held that mechanical imitation was desirable in literary creation. 'Plagiarism and imitation. (*p'iao-ch'ieh mo-ni*), as he put it, 'are the great faults of poetry' (*shih chih ta-ping*).[47] He further postulated that the supreme poetic quality could only be achieved when a poet was not enslaved by ancient works.[48] It was with this belief in mind that Wang Shih-chen severely criticized some of Li Meng-yang's imitative work as 'robbery and theft' that made him want to 'vomit.'[49] Wang Shih-chen's opinion of Li P'an-lung (1514–70), the leader of the Latter Seven Masters, was just as critical. He sarcastically pointed out that Li's imitative works of ancient *yüeh-fu* were indeed 'excellent' (*ching-mei*); however, when these works were compared with authentic *yüeh-fu*, their faults became apparent.[50] Wang Shih-chen was also quite aware of the general weakness of Ming poetry. In a preface to a collection of poetry, he offered this criticism:

> The development of [Ming] poetry started in the periods of Hung [-chih] and Cheng [-te] and flourished in the periods of Lung [-ch'ing] [1567–72] and Wan [-li] [1573–1619]. The superior poets of these periods promoted themselves by using style and resonance; their works were not based on genuine emotion and reality. Although their works sounded perfect and appeared well structured, upon close examination, we find nothing in their poetry.[51]

Wang Shih-chen was clearly dissatisfied with the direction of Ming poetry.

With regard to literary models, Wang Shih-chen no longer confined himself to the prose of the Ch'in and Han dynasties and the poetry of the High T'ang period; he included the Sung as a period of accomplishment in poetry worthy of study. In *I-yüan chih-yen* he identified Po Chü-i (772–846), Su Shih (1037–1101) and Lu Yu (1125–1210) as three great masters of poetry.[52] In a preface to his compilation of selected works by Su Shih, *Su Ch'ang-kung wai-chi*, he compared Su Shih with Han Yü (768–824), Liu Tsung-yüan (773–819) and Ou-yang Hsiu (1007–72):

> Su Shih's talents were extremely great, and his learning extremely broad. However, he expressed himself in a very direct and simple way. The greatness of these three masters [i.e. Han, Liu and Ou-yang] can be exhaustively comprehended from reading their collected works, yet the greatness of Su Shih cannot be exhausted in his works.[53]

His admiration for Su Shih is apparent. From Liu Feng's preface to Wang Shih-chen's *Yen-chou shan-jen hsü-kao* (a sequel to *Yen-chou shan-jen ssu-pu kao*), we learn that even just before his death, Wang Shih-chen was reading a volume of Su Shih's works.[54] Li Wei-chen (1547–1626) also noted: 'As for T'ang poets, Wang Shih-chen was fond of Po Le-t'ien [Chü-i], [and] for Sung poets [it was] Su Tzu-chan [Shih].'[55] Wang Shih-chen himself confessed that his opinion of Su Shih underwent a significant transformation:

> When I was young, I studied classical prose with Yü-lin [Li P'an-lung], and I was not able to appreciate the works of the four writers [i.e. Han Yü, Liu Tsung-yüan, Ou-yang Hsiu and Su Shih]. When I became older, I felt at ease with their works. I cherished Su Shih's prose; as for his most unconventional poems, although I could not take them as my models, I still treated them as a resource [for my writing].[56]

Wang Shih-chen's fondness for Po Chü-i and Su Shih demonstrated that the prose of the Ch'in and Han dynasties and the poetry of the High T'ang period could no longer satisfy an open-minded 'Archaist Master.' This was a significant deviation from one of the major principles of archaism established by Li Meng-yang: that in prose one must follow the works of Ch'in and Han, and in poetry the works of the High T'ang. This deviation further narrowed the gap between the Archaist and Kung-an schools, and prepared the way for the emergence of such freethinking ideas about literary creativity as those expounded by the three Yüan brothers. The taking of a broader perspective toward the past of Chinese literature and the elevating of the value of the works of the Sung period both later became essential components of the Kung-an school's literary theory.

The modern Japanese scholar Matsushita Tadashi actually considered Wang Shih-chen's theory to be one of the sources from which Yüan Hung-tao derived his ideas on literature. In his article 'En Kōdō no seireisetsu no hōga' ('The Initial Stage of Yüan Hung-tao's Theory of *hsing-ling*'), Matsushita argues convincingly that some of the basic literary concepts in Yüan's theory had already been developed in Wang Shih-chen's writings: 'innate sensibility' (*hsing-ling*), the hallmark of the Kung-an school, appeared frequently in Wang Shih-chen's works and was valued highly. Furthermore, as Matsushita has pointed out, there were quite a few phrases and concepts which were first contrived by Wang Shih-chen and later adopted by Yüan Hung-tao.[57] The change in Wang Shih-chen's perspective on literature marked a turning point in the development of late Ming literary criticism. He so substantially modified the standards of literary excellence set by Li Meng-yang and early archaists that he brought the Archaist movement to an end and at the same time planted the seeds for a great flowering of self-expression.

The development of literary criticism from Li Meng-yang through Hsieh Chen to Wang Shih-chen was characterized by a gradual relaxation of formalistic rules and by an increasing awareness of the expressive nature of literature. This change foreshadowed the direction of literary development in the late sixteenth and early seventeenth centuries. Moreover, although the influence of the three Yüan brothers has often been interpreted as the main force behind the decline of the Archaist school, as we have observed in Wang Shih-chen's case, it would be more appropriate to say that the decline of the Archaist movement was a spontaneous development initiated by its own members rather than a result of attacks launched by the Kung-an school. In this light the literary theories of the Kung-an school take on new import. They were not radical in the sense that they have often been represented, but they were innovative and provocative.

The predecessors of the Kung-an school

The literary theories of Li Meng-yang, Hsieh Chen and Wang Shih-chen illustrate that, notwithstanding the strong influence of archaism and formalism, the expressive trend never lost its momentum and continued to flourish. The theories of three more critics will be examined in this section. They are T'ang Shun-chih (1507–60), Hsü Wei (1521–93) and Li Chih (1527–1602). Each of these men either directly influenced the three Yüan brothers through their ideas on literature, or indirectly gave an impetus to the formation of the Kung-an school. Study of these critics not only enables us to see in what direction the expressive trend developed, but also affords us some understanding of the more important sources for the three Yüan brothers' literary theories.

T'ang Shun-chih, a contemporary of the Latter Seven Masters, has often been called the founder of the *T'ang Sung p'ai*, or the 'T'ang Sung school,' in the history of Chinese literature. Li Chih, a most rigorous and cynical critic, portrayed T'ang as a righteous official of great integrity.[58] As for his literary achievement, Li considered T'ang's prose to be on a par with that of Ssu-ma Ch'ien (*c.* 145–135 BC) and Pan Ku (AD 32–93), the two greatest prose writers of the Han dynasty. He compared his poetry with that of Li Po (701–62) and Tu Fu (712–70).[59] It was quite unusual for Li Chih to offer such unreserved praise of a contemporary. Such unrestrained praise for T'ang Shun-chih's literary ideas and works suggests that they pleased Li Chih, and that Li regarded T'ang as a comrade in the campaign for self-expression.

T'ang Shun-chih believed that the works of the Ch'in and Han dynasties were too far removed from the present for people to follow as models, and owing to the subtlety of the *fa* (rules) contained in these works, one could never truly recapture the spirit of the Ch'in and the Han. The secrets of the methods of composition or *fa*, as T'ang Shun-chih indicated, were more tangible in the T'ang and Sung dynasty works, and he therefore advocated studying the works of the T'ang and Sung as the path . to literary excellence.[60] In this regard, even though the models were changed from the Ch'in and Han works to those of the T'ang and Sung, there was no fundamental difference between his opinions and those of the Archaist Masters because T'ang Shun-chih also advocated the same method – an imitative approach to writing.

T'ang Shun-chih's dramatic transformation from a formalist to an expressionist occurred at the age of forty. Only then did he realize that literature was created not by imitating previous works, but by the art of a creative individual. On the basis of this realization he advanced the critical concept of *pen-se* (original color), in which he stressed the importance of originality and straightforwardness in writing. In a letter to Mao K'un (1512–1601) T'ang defined *pen-se* by comparing two kinds of writer:

> Now there are two people: one has a transcendent mind, the so-called person with great insight. He has never set pen to paper nor read aloud in order to learn how to write a composition, but relies simply on his own feelings, and writes with uninhibited hand, as if he were writing a family letter. His works might be crude and unadorned but they definitely do not contain affectations or stale

clichés and hackneyed expressions. This is, after all, the best writing in the world.

The second person is but an ordinary man, who concentrates on learning literary writing, and complies perfectly with rules and formal structure. However, what we find in his writings is nothing but bromides and truisms. We vainly seek in his writing any authentic spirit and eternal, imperishable insights. Even though his writings are perfectly composed, they cannot avoid being considered 'low grade' (*hsia-ko*). This [explains the concept of] the 'original color' of literature.[61]

T'ang Shun-chih further elaborated on the significance of *pen-se* by taking T'ao Yüan-ming (365/372/376–427) and Shen Yüeh (441–513) as examples exemplifying respectively the possession and the absence of this quality. T'ang indicated that T'ao did not pay special attention to versification and diction. He simply wrote his poems casually, but they nevertheless represent poetry of the highest quality. This is because his works are rich in 'original color.' On the other hand, 'ever since the inception of poetry,' T'ang Shun-chih observed, 'no one has labored more painfully on versification and diction, nor has anyone established stricter rules in poetry than Shen Yüeh.' However, 'when one reads his poetry, the only thing one sees is fetters and bonds. In his piles of works he did not write even one or two worthy lines. This is because there is such a low level of "original color" in his writings.'[62] In T'ang Shun-chih's critical system the level of 'original color' was the sole criterion to be used in judging the quality of literature. From T'ang's interpretation of T'ao Yüan-ming and Shen Yüeh we observe that 'original color' refers to a combination of originality in creation and freedom in writing. Hence this idea of *pen-se* is very similar to *hsing-ling* (innate sensibility), which is the principal critical construct of Kung-an literary theory. (The meaning of *hsing-ling* will be discussed at length in Chapter 2.)

In another letter, to Hung Fang-chou, in which he specially emphasized directness of self-expression, T'ang Shun-chih again explained the significance of 'original color':

> Recently I have felt that poetry and prose are simply a reflection of one's heart and mind. As the proverb says, 'when a person opens his mouth, his throat is also revealed' (*k'ai-k'ou chien hou-lung*). [In a similar way], when later generations read his works, it is like seeing the true face of the author. Merits and flaws cannot be concealed. This is what is meant by the phrase 'original color.'[63]

From the above quotation, it seems that the term 'original color' describes a quality of the writer's mind. Accordingly, the proverb that T'ang cited in his letter implies that to achieve this quality a writer must be direct and unreserved in his expression. A similar fondness for forwardness was shared by the three Yüan brothers many years later.[64]

T'ang Shun-chih died in 1560, and Yüan Hung-tao was not born until 1568. T'ang obviously had no direct personal influence on the Yüan brothers. However, T'ang's idea of 'original color' was largely taken over by Hsü Wei, the Ming poet most esteemed by Yüan Hung-tao. Consequently, in this regard T'ang's ideas about literary criticism provided one important antecedent for the later formulation of the Kung-an school's literary theories.

Hsü Wei, a man with a rare talent for poetry, prose, drama, calligraphy and painting, was Yüan Hung-tao's contemporary for the last twenty-six years of his life. Throughout his lifetime, Hsü Wei was known as a professional writer, painter and military strategist. His posthumous fame in poetry and prose resulted for the most part from Yüan Hung-tao's publication of his biography and works. Ch'ien Ch'ien-i wrote in *Lieh-ch'ao shih-chi hsiao-chuan*: 'without Yüan Hung-tao, how would the world again know [of] Wen-ch'ang [Hsü Wei]?'[65] This comment reveals how important Yüan Hung-tao was in promoting Hsü Wei as an independent poet and essayist.

Hsü Wei had a very congenial relationship with T'ang Shun-chih, even though T'ang was thirteen years his senior. They first met each other in 1552, when Hsü was thirty-two years old.[66] According to T'ao Wang-ling's biography of Hsü Wei, T'ang was greatly impressed by Hsü's achievements in literature and spoke highly of him.[67] Hsü Wei in turn regarded T'ang as the only person who truly knew and understood him. Forty years after T'ang's death, Hsü Wei, then aged seventy-three, was still very grateful for T'ang's encouragement and assistance.[68]

In the preface to *Hsü Wen-ch'ang chi*, Yü Ch'un-hsi (*chin-shih*, 1583) indicated that Hsü Wei and T'ang Hsien-tsu (1550–1616) were the only two writers who did not cooperate with Wang Shih-chen and Li P'an-lung during the heyday of the Latter Seven Masters.[69] With this in mind, Hsü Wei should be considered as an early challenger of the dominant influence of the Archaist school.

Even though Hsü Wei and Yüan Hung-tao were contemporaries for twenty-six years, Yüan did not hear of Hsü Wei until 1597, four years after Hsü's death. In the spring of that year, Yüan resigned from the magistracy of Wu-hsien, Kiangsu province (modern Soochow), and traveled in the area southeast of the Yangtze for three months. During this period he visited T'ao Wang-ling (1562–1609) in Shao-hsing, Chekiang province, and accidentally discovered Hsü's works in T'ao's house. This discovery greatly affected Yüan's career as a writer and as a critic. At the start of Yüan's biography of Hsü Wei he recalls the intense pleasure that Hsü's poetry collection afforded him:

> One night I was sitting in Grand Historian [T'ai-shih] T'ao's chamber. By chance, I took a few books off the shelf and came across an incomplete collection of poetry. The quality of paper and the clarity of the calligraphy were very poor, and the book was blackened with coal smoke. I could barely make out the characters. I took the book over by the lamp and began reading; after having read a few poems, I could not but jump with excitement. Hurriedly I called Chou-wang [T'ao Wang-ling] into the room and asked: 'Who wrote these verses? Was he a modern or ancient poet?' Chou-wang said: 'This work is that of Hsü Wen-ch'ang, a native of my home town.' [At that moment] both of us jumped up. We read the poems under the lamplight and cried out; we cried out and then read them again, waking up all the sleeping servants. Only now, when I am thirty years old, have I found out there is a Mr Wen-ch'ang in the world! Oh! Why did it take so long for me to hear about him?[70]

Yüan Hung-tao's admiration for Hsü Wei and his excitement upon finding Hsü's works are clearly documented in his writings. Yüan never identified himself so closely with any of his contemporaries as he did with Hsü Wei. Nor did he ever praise another Ming writer so effusively. Yüan said in a letter to his friend that Hsü Wei was both the Li Po and the Tu Fu of the present time.[71]

   Hsü Wei's biography is one of Yüan Hung-tao's most famous essays. It was included in *Ku-wen kuan-chih*,[72] a prose anthology compiled in the K'ang-hsi reign (1662–1722), and widely used as a textbook for several centuries. This biography, however, is not historically accurate in many aspects, as Liang Jung-jo has demonstrated.[73] Yüan Hung-tao referred to this in a letter to T'ao Wang-ling: 'Even though the biography of Hsü Wei is not very accurate, it has greatly elevated Wen-ch'ang's status.'[74] But the historical facts about Hsü Wei's life were never Hung-tao's major concern. His purpose in writing the biography was to re-evaluate Hsü's achievements so that he could mold Hsü into a figure who appeared to champion his own causes. Therefore the emphasis in Hsü's biography fell on his personality and the unconventional quality of his poetry, rather than on the events of his life. Yüan Hung-tao portrayed Hsü Wei as a man with 'a strong mind and iron bones' (*ch'iang-hsin t'ieh-ku*).[75] He described Hsü as 'breaking all the conventional stereotypes, and writing with his own ideas and insights.'[76] Yüan Hung-tao summed up Hsü's biography in one word, *ch'i*,[77] which means unique, rare and surprising. He wrote Hsü's biography with mixed feelings of profound sympathy and admiration. He deeply regretted that he had not known Hsü Wei earlier, and he was anxious to establish Hsü as a forerunner of the Kung-an school. In the biography Yüan wrote: 'When [I discovered Hsü Wei's works] I introduced Hsü Wen-ch'ang to the others in person and through writing . . . In a short period of time [Hsü Wei] became well known among officials and scholars.'[78] Yüan Hung-tao also actually used examples from Hsü Wei's works to support his own arguments about literature.

The discovery of Hsü Wei's works tremendously strengthened Yüan Hung-tao's confidence both in theory and in practice. Even though Yüan never knew Hsü personally, the influence of Hsü's works and the encouragement they afforded him should not be underestimated. In 1597, which was still an early stage in the development of the Kung-an literary movement, Hung-tao found very few supporters and received little encouragement from his friends. Therefore he especially treasured the knowledge that such an accomplished poet as Hsü Wei held opinions similar to his own. In fact, the editor of *Ssu-k'u ch'üan-shu tsung-mu t'i-yao* considered Hsü Wei one of the important predecessors of the Kung-an school.[79]

The underlying theme of Hsü Wei's views on literature is that emotion is the essence of a literary work and that poetry is a refined verbalization of emotion. He elaborated on this point in the following manner:

> The poetry of ancient people was based on their emotions, and these emotions were not fabricated; therefore there was poetry but no poets. Only in later times did poets emerge. Nowadays the topics and styles of poetry are numerous. However, most of these poems are not based on true emotion. The purpose of writing poetry with fabricated emotion is to seek fame. If one searches for fame in poetry, then one inevitably ends up imitating poetic styles and plagiarizing diction. When this happens, the substance of poetry is lost.[80]

On the basis of this belief Hsü Wei gave a new interpretation to the four functions of the *Book of Poetry* first mentioned by Confucius – to inspire, to observe, to make oneself fit for company, and to express grievance (*hsing kuan ch'ün yüan*).[81] He contended that if a poem makes a reader feel as if 'cold water was being poured over his back, suddenly shocking him,'[82] it is a poem that fulfills these four functions. In other words a good poem must have a quality of freshness and uniqueness that can penetrate the reader's heart, so that the reader will be insensibly seized by a sudden feeling. In this case Hsü Wei was not so much concerned with the type of reaction as with the intensity of the reaction. As long as the feeling caused by a poem is strong, no matter whether the feeling is pleasant or unpleasant, happy or sad, the poem should still be considered a good poem.

In the preface to the *Romance of the Western Chamber* (*Hsi-hsiang chi*), Hsü Wei posited that there existed both a 'true nature' (*pen-se*) and an 'apparent nature' (*hsiang-se*) in literature, imitation in writing was tantamount to replacing the 'true nature' with the 'apparent nature,' and that this could never be successfully done.[83] In the preface to Yeh Tzu-su's poetry ('Yeh Tzu-su shih hsü'), Hsü Wei explained why:

> If a man imitates the sound of a bird, and his voice even becomes like that of a bird, his nature, however, is still that of man. Likewise, if a bird imitates a human voice, and it does sound like a human's, its nature is still that of a bird. This can be used as a criterion to distinguish a man from a bird. What is the difference between this and the people who write poetry today? [Their poetry] is not derived from what they truly know; they simply pilfer what people have already said. They say: 'A certain sentence resembles that of a certain person, and another does not.' Although these writings are extremely refined, they are merely imitations of others' [works]. This is no different from the bird that tries to imitate human language.[84]

He concluded that it is futile to imitate others' works. No matter how closely one might try to imitate, the likeness does not change the true nature of the writer.

In order to keep the 'true nature' intact, Hsü opposed using archaic expressions in contemporary writings. He especially decried writing drama in the *pa-ku wen* (eight-legged essay) style. In a one-*chüan* pamphlet entitled 'Nan-tz'u hsü-lu,' he stated: 'The Classics should not be used even in poetry, let alone in drama.'[85] At the end of this passage, Hsü summed up his ideas in two lines: 'It is better to be vulgar and easily understood than to be elegant and incomprehensible.'[86] Hsü Wei was one of the few scholars who was both well versed in classical literature and devoted to writing dramas.[87] His comments on drama are thus especially significant. Given his basic views on literature, it is not surprising to find that Hsü Wei praised folk songs. He also wrote a considerable number of jokes, riddles and Buddhist chants which are included in *Hsü Wen-ch'ang i-kao*. The editor of the *Ssu-k'u ch'üan-shu tsung-mu t'i-yao* criticized these works as 'vulgar, obscene and trivial' (*pi li wei tsa*).[88] However, these works demonstrated precisely how seriously Hsü Wei was committed to introducing literary works in popular and colloquial language. This attitude was later for the most part shared by the Yüan brothers.

In the 'Fourth Essay on Lun Chung' ('Lun-chung ssu')[89] Hsü Wei presents his most important ideas about literature. The similarity between this essay and Yüan Hung-tao's 'Hsüeh-t'ao ko chi hsü'[90] is striking. In fact, some of the examples used in the two essays are identical. The latter was written between 1598 and 1600, immediately following Yüan Hung-tao's discovery of Hsü Wei's works. Therefore the similarities between these two essays can hardly be coincidental. The extent of Hsü Wei's influence on Yüan Hung-tao can readily be seen in such comparisons.

Although Hsü Wei's posthumous fame resulted in large measure from Yüan Hung-tao's promotion, Hsü Wei also contributed a great deal to the rise and success of the three Yüan brothers. He not only inadvertently became the ideal model for the Kung-an school; he also participated in crucial debates in the field of literary theory against the Archaist school before the three Yüan brothers had even appeared on the literary scene.

Li Chih, one of the most controversial intellectuals in the late Ming period, was regarded as a heretic by such traditional Confucianists as Ku Yen-wu (1613–82)[91] and Wang Fu-chih (1619–92),[92] but as a hero by such other-minded scholars as Yüan Hung-tao[93] and T'ang Hsien-tsu (1550–1616).[94] Li Chih considered himself more a philosopher and historian than a poet or literary theorist. However, his impact on late Ming literature in general and on the three Yüan brothers in particular was greater by far than that of any other writer. Ch'ien Ch'ien-i held that Li Chih was the one who cleared the way for the three Yüan brothers. He wrote in the preface to *Tun-yüan chi*:

> Near the end of the Wan-li [1573–1619] reign, everyone criticized Wang [Shih-chen] and Li [P'an-lung], and venerated Le-t'ien [Po Chü-i] and Tzu-chan [Su Shih]. This trend was initiated by the Yüan [brothers] from Kung-an. However, Chung-lang [Yüan Hung-tao] and Hsiao-hsiu [Yüan Chung-tao] were both students of Li Cho-wu [Chih], and this idea actually originated with Cho-wu.[95]

Li Chih's iconoclastic philosophy, his praise of the 'childlike mind' (*t'ung-hsin*),[96] his appreciation of the novel and drama, and his historical approach to literature, both anticipated and fostered the emergence of more individualistic and expressive styles in literary writing.

Li Chih's biography, philosophy and his relationship with the Yüan brothers have been widely studied in Chinese, Japanese and English.[97] I will not explore these areas in detail, but will rather give a brief account of his literary views insofar as they directly bear on those of the three Yüan brothers.

Li Chih's view of literature hinges on his concept of the 'childlike mind.' The 'childlike mind,' as he interpreted it, is 'the beginning of the mind.' It represents the state of mind that exists before the mind receives impressions gained from experience and book-learning. He believed that as long as this natural state of mind could be preserved, everyone had the potential to become a great poet, essayist, dramatist, or even a writer of eight-legged essays. He further indicated that the growth of falseness was synonymous with the loss of the childlike mind. Thus, what the childlike mind stands for is genuineness. In Li Chih's opinion, all great literary works shared this pristine quality of mind.[98]

The nature of the childlike mind, as Li Chih describes it, is sometimes vulnerable to knowledge and experience. However, this does not mean that Li Chih was anti-intellectual. For 'the ancient sages,' he wrote, 'read many books, but only to protect their childlike mind, and to keep it from being lost.'[99] In this respect book-learning could be helpful to the child-like mind. What Li Chih considered harmful was not knowledge itself, but what knowledge could do to the childlike mind. In other words, if knowledge could function as a complement to the childlike mind, then knowledge would protect it; however, if knowledge were to overshadow or even replace the childlike mind, then knowledge would be harmful. Based on what Li Chih said in his essay 'On the Childlike Mind,' one may safely assume that he believed literary creation was primarily an emotional rather than an intellectual activity.

As far as the process of writing is concerned, Li Chih contended that a writer should not write unless he feels an uncontrollable, compelling force in his mind that is driving him to write. Writing in his opinion should not be the result of contemplation or premeditation; rather, it should be a sudden and violent display of one's true or genuine emotion. This drive can be so strong that a 'true' writer would have to write even at the expense of his own life. Only under such conditions, Li Chih contended, could a truly great work be written.[100] This idea is further elaborated in Li Chih's definition of a 'writer.' 'What we call a writer,' Li Chih wrote, 'is one who is aroused by his feeling, whose mind cannot stop acting, or one, whose emotions having been stimulated, cannot restrain himself from revealing these emotions in words.'[101]

Since the process of writing was so spontaneous the writer was totally overwhelmed by his feelings, and writing simply served as a release for an emotional outburst. Under such circumstances, the writer could by no means be concerned with technique or form. Li Chih held that any aesthetic achievement gained at the expense of spontaneity had to be considered a loss. He called those who were restrained by metrical rules 'slaves to poetry' (*shih-nu*).[102]

'Contrived structure and verbal parallelism,' Li wrote, 'can only be used in common literary works; no such rules have any place in truly superior works.'[103] The ultimate literary achievement, as Li Chih described it, was *hua-kung*, or the 'transcendence of art.' This refers to a work in which technical skill cannot be observed. Li Chih used the growth of flowers to illustrate his idea of *hua-kung*. In the essay entitled 'Miscellaneous Talks' ('Tsa-shuo') he wrote: 'Heaven and earth produce hundreds of flowers, everyone who sees them likes them; however, one who searches for the technique [of producing these flowers] finds nothing at all.'[104] This analogy suggests that the art of nature is artless, and that the supreme work leaves no observable trace of technique. Nevertheless, the absence of observable technique is quite different from the actual absence of technique. In other words, Li Chih was not opposed to technique; what he opposed was the pursuit and use of technique in an artificial way. Any work in which the effort to affect a certain manner is evident, no matter how dexterously wrought, falls into an inferior category. Li Chih designated this kind of work by a different term, also pronounced *hua-kung*, but which means 'artifice.'[105] Yüan Hung-tao was very much influenced by Li Chih's attitude toward literary technique, and this influence is evidenced in the casual manner of Yüan's writing, which was one of the most distinctive characteristics of Kung-an style.

Li Chih's historical view of the development of literature also influenced the Yüan brothers. Yüan Hung-tao's sharp criticism of the imitative approach to writing was based in large measure on Li Chih's evolutionary concept of literature. In the postscript to a collection of eight-legged essays ('Shih-wen hou-hsü') Li Chih indicated that the notion of antiquity was relative rather than absolute:

From today's point of view, antiquity certainly is not the present; however, from a future point of view, today will one day become antiquity as well ... When five-character verse first appeared, four-character verse became old; when T'ang poetry first appeared, five-character verse became old again. Since poetry in the T'ang style is considered ancient [by contemporary writers of] 'modern style' verse, we can infer without doubt that ten thousand generations from now we will be like the T'ang [is now].[106]

On the basis of this assumption, he challenged the supremacy of pre-Ch'in prose and High T'ang poetry: 'Why must poetry be selected from the ancient period? And why must prose be confined to the pre-Ch'in period?' He wrote in his essay 'On the Childlike Mind':

> Time passed, there came the Six Dynasties, and the modern style of poetry was formed. Literature evolved further and the *Ch'uan-ch'i* appeared, then the *Yüan-pen*, the Yüan play, the *Romance of the Western Chamber*, the *Water Margin*, and today's eight-legged essay. All are the first literature of the past and present. [The value of these works] should not be judged in terms of their early or late [appearance] in time.[107]

This preliminary concept of the evolution of Chinese literature was better developed in Yüan Hung-tao's theory, and it became a fundamental concept advocated by members of the Kung-an school.

By drawing on his 'childlike mind' theory, Li Chih was able to enlarge the scope of what might be considered literature: drama and fiction were no longer excluded from the literary realm. In fact, Li Chih was the first scholar who was broadly learned in classics and history, and yet openly praised drama and novels. He referred to the *Romance of the Western Chamber* and *Worshipping [the] Moon Pavilion* (*Pai-yüeh t'ing*) as works of 'transcendent art'[108] that would 'endure as long as heaven and earth.'[109] He also contended that drama had the same functions as the *Book of Poetry*. He stated this idea in a rhetorical question: 'Who says that *ch'uan-ch'i* cannot be used to inspire, to observe, to make you fit for company, and to express grievances?'[110] As was indicated in the last section, these are four functions that Confucius believed only the *Book of Poetry* could fulfill. Li Chih was attempting with this remark to elevate the position of drama to the same level as the *Book of Poetry*.

The more progressive critics of the late Ming generally favored the use of colloquial language. Li Chih once said that he was 'fond of observing simple language' (*hao-ch'a erh-yen*), by which he meant 'people's daily language' (*pai-hsing jih-yung chih erh-yen*).[111] He held that scholars' refined but insincere words were not as attractive to him as those of commoners because the latter talked only about what they did and what they knew. He contended that one should not write about anything that one did not truly know of or believe in: 'The businessmen should talk only about business, and farmers should talk only about farming.'[112] Li Chih considered this kind of plain language 'words of virtue' (*yu-te chih-yen*).[113]

Noting Li Chih's idea of the childlike mind and his emphasis on spontaneity in writing, one might think of his ideas on literature as individualistic and expressive. However, when Li Chih praised the value of *Shui-hu chuan*, his attitude became more pragmatic than expressive. In his preface to *Chung-i Shui-hu chuan* (*The Water Margin of Loyalty and Righteousness*), the novel's literary value was not his concern. What he focused on was the righteousness and loyalty depicted throughout the novel.[114] Li Chih believed that the authors' motive in writing this novel was nothing but patriotism. 'Even though Shih [Nai-an] and Lo [Kuan-chung] [*c.* 1330–1400] lived in the Yüan dynasty,' Li wrote in the preface, 'their hearts were in the Sung dynasty.'[115] Li Chih further indicated that *Shui-hu chuan* contained great moral teachings and that reading this novel would arouse feelings of loyalty and righteousness:

> He who rules the country must read this book; once he reads it, loyalty and righteousness will not be in the water margins but all around the emperor. The capable prime minister must read this book; once he reads it, loyalty and righteousness will not be in the water margins, but in the court. Military advisors at the capital and generals in the frontier must read this book; once they read it, loyalty and righteousness will not be in the water margins, and they will become the most loyal and reliable people to the country.[116]

The preface to *The Water Margin of Loyalty and Righteousness* illustrates that the aesthetic qualities of the novel were completely ignored, while its social and political value was strongly affirmed.

Li Chih's commentary to the *Water Margin* may be seen as a further example of how he put his theory into practice. In the commentary, criticism against the government and his sarcastic gibes at Neo-Confucianists appear repeatedly.[117] As far as Li Chih was concerned, novels were, after all, only a means for attaining certain social ends.

Does such a practice seem to contradict Li's individualistic and expressive remarks on literature? My answer is that recognizing the social and political functions of a novel is quite different from regarding literature as nothing but a vehicle for promoting Confucian teachings. Although Li Chih asserted that the emotions of loyalty and righteousness could be aroused by reading the *Water Margin*, he never claimed that this should be the sole purpose of writing a novel. This kind of theoretical mixture of pragmatic and expressive viewpoints was also exhibited by Yüan Hung-tao in his comments on the *Chin P'ing Mei*, which will be discussed in detail in Chapter 2.

Of the three critics discussed above, Li Chih was the only one with whom the three Yüan brothers had a personal relationship. Li Chih was not only a precursor of the Kung-an school, but was also the Yüan brothers' personal teacher. He influenced their opinions deeply and decisively both in philosophy and in literature. The subsequent achievements of the Kung-an school should then to a certain extent be credited to Li Chih.

2

THE LITERARY THEORIES OF THE THREE YÜAN BROTHERS

The Kung-an school of the late Ming derived its name from Kung-an hsien in Hupeh province, where the three Yüan brothers came from. The most active period of this school only lasted for about six years, from 1595 – when Yüan Hung-tao was appointed magistrate of Wu-hsien, Kiangsu province – until the death of Yüan Tsung-tao in 1600. Wu-hsien, at the heart of Soochow Prefecture, was the cultural center of the Yangtze valley. After serving as the magistrate of Wu-hsien for two years, during which time he resided in Soochow city, Yüan Hung-tao became disillusioned with bureaucratic life. Yet his tenure in office gave him a unique opportunity to share his ideas on literature with his friends in this area. Among them, Chiang Ying-k'o (1556–1605) and T'ao Wang-ling (1562–1609) were his two most enthusiastic supporters.

In 1598 Yüan Hung-tao joined his two brothers in Peking to accept a new appointment as an instructor in the Metropolitan Prefectural School (*Ching-chao chiao-kuan*). In the same year the Grape Society (*P'u-t'ao she*), a literary group led by the three Yüan brothers, was established at Ch'ung-kuo temple in the western suburbs of Peking. Its members included high officials and well-known scholars in the area around the capital. In addition to T'ao Wang-ling and Chiang Ying-k'o, Huang Hui (1554–1612), Hsieh Chao-che (1567–1624) and P'an Shih-tsao (*chin-shih*, 1583) comprised the central figures in this society.[1] After the establishment of the Grape Society, the activities of the Kung-an school expanded until 1600, the year of Yüan Tsung-tao's death, and even though the active period of the Kung-an school was quite short, it nonetheless exerted a great influence on the development of late Ming literary criticism. Self-expression through literature had been a goal sought by men of letters since the early sixteenth century. However, it was not until the rise of the three Yüan brothers that self-expression, combined with an individual voice, emerged as a major movement in the literary world of the late Ming period.

The three Yüan brothers were more often regarded as a group than as individuals writing independently, since they shared many similar ideas. It would, however, be a mistake to assume that their literary theories contained no contradictions. Modern scholars are in general sympathetic to the three Yüan brothers and their ideas about literature. As a result of this sympathetic disposition, the Kung-an school has not been treated critically in the twentieth century, and the mutually contradictory opinions in the works of the three Yüan brothers have for the most part been ignored by modern critics. In this chapter the literary theories of the three Yüan brothers will be treated separately, with particular attention being given to their theoretical differences.

Yüan Tsung-tao: the founder of the Kung-an school

Yüan Tsung-tao was born in 1560 and was the eldest of the three brothers. He received his *chü-jen* degree in 1579 and took first place in the metropolitan examination in 1586 at the age of twenty-six. He had the most successful official career of the three brothers. After passing the metropolitan examination, he was immediately appointed bachelor in the Han-lin Academy (*Han-lin yüan shu chi-shih*). In the last three years of his life he served as a tutor (*Tung-kung chiang-kuan*) to the emperor's eldest son, Chu Ch'ang-lo.[2] His two younger brothers, Hung-tao and Chung-tao, were deeply influenced by him in their early years, both in literature and philosophy.[3] Li Chih once described him as 'stable and solid' (*wen-shih*).[4] Ch'ien Ch'ien-i did not speak highly of him but acknowledged him as the founder of the Kung-an school. In *Lieh-ch'ao shih-chi hsiao-chuan*, Ch'ien remarked: 'Though he [Tsung-tao] was not as talented as his two brothers, the Kung-an school was actually started by him.'[5]

The Kung-an literary movement has often been described as a movement concerned with poetry, yet Yüan Tsung-tao's interest lay more in prose than in poetry. His two most important writings on literature are entitled 'On Prose' ('Lun-wen'). In these two essays he emphasized the importance of comprehensibility and scholarship in literary writing. Yüan Tsung-tao believed that the primary function of language was to communicate, and he therefore held up comprehensibility as the most important quality in writing. Anything that diminished comprehensibility was undesirable.

He also stressed that language was constantly changing with the passage of time. What made the classical language difficult to understand, he pointed out, was not that it was more abstruse than the modern language; rather, it was the distance in time between the people who wrote it and those who read it afterwards that made the classical language incomprehensible.

In the first part of his essay 'On Prose' he indicated that the classical language actually comprised colloquial expressions of ancient times:

> Speech represents one's intent, and writing is an alternative form of speech. [Writing] is separated and removed from [intent], and even though [one] writes fluently and clearly, it must be less so than what comes from the mouth and tongue, and much less than what is stored in the mind. Therefore when Confucius discussed literature, he said: 'Words communicate, and that is all.' Whether intelligibility is achieved or not decides whether it is literature. [Originally] none of the works of T'ang, Yü and the Three Dynasties [i.e. Hsia, Shang and Chou] was incomprehensible. Since modern people cannot understand ancient books easily, they therefore conclude that the ancient writings were difficult and obscure, and modern people should not write in a plain and straightforward style. Time moves from the past to the present and language evolves accordingly. How do we know that what is incomprehensible to modern people was not the street talk of ancient times.[6]

In the same essay Yüan Tsung-tao cited many historical examples to support his argument. By comparing different words referring to the same object in the *Shang-shu* (*Book of History*), the *Tso-chuan* (Tso Ch'iu-ming's commentary on the *Spring and Autumn Annals*), and the *Shih-chi* (*Records of the Grand Historian*), he was able to demonstrate that the language of *Shang-shu* (the oldest text) was no longer used in the *Tso-chuan*, and the language in the *Tso-chuan* was no longer used in *Shih-chi* (the latest of the three texts).[7] Based on his findings, he attacked the adoption of archaic expressions in modern writing:

> The time when Tso [Ch'iu-ming] lived was not very distant from [high] antiquity; however, the language in the *Tso-chuan* does not resemble that of the *Shang-shu*. Ssu-ma [Ch'ien's] [c. 145 BC or 135 BC–?] time, likewise, was not too long after Tso's, yet the language in the *Shih-chi* is not like that in the *Tso-chuan*. As for today, we are trying to go back to [using the expressions of] the former Han dynasty [206 BC–AD 22], which are over a thousand years old. If even Ssu-ma could not emulate Tso, how absurd it would be if modern people tried to be like Tso and [Ssu] Ma![8]

Yüan Tsung-tao criticized archaistic imitation in literary writing by drawing an analogy. 'To adopt ancient words and phrases into one's own works,' he said, 'is no different from sticking animal skins and tree leaves in one's [modern] dress or throwing raw meat [dripping] with blood into delicacies.'[9] However, he did not oppose learning derived from ancient

works. What should be gleaned from the ancients, he believed, was their
creative spirit and the comprehensibility of their language, not their
words and sentences *per se*. This idea was further clarified in the following
dialogue:

> Someone asked me: 'If what you have said [i.e. that language
> changes from time to time] is true, then do you mean that we do not
> have to learn from antiquity?' I responded: 'Ancient literature
> values comprehensibility; studying comprehensibility is what [I
> mean by] studying antiquity. We should learn the idea [from the
> ancient works] and not get bogged down in words and senten-
> ces'. . . . Generally speaking, the first priority in the writings of the
> ancients was to convey [their ideas] directly, and the first priority of
> today's writers is to convey their ideas by indirection. To study
> comprehensibility through incomprehensibility – can this be called
> learning from antiquity?[10]

Yüan Tsung-tao affirmed the value of 'learning from antiquity' (*hsüeh-
ku*), but only if one knew what to learn and how to learn it.

From the preceding remarks, one might conclude that Kung-an literary
theory was anti-archaic and anti-imitative. However, such a generaliz-
ation might lead one to believe that the adherents of the Kung-an school
viewed antiquity as a period of no value, and felt that imitation was a
useless practice in writing. It is important to note that 'restoring antiquity' (*fu-ku*) and imitation (*mo-ni*) are different: the former term denotes
a judgement of literary value, whereas the latter is more technical.
'Restoring antiquity' was a goal, while imitation was merely a means by
which to reach this goal. Although the Yüan brothers repeatedly claimed
that a writer should use the language of his own time and should not
imitate the works of the previous dynasties, it does not follow that they
did not respect ancient writers. On the contrary, the very reason that they
opposed imitation was that in their opinion the quality of ancient works
was so superior that imitation could not produce works of comparable
quality.

For the Former and Latter Seven Masters, antiquity was quite tangible;
it referred to the Ch'in and Han dynasties in the area of prose, and to the
High T'ang in poetry. For the three Yüan brothers, antiquity no longer
represented a specific period in history, but rather the highest attainments
of literature. They often used the term *ku-jen* (the ancients) or *ku* (antiquity) to describe the 'perfect' writer or ideal literary works. In his essay
'On Prose,' Yüan Tsung-tao contended that in their works the ancients
sought only intelligibility, whereas modern writers sought unintellig-
ibility. The superiority of the ancients was to him quite obvious.

Yüan Hung-tao had an extremely overbearing personality. Once he described his contemporaries as 'chickens in a jar' (*weng-chung chi*), and himself as 'the crane in the clouds' (*yün-chung ho*).[11] However, while he compared himself with the ancients, he humbly said that 'My talents are not on a par with those of the ancients (*ku-jen*), yet I presume to write.'[12] As for ancient writers, Yüan Hung-tao praised them saying that 'they cast aside ornaments and sought substance' (*k'an hua erh ch'iu chih*).[13] 'The ancients' thus became models for 'modern people' (*chin-jen*).

Disagreements on the meaning of 'restoring antiquity' between the Archaist Masters and the Yüan brothers focused not on the value of antiquity and ancient styles of writing, but on the feasibility of 'restoring' them. For the Archaist Masters, 'antiquity' was not only a valuable quality but also an attainable one – through an imitative approach. Antiquity remained a valuable quality for the Yüan brothers, but it was not attainable, and certainly not through an imitative approach. Yüan Hung-tao clearly stated in the preface to Chiang Ying-k'o's *Hsüeh-t'ao ko chi* (*Collected Works from the Snow-Wave Study*), that what he opposed was not the idea of restoring antiquity *per se*, but the slavish, imitative approach that this notion fostered in some writers.[14]

This disagreement between the Kung-an critics and the Archaist Masters centered not on whether a writer should learn from his predecessors, but rather on what he should learn, how he should learn it, and whom he should model himself on. Yet there are anomalies in the Yüan brothers' precepts. For example, for a poet to imitate Li Po (701–62) and Tu Fu (712–70) was for the Yüan brothers absolutely unacceptable; however, to emulate Po Chü-i (772–846) and Su Shih (1037–1101) was quite permissible. In a letter to T'ao Shih-k'uei, Yüan Tsung-tao clearly revealed his double standards in judging imitation:

> I heard that [Wang Shih-chen's] works written during his late years were not appreciated by his contemporaries. However, that which was not appreciated by his contemporaries is most likely highly regarded by us. Formerly, Fan Ning-yü had a copy [of Wang Shih-chen's works]. I borrowed it and read them. Only then did I realize that this old man [i.e. Wang Shih-chen] entirely modeled himself on [Su] Tung-p'o. In the end, however, [Wang Shih-chen's works] do not resemble [those of Su Shih].[15]

Yüan Tsung-tao's ambivalence about Wang Shih-chen's emulation of Su Shih is reflected in his mixed tone of praise and contempt. As far as Yüan Tsung-tao was concerned, it was permissible for Wang Shih-chen to imitate Su Shih; however, at the same time, it was regrettable because Wang's imitation did not quite resemble Su Shih's style. Obviously, when he made this comment, he forgot that it was precisely the dissimilarity between a poet and his predecessors that made the poet unique. His remarks on the lack of resemblance between the works of Wang Shih-chen and those of Su Shih thus somewhat contradict his earlier views on the issue of imitation.

In the Ch'ing dynasty the three Yüan brothers were often regarded by such critics as Ch'ien Ch'ien-i and Shen Te-ch'ien (1673–1796) as wild rebels fighting against the orthodox tradition.[16] A careful study of the theories of the three Yüan brothers does not support this interpretation. They never denied the value of studying the best writers of the past, nor was their attitude toward the Former and Latter Seven Masters altogether hostile.[17] This sentiment is particularly evident in Yüan Tsung-tao's comments on Li Meng-yang's writing. While criticizing contemporary literature, he showed great respect and sympathy for the leader of the Former Seven Masters:

> K'ung-t'ung (Li Meng-yang) fails to realize [that great literature does not arise solely from imitation] and he writes every piece of his work through imitation, calling this practice 'returning to the orthodox' (*fan-cheng*). Later the writers regarded this practice as a fixed rule and respected it as an axiom. When there was a single phrase not resembling that of the ancients, the writer was reprimanded for using an unorthodox style. What they do not perceive is that K'ung-t'ung's imitation was the innovation of one person, and is therefore not so seriously at fault. However, as time went by, and hundreds of his followers compounded the error, their writing became even more debased. Their works are not even worth reading. Moreover, K'ung-t'ung's essays still contain many of his own ideas, and his accounts of events and feelings are often quite realistic. What is especially praiseworthy in his writing is the adoption of modern place names and official titles. Nowadays [people feel] that it is not elegant if they use modern titles and place names in their writings. Therefore they use the official titles and place names of the Ch'in and Han [dynasties] in order to sound more refined. If one does not search them out in the historical gazetteers, one will never know where these places were.[18]

Yüan Tsung-tao believed that writing must reflect the language of the time, and this is why he praised Li Meng-yang for using modern official titles and geographical names. Even though he did not agree with Li's imitative approach in writing, he respected him as an independent writer with original thoughts. Li Meng-yang was not held to be entirely responsible for the decline of Ming poetry. What antagonized Yüan Tsung-tao was the attitude expressed by many of Li's followers, who espoused the slavish imitation of ancient writers. His two younger brothers to a large extent agreed with him on this point. Yet in the final analysis the theoretical confrontation between the Kung-an and the Archaist schools was really not as sharp as many literary historians have suggested.[19]

The first part of Yüan Tsung-tao's essay 'On Prose' demonstrates the importance that he attached to comprehensibility and the use of contemporary language, as well as his opposition to the use of archaic idioms. These ideas were later more fully developed in Yüan Hung-tao's theory. It was for the most part these ideas that made the Kung-an school of interest to modern writers and made the three Yüan brothers heroes in the vernacular movement of the early twentieth century.

The second part of 'On Prose' stresses the significance of learning in literary writing. Yüan Tsung-tao held that only those who were truly learned could produce great literature. The root of the problem with contemporary writers, he pointed out, was not imitation *per se*, but, rather, a lack of insight and erudition. His prescription for the 'illness' of imitation was that 'a scholar must first have substantial insights and knowledge and only then add refinement' (*Shih hsien ch'i-shih erh hou wen-i*).[20]

Yüan Tsung-tao believed that, if one truly had a philosophy, then one's language and style of writing would develop naturally out of it. This, as he put it, was similar to what happened when people were genuinely happy and sad: they could not but laugh and weep. However, he went on, for those who acted on the stage, since there was no genuine emotion in their minds, they had to force laughter or fake tears; and the only way for them to achieve that was by imitating genuine emotions. Yüan Tsung-tao then criticized his contemporaries for being deficient in scholarship and yet trying to produce writings worth saving for posterity. In order to fulfill such an unrealistic dream, authors inevitably had to resort to plagiarism.[21] 'If someone's mind were filled with penetrating insights,' continued Yüan, 'he would not even have time to grind ink and wield his brush: he would only fear that he could not capture his ideas in time. How could he find the time and energy to use the phrases and sentences of the ancients?'[22] He then concluded that 'if a writer could distill a philosophy from what he has learned and write on the basis of that philosophy, even if he were driven to imitate, he would not do it.'[23]

One of the common charges made by Ch'ing critics against the Kung-an school was that the three Yüan brothers were writers without scholarship.[24] Their emphasis on the spontaneous expression of true emotion and their underplaying of the importance of studying the works of the Ch'in, Han and High T'ang periods were interpreted by Shen Te-ch'ien as the major cause behind the development of a certain vulgarity and shallowness in late Ming poetry.[25] If one examines the writings of the Yüan brothers, it becomes obvious that scholarship and learning were not at all ignored by the Yüan brothers and that the charge is exaggerated if not altogether groundless.

A particular fondness for the writing of Po Chü-i and Su Shih, one of the characteristics of the Kung-an school, was also initiated by Yüan Tsung-tao. Just as Li Po and Tu Fu were ideal models for the Archaists, Po and Su were literary heroes for the Kung-an school. Yüan Tsung-tao not only named his study *Po Su chai* (The Study of Po Chü-i and Su Shih), but also entitled his collected works *Po Su chai lei-chi* (*The Collected Works from the Po and Su Study*).[26] In a long letter to his brother, Chung-tao, he compared himself to Po Chü-i in many personal aspects. Even though he modestly denied that his career and achievements were comparable to Po Chü-i's, his close identification with Po can easily be sensed.[27] His fondness for Po and Su greatly influenced his two brothers and became a tradition of the Kung-an school.

In the history of Chinese literature, Po Chü-i is best known as a committed social and political poet. He advocated that poetry should reflect the contemporary political and social situation and serve as a vehicle to express that to which the popular will inclined. In his famous letter to Yüan Chen (779–831), 'Yü Yüan chiu shu,' he clearly indicated that 'Prose is written for the time in which the writer lives, and poetry is composed for public affairs.'[28] This idea was put more forcefully in his preface to *Hsin yüeh-fu*: 'To sum up, these poems have been written for rulers, for officials, for people, for objects, and for events. They are not written for the sake of literature.'[29] As far as these opinions are concerned, we find little similarity between Po Chü-i and Yüan Tsung-tao. Social and political issues were hardly a major concern for the Kung-an school. On what basis, then, did Yüan Tsung-tao identify himself with Po Chü-i?

Po Chü-i was also known as a poet who frequently used colloquial expressions in his works. The most celebrated legend about his commitment to writing colloquial poems recounts that whenever he composed a poem he would ask an illiterate old woman to explain the meaning of the poem in order to see whether she could understand it. If she did, he would be satisfied; if she did not, he would revise the poem.[30] Of course, one should not take this story too literally, or regard it as Po Chü-i's normal method of composition. However, it does underscore Po Chü-i's effort to write poetry that was comprehensible. In his preface to *Hsin yüeh-fu* he asserts that 'the language of poems should be plain and direct, in the hope that they will be understood easily.'[31] It was Po Chü-i's plainness and straightforwardness of language that Yüan Tsung-tao admired.

Yüan Tsung-tao's admiration for Po Chü-i underscored his commitment to clarity of language; his esteem for Su Shih reflected his desire to pursue freedom in writing as well as in life. However, the desire for freedom and the praise for Su Shih were expressed much more strongly in Hung-tao's writing. This will be discussed in the following section.

Even though Yüan Tsung-tao did not present himself as a comprehensive literary theorist during the initial stage of the Kung-an movement, he laid the theoretical basis for the later development of the Kung-an school. As the founder of this school, Yüan Tsung-tao's major contribution to it was his realization that language changed with the passage of time. In order to write intelligibly, one's writing had to take into account the organic nature of language. In other words, the written language could not be completely isolated from the spoken language. This linguistic approach to literature later became the most efficient and powerful argument in the Kung-an school's debates with the Archaist school.

Yüan Hung-tao: the leader of the Kung-an school

Yüan Hung-tao, the leader and principal spokesman of the Kung-an school, was nine years younger than Tsung-tao, but his influence on the development of the school surpassed that of his elder brother. Moreover, his literary theory has attracted more attention from critics of the past three and a half centuries than his brothers' theories have. Yüan Hung-tao had already demonstrated his leadership and aptitude for literature by the age of sixteen. According to his biography in the *Official History of the Ming Dynasty* (*Ming-shih*), he organized a literary society in his home town, and all of the members up to the age of thirty came under his sway. He was said to have been good at writing 'eight-legged essays' while still a child. He passed the *chü-jen* examination in 1588, and the *chin-shih* examination in 1592 at the age of twenty-four. Although he was considered a capable administrator by his biographers,[32] he showed little interest in politics. He devoted most of his life to promoting his ideas about literature. Since these ideas were presented through his poetry, essays, and letters to friends, they may seem fragmentary and unstructured. However, if all of these small pieces are put together, it proves not too difficult to outline the framework and underlying themes of Yüan Hung-tao's literary theory.

Yüan Tsung-tao's two essays 'On Prose' served as a manifesto for the

Kung-an literary movement. They did not, however, put forth a comprehensive literary theory. It was Yüan Hung-tao's writing that provided the Kung-an movement with a coherent and comprehensive theory of literature.

Yüan Hung-tao's dominant position in the Kung-an school was beyond cavil; his influence reached the senior members of the school and changed their poetic styles. In the winter of 1598 Yüan Chung-tao joined his two brothers in Peking, and Huang Hui also came from Szechwan to the capital. In a postscript to Huang Hui's collected works Yüan Chung-tao recorded their relationship during this period:

> In order to break the current conventions, Chung-lang [Hung-tao] wrote poetry that contained skillfully crafted lines of the utmost sincerity. Po-hsiu's [Tsung-tao's] poetry was characterized by stability and clarity (*wen erh ch'ing*), while Shen-hsüan's [Huang Hui's] poetry sought uniqueness and ornament (*ch'i erh tsao*). Under the influence of Chung-lang, both somewhat deviated from their original practices.[33]

Huang Hui was fourteen years older than Yüan Hung-tao. He and Yüan Tsung-tao established the Kung-an school. After Yüan Hung-tao arrived in Peking in 1598, he not only stimulated the original members of the school, but also reoriented the direction of the movement from prose to poetry.

Yüan Hung-tao was himself very much aware of the leading role that he was playing. In a letter to Li Hsüeh-yüan (*chü-jen*, 1600) written in 1599, Hung-tao called himself the pioneer of the Kung-an literary movement: 'Even though I am poor in talent, I claim to be a forerunner in cleaning up the debased practices in contemporary poetry. I am also the first person to defend Han [Yü] [768–824] and Ou [-yang Hsiu] [1007–72].'[34] Of course, such men as Li Chih and Hsü Wei were the important precursors of the Kung-an school – especially Li Chih, who had a tremendous impact on Yüan Hung-tao. However, anti-archaic sentiments did not appear until Yüan Hung-tao had developed his literary theory.

Historical perspective of literature

At the core of Yüan Hung-tao's literary theory was his historical perspective on the development of literature. He believed that literature evolved over time and that literary works were the product of the age in which the writer lived. Therefore, according to him, no writer could escape the influence of his time. Any attempt to defy this condition would have to end in failure, and any literary work created in opposition to this condition could not endure. Since times differ from one dynasty to the next, the form and style of literature does not remain unchanged. It was from this standpoint that Yüan Hung-tao launched his attacks against the imitative approach advocated by the Archaist school.

Li Chih was the first critic to shed some light on the relative merit of antiquity in literary works. Yüan Hung-tao's historical approach to literature was an elaboration of Li Chih's ideas, but Yüan placed more stress on the irreversibility of the process of development. No matter how glorious the past may have been, it could never be brought into existence again. No matter how closely a writer might imitate the ancients, his work would be no better than a fake antique. In his preface to *Hsüeh-t'ao ko chi*, he wrote:

> It is time (*shih*) that propels literature from antiquity to modern times. The criterion of beauty and ugliness follows time, not people's eyes . . . Those who adhere to ancient language and pretend to be ancient are like those who wear summer clothes in a severe winter.[35]

Yüan Hung-tao further expressed this idea in a letter to Chiang Ying-k'o. Here he identified *shih*, which means a natural force or tendency, instead of *shih*, time, as the vital cause of the inevitable change in the development of literature. He remarked: 'It is a natural tendency (*shih*) that the ancient cannot be the modern.'[36] He also realized that modern people's inability to write like the ancients was due to the mutation of language. In the same letter to Chiang Ying-k'o, he elaborated on this idea:

> The chapters 'Ta-kao' and 'To-fang' in the *Chou-shu* [sections of the *Book of Documents*] were official announcements in the ancient times. Could they still be used as announcements today? The poems from the states of Cheng and Wei in the *Mao-shih* [i.e. the *Book of Poetry*] were ancient erotic literature. Could such contemporary folk songs as 'Yin liu-ssu' and 'Kua chen-erh' copy a single word from [these ancient erotic songs]? Since the way of the world has changed, literature has followed accordingly. That the modern need not model itself on the ancient is also the result of natural forces and tendencies.[37]

The development of literature was viewed by the Archaist school as a process of successive deteriorations. They believed prose had reached its apogee in the Western Han, and poetry in the High T'ang, and that the quality of these two genres had been deteriorating ever since. In order to revive the vitality of poetry and prose they felt that models for imitation had to be established. These models were none other than the prose of the Western Han and the poetry of the High T'ang periods. Yüan Hung-tao argued for a historical approach to literature in reaction to the masters of the Archaist school, who had previously laid down strict rules dictating which periods of literature were to be imitated. Since time moves on and literature changes accordingly, the 'antiquity' of literature becomes relative, and no models can be recognized as everlasting or absolute. Only on the basis of this belief can one declare that the quality of literature has nothing to do with its antiquity. More ancient is not necessarily more excellent; likewise, more recent is not necessarily more deplorable.

Yüan Hung-tao contended that the quality of literature could never be enhanced through an imitative approach. As a matter of fact he regarded mere imitation as the principal cause of the deterioration of literature in Ming times. He severely criticized this defect in his preface to Yüan Chung-tao's poetry:

> In recent years poetry and prose have reached their lowest ebb.
> Prose must be based on the standards of the Ch'in and Han periods;
> and poetry must be based on those of the High T'ang. [Modern
> writers] plagiarize and imitate [them], following their every step like
> shadows and echoes. When they see other writers use a word which
> does not resemble [those of the Ch'in, Han and High T'ang], they
> curse them as 'wild fox heretics' (*yeh-hu wai-tao*). What they do not
> realize is this: suppose we regard Ch'in and Han prose as our
> standard; does that mean they [i.e. Chin and Han writers] copied
> every single word from the *Six Classics*? Suppose we regard High
> T'ang poetry as our standard; does that mean that they [i.e. the
> High T'ang poets] copied every single word from [the poets] of the
> Han and Wei? If [those writers of] the Ch'in and Han modeled
> themselves on the *Six Classics*, would there be the prose of the Ch'in
> and Han? If [the poets] of the High T'ang imitated the poetry of the
> Han and Wei, would there be High T'ang poetry? Since dynasties
> rise and fall, the standards [of literature] do not remain unchanged.
> It is inexhaustible mutation that makes literature so valuable.
> Therefore [literature of different periods] should not be judged in
> terms of superiority and inferiority.[38]

A literary work, Yüan Hung-tao asserted, should be judged on its own merits, not on its similarity to the works of another period. He remarked: 'The greatness of T'ang poets lies precisely in the absence of imitation'

(*T'ang-jen miao-ch'u cheng tzai wu-fa erh*).[39] It was the poets' unwilling-
ness to imitate that made the T'ang a supreme period of Chinese poetry.

Nevertheless, Ming Archaists who believed in the imitative theory tried
to achieve literary excellence through emulation, and thus modeled
themselves after the very T'ang poets who detested emulation.[40] This was
the reason the Archaists could never attain the true spirit of T'ang poetry.
In the preface to *Chu-lin chi* (*Bamboo Grove Collection*), Yüan Hung-tao
wrote:

> Those who are skilled in poetry learn from the myriad phenomena
> of the universe, and not from their predecessors. Learning from the
> T'ang [poets] does not mean emulating their metrical rules and
> exact words and sentences. It means emulating the independent
> spirit [that the T'ang poets possessed] of not being like the [the
> poets of] the Han, Wei and the Six dynasties.[41]

In a letter to Ch'iu T'an, Yüan Hung-tao argued that the greatness of
periods and poets lay in their dissimilarity of their predecessors and not in
their similarity:

> The T'ang has its own poetry, and it is not necessarily similar to that
> in the *Wen-hsüan*. The four periods (i.e. Early, High, Middle and
> Late) of T'ang poetry have their own styles; one need not model
> oneself after the Early and High [periods]. From Li [Po], Tu [Fu],
> Wang [Wei], Ts'en [Shen], Ch'ien [Ch'i] and Liu [Ch'ang-ch'ing]
> down to Yüan [Chen], Po [Chü-i], Lu [T'ung] and Cheng [Ku],
> each had his own style, and they did not have to model themselves
> after Li and Tu. The Sung period was also like this. In the poetry of
> Ch'en [Shih-tao], Ou [-yang Hsiu], Su [Shih] and Huang [T'ing-
> chien], could one word be found in which they imitated one anoth-
> er? The reason their poetry cannot be like that of the T'ang is
> probably that each era has its own prevailing spirit (*ch'i-yün*). It is
> the same as saying the T'ang style cannot be like that of the *Wen-
> hsüan*; the *Wen-hsüan* style cannot be like that of the Han and Wei
> dynasties.[42]

Ch'i-yün was another term that Yüan Hung-tao used to explain the
cause of inevitable change in literary development. Basically 'the times'
(*shih*), 'the circumstances' (*shih*) and 'the resonance of the atmosphere'
(*ch'i-yün*) are all used synonymously in Yüan Hung-tao's writing, all
referring to the characteristic sentiment of an age which manifests itself in
literature. Of course, these vague terms are much too general to explain
changes in literature; this kind of thinking, however, suggests that Yüan

Hung-tao realized that the development of literature was not divorced from social change. Even though he did not indicate precisely what effect social change had on literary development, this realization provided him with a broad and realistic perspective on the history of Chinese literature. In the same letter to Ch'iu T'an he remarked that the antiquity of literature was only a relative concept:

> Nowadays scholars desire to make every poem in the world like those of the T'ang dynasty. Moreover, they criticize Sung poetry because it is not like T'ang poetry. Since they criticize Sung poetry for not being like that of the T'ang, why do they not criticize T'ang poetry for not being like that in the *Wen-hsüan*, the *Wen-hsüan* for not being like that of the Han and Wei, the Han and Wei for not being like the *Book of Poetry*, and the *Book of Poetry* for not tying knots for records and not relying on bird tracks?[43]

This is a strong and persuasive argument against the imitative approach to writing prose and poetry. In assessing the value of literature, resemblance to antiquity was never Yüang Hung-tao's chief concern.

The scope of the literary models set up by the Archaist Masters (the prose of the Ch'in and Han dynasties and the poetry of the High T'ang) was much too narrow for the Yüan brothers. Kung-an critics also valued the works of the late T'ang, and the Sung and Yüan dynasties. In order to counterbalance the veneration accorded to the models of the Archaist school, Yüan Hung-tao expressed strong doubts about the superiority of Han prose and T'ang poetry. In a letter to Chang Hsien-i, Yüan Hung-tao put it this way:

> People of today praise the T'ang, but I say the T'ang has no poetry; people of today praise the Ch'in and Han, but I say the Ch'in and Han have no prose. People of today despise the Sung and cast aside the Yüan, but I say that the best poetry and prose may be found in the works of great writers of the Sung and Yüan dynasties.[44]

In making such a statement, Yüan Hung-tao intentionally took an extreme position to correct a mistaken view; his aversion to using the prose of the Ch'in and Han and the poetry of the High T'ang as the only standard for good writing is also clearly revealed in this passage.

One of Yüan Hung-tao's strategies in attacking the reverence for High T'ang poetry was to elevate the value of Sung poetry and to praise the greatness of Su Shih. In a letter to Li Chih, he articulated this view:

> I find nothing more delightful these days than writing marginal comments to, and punctuating the works of, Ou [-yang Hsiu] and

Su [Shih]. There is no need to discuss the merits of Ou's prose. His prose is like the flowing of the Yangtze to the sea. His achievements are almost comparable to those of Shao-ling [Tu Fu]. It is a spectacular phenomenon in the universe. What I resent is that modern people's minds are preoccupied by doggerel; they are not able to read [the works of Ou-yang] with open minds. Su [Shih's] poetry is not as lofty and as classical as that of Old Tu, yet it surpasses [Tu's] insofar as it transcends the secular and is unique. Since the time that heaven and earth were formed, there has been no other like him. I often remark that there was no poetry during the Six Dynasties' period; only T'ao [Yüan-ming's] poetry has poetic charm, and only Hsieh [Ling-yün's] poetry has poetic content. The rest are all mediocre poets whose works are not worth reading. Not until Li [Po] and Tu [Fu] did poetry flourish. Han [Yü], Liu [Tsung-yüan], Yüan [Chen], Po [Chü-i] and Ou [-yang Hsiu] were sages (*sheng*) of poetry, Su [Shih] was the God (*shen*) of poetry. Those who say that Sung poetry is inferior to that of the T'ang have the views of a spectator. How could they possibly know what poetry is?[45]

In this letter Yüan Hung-tao not only denies that T'ang poetry is superior to Sung poetry, but also contends that Tu Fu's achievements in poetry are not necessarily greater than Su Shih's. In fact, he points out more than once that Su Shih was the only one who truly mastered the art of poetry and that no one could ever surpass him. On another occasion Yüan Hung-tao again compared Su Shih with Li Po and Tu Fu in a more explicit way:

> Every word in Master Su's poetry is good! Ch'ing-lien [Li Po] was good at depicting the abstract (*hsü*), while Kung-pu [Tu Fu] was good at depicting the concrete (*shih*). Since Ch'ing-lien concentrated on the abstract, he often ignored the realistic scene right in front of him. Since Kung-pu was absorbed by the concrete, his poetry succeeded with human affairs, but not with nature. His [Tu Fu's] poetry is great, transcendent, but not divine. As for the Master Su's poetry, it transcends the human world and it penetrates the human world, it uses sketchy expressions and it uses fine details, and the overall force of it is wonderful and profound . . . This was due to the fact that Master Su was highly talented, and his learning and insights were far superior to those of Li Po and Tu Fu. No wonder he was the greatest [poet] in history.[46]

Yüan Hung-tao's real motive in challenging the superiority of Li and Tu was not to discredit Li and Tu as great masters of poetry, but to defy the authoritarian rules laid down by the Archaist school in the sixteenth century, which held that there was nothing of value in the corpus of Sung poetry. The theoretical differences between the Kung-an and the Archaist schools were, to a certain extent, articulated in debates over whether T'ang or Sung poetry was superior.

Yüan Hung-tao, however, did not blindly praise Sung poetry. In his preface to *Hsüeh-t'ao ko chi*, he objectively pointed out its merits and flaws:

> During the Sung dynasty, writers like Ou[-yang Hsiu] and Su [Shih] appeared; they changed the practice of late [T'ang] to a large extent. As for subjects (*wu*), there was not one that they did not deal with; as for poetic methods (*fa*), there was not one they did not include; as for emotions (*ch'ing*), there was not one they did not explore. [Sung poetry] was as boundless and extensive as rivers and lakes . . . However, the fault of [Sung poets] is that they made poetry out of prose; or worse, out of Neo-Confucianism (*li-hsüeh*); or worse, out of ditties (*ko-chüeh*); or worse, out of Buddhist chants (*chieh-sung*).[47]

What Yüan Hung-tao appreciated about Sung poetry was its broad scope and richness of content. As a result of these qualities, however, the boundary between poetry and prose became blurred, and he looked upon this fact as a sign of degeneration in Sung poetry. It is, however, ironic that what Yüan Hung-tao lamented about Sung poetry later became characteristic of his own poetry. This will be discussed further in the chapter on Yüan Hung-tao's poetry.[48]

The key terms in Yüan Hung-tao's historical perspective on literature are 'time' (*shih*), and 'current' (*shih*). The significance of this theoretical construct is that it confirms the value of contemporary literature. Yet Yüan Hung-tao sometimes went to extremes and became obsessed by the 'newness' of a literary genre. In the 'Preface to a Collection of Eight-Legged Essays' ('Shih-wen hsü), Yüan Hung-tao clearly stated the importance of 'newness': 'If [something] is not contemporary, it is not pre-eminent; if [something] does not exhaust the possibilities of novelty and innovation, it is not contemporary.'[49] With this credo in mind, he praised eight-legged essays as a great literary achievement of the Ming dynasty. In a letter to his friend he strongly defended this infamous literary genre:[50]

> True literature is dying out in the world, only the words of the scholars with profound learning [*po-shih chia*, i.e. the eight-legged essayists] are still worth reading. Its [i.e. the eight-legged essay's]

style is unprecedented; its diction reaches the limits of a talented
writer; its tune changes with the passage of years and months.
[Every writer] is able to demonstrate his unique talent [through the
eight-legged essay] with different techniques. In the past two
hundred years, this [the eight-legged essay] has been the only
literary device that the government has relied on to select talented
scholars, and in turn the scholars have expressed their intentions
[through this literary device]. Those who despise the present regard
[the eight-legged essay] as unorthodox and discard it. Thus it has
not been accepted in literary circles. Alas! those who do not understand [the change of] time, how could they know literature?[51]

Yüan Hung-tao considered the eight-legged essay a much more 'lively'
genre than poetry. He remarked in the preface to a friend's poetry
collection:

> Nowadays those who write poetry usually do it with the energy that
> they have left over from writing eight-legged essays. Or, owing to
> their poor talents, they use poetry to cover up their weaknesses.
> Therefore poems are not usually well composed. In respect of the
> eight-legged essay, people study it from childhood, and it has
> attracted attention from everybody in the world, so that the variety
> and liveliness of the eight-legged essay is a hundred times more than
> that of poetry.[52]

It is surprising and disturbing to some that such wholehearted praise of
the eight-legged essay was actually written by the free-spirited Yüan
Hung-tao, the same man who championed innate sensibility (*hsing-ling*)
and spontaneity in his literary theory. The eight-legged essay was regarded by many well-known Ming scholars, including Ku Yen-wu
(1613–82) and Huang Tsung-hsi (1610–95), as the most rigid literary
device ever created, a genre full of hackneyed expressions and clichés. It
was even viewed by Ku Yen-wu as one of the major factors contributing
to the downfall of the Ming dynasty.[53]

   Given the rigid restrictions governing the composition of the eight-
legged essay, Yüan Hung-tao might have been critical of this new genre,
for it appeared to deny the spontaneity and unrestrained self-expression
that he also espoused. However, he made no adverse critical comments
whatsoever about this literary genre. On the contrary, he quite favored
this strict, Confucian style of essay-writing. Yüan Hung-tao was a
proponent of the tradition that 'literature expresses one's intent' (*shih yen
chih*). Yet the eight-legged essay was the typical model for the idea that
'literature is a vehicle for the *Tao*' (*wen i tsai-Tao*). This contradiction in

his writing has been largely overlooked by modern scholars. The only reason that Yüan Hung-tao defended the eight-legged essay so passionately, as far as I can see, was that it comprised a new literary genre which truly belonged to the Ming dynasty. It would not be too far-fetched to say that in order to challenge the deeply rooted conviction that 'the past is superior to the present,' Yüan Hung-tao had to say that 'anything that is current is valuable.' The faults of these two premises are identical in that both allow the judgement of a literary work to be based on *when* it was written, rather than on *what* was written or *how* it was written.

Essential concepts of literature

Individuality and freedom. Yüan Hung-tao's most celebrated dictum was: 'uniquely express [one's] personality and innate sensibility without being restrained by convention and form' (*tu-shu hsing-ling pu-chü ko-t'ao*).[54] The first half of this ideal refers to content, in which the importance of individuality and the genuineness of emotion are emphasized; the second half refers to form, in which freedom of style is stressed. He believed that only when one expressed oneself freely could one's real feelings and true emotions be revealed. The Kung-an school is also known as the 'School of Innate Sensibility' (*Hsing-ling p'ai*). *Hsing-ling* became in fact the hallmark of Yüan Hung-tao's literary theory.

Since *hsing-ling* is the most distinctive characteristic of the Kung-an school, it would be useful to examine its origins and to investigate its meaning. As early as the sixth century Liu Hsieh (d. *c*. 523) used this term in the first chapter of *Wen-hsin tiao-lung*, where he meant, as James J. Y. Liu has translated it, 'natural spiritual powers.'[55] It seems to suggest that *hsing-ling* is being regarded as one of the vital elements constituting literature. On another occasion Liu Hsieh used the same term in a different sense. In Chapter 3, 'Tsung-ching' ('The Classics as Literary Sources'), he defined the Classics and their functions:

> The works dealing with the universal principles of the Great Trinity [heaven, earth, and man] are known as *ching* . . . They help to articulate the order of things and to set up the rules governing human affairs. In them is found both the secret of nature and of spirit (*hsing-ling*), and the very bone and marrow of fine literature.[56]

Here *hsing-ling*, as Vincent Shih has translated it, means 'nature and spirit.' It does not have the metaphysical meaning of the term as Liu Hsieh used it in the first chapter of *Wen-hsin tiao-lung*. In Chapter 31, 'Ch'ing-ts'ai' ('Emotion and Literary Expression'), Liu Hsieh used the same term again to mean 'inner spirit' as opposed to external 'physical object.'[57]

Hsing-ch'ing and *ch'ing-hsing* are the two terms found in the sixth century that have a meaning very similar to *hsing-ling*. In the introduction to Chung Jung's (fl. 483–513)[58] *Shih-p'in* (*Classes of Poetry*) they both mean 'personal nature,' or 'personal feelings.'[59] Later in the same introduction Chung Jung seems to define *hsing-ch'ing* as spontaneous, individual expression, and he writes: 'In expressing one's nature and one's feelings, what value is there in using allusions?'[60]

In the seventh century the meaning of *hsing-ling* was clearly established as 'personal nature,' and the term lost its original metaphysical sense. Yao Ssu-lien (d. 637), an early T'ang historian, used this term in the following context: 'Literature is what miraculously expresses one's personal nature and uniquely draws forth what lies in one's bosom' (*Fu wen-che miao-fa hsing-ling, tu-pa huai-pao*).[61] Up to this point we may conclude that, in the *Wen-hsin tiao-lung, hsing-ling* contained two levels of meaning: one was metaphysical and meant 'natural spiritual powers'; the other meant 'personal nature and spirit.' The former meaning was not adopted by the later literary theorists, while the second meaning was developed into a major theme of expressionism.

During the Sung dynasty the term *ch'ing-hsing* was often used interchangeably with *hsing-ch'ing* or *hsing-ling*. In the *Ts'ang-lang shih-hua*, for example, Yen yü (1180–1235) states: 'Poetry is the expression of one's nature (*ch'ing-hsing*).'[62] Here *ch'ing-hsing* is simply an alternative expression for *hsing-ch'ing* or *hsing-ling*.

The interpretation of *hsing-ch'ing* given by Neo-Confucians was quite different from that given by men of letters. Shao Yung (1011–77), a leading scholar of Neo-Confucianism in the Sung dynasty, defined *hsing* and *ch'ing* as two separate words, rather than as a single term. He stated: 'To view things from the viewpoint of things is *hs'ing*; to view things from the viewpoint of the viewer is *ch'ing*. *Hsing* is clear (*ming*) and open (*kung*); *ch'ing* is dark (*an*) and closed [or 'secret,' 'surreptitious'] (*t'ou*).'[63] Thus, in the literary criticism of the Sung dynasty, certain moral overtones were ascribed to *hsing* and *ch'ing*; but these moral overtones were totally absent when the terms *hsing-ling* or *hsing-ch'ing* were used in Yüan Hung-tao's literary theory. In the preface to Chung-tao's poetry, Yüan Hung-tao writes:

> A great many of my younger brother Hsiao-hsiu's poems have been lost. Those that are extant are no more than are found here . . . The great majority [of his poems] uniquely express his personality and

innate sensibility (*hsing-ling*) without being restrained by convention and form. He would not compose unless it flowed from his bosom. Sometimes, when he wrote, emotion and scene merged together. In an instant a thousand words, flowing like a river, stun his readers. Among his works we find good lines and flawed ones. The good ones need no comment; even the flawed ones possess great originality and creativity. However, it is the flawed lines that I truly take delight in. Yet even among the so-called good lines it is regrettable that we find flowery language and hackneyed expressions, the reason being that he could not completely shake off the prevalent style of modern writers.[64]

Even though Yüan Hung-tao did not clearly define *hsing-ling*, a few points can be deduced from this passage. *Hsing-ling* is the personal nature that lies intrinsically within one's bosom. This innate quality is revealed through spontaneous outbursts and not through deliberate contemplation. *Hsing-ling* is not only a combination of personality and spirit, but also a synthesis of feeling (*kan-chüeh*) and emotion (*kan-ch'ing*). In this preface originality in idea and simplicity in diction were applauded. He held that as long as a poem reflects one's *hsing-ling*, flaws can be tolerated, and that refinement of diction should not outweigh true originality and creativity.

Lin Yutang (1895–1976) once defined the *hsing-ling* of the Kung-an school, using modern terminology:

> At the end of sixteenth century the three Yüan brothers established the so-called 'School of Innate Sensibility' (*Hsing-ling p'ai*) or the 'Kung-an school' (*Kung-an p'ai*). This school was actually a school of self-expression (*tzu-wo piao-hsien*). *Hsing* refers to one's character (*ko-hsing*), and *ling* refers to one's soul (*ling-hun*) or spirit (*ching-shen*).[65]

The true significance of *hsing-ling*, in my opinion, is the determination to be oneself and the realization of individuality. With this definition in mind it is possible to outline the basic principles of Yüan Hung-tao's theory of poetry.

Yüan Hung-tao believed that a good poem revealed the poet's personality and inner feeling. And it was the 'I' in the poem that made the work unique and special. In his theory poetry and personality were inseparable. He stated in the preface to his friend Liu Yüan-ting's poetry: 'The poetry of Yüan-ting is a footnote to him as a person . . . Those who do not know Yüan-ting read his poetry [as a way of knowing him]. And those who do not know Yüan-ting's poetry observe him [as a way of knowing his poetry].'[66] This thought, of course, is a banality; nonetheless, it underscores the self-consciousness of the Kung-an poets, that is to say poetry and personality were considered to be two sides of the same coin, and divergent personalities were expected to produce different poetry. If every poet imitated the same ancient model and used the same techniques, poetry would no longer reflect the poet's personality and would thus stifle one's innate sensibility. The imitative approach to literature, in which ancient models were closely followed, was consequently not acceptable to him. He rejected the 'debased practices' of the Archaist Masters, which he identified in his letter to Li Yüan-shan.[67]

The significance of *hsing-ling* lies in the determination to be oneself. This, as Yüan Hung-tao contends, means being genuine and unique. He writes in a letter to Ch'iu T'an: 'Generally speaking, things that are genuine are precious. If it is genuine then my face cannot be the same as yours, let alone [the same as] the faces of the ancients.'[68] Uniqueness is a natural result of being genuine. It is the inevitable difference between oneself and others which identifies who the 'I' is. Therefore the loss of uniqueness means the loss of one's identity. In the preface to Chung-tao's poetry, Yüan Hung-tao again stresses this point:

> Of all the things in the world it is the singular acts [of individuals] which we can by no means be without, and since we cannot be without them, even if we wished to eradicate them we could not. Striking similarities, on the other hand, are dispensable, and since they are dispensable, even if we wished to perpetuate them we would not be able to do so.[69]

In a letter to Chang Yu-yü, Yüan Hung-tao elaborated upon this idea with the examples of Lao-tzu, Chuang-tzu and Hsün-tzu:

> Lao-tzu wanted to put the sages to death, and Chuang-tzu ridiculed Confucius, and yet their works are still read today. Hsün-tzu talked of innate evil, but his biography was placed alongside that of Mencius [who held the opposite view].[70] Why? Because their views were derived from themselves without so much as a shred of reliance on any ancient person. Thus they attained their inviolable greatness. Although people of today can ridicule them, they cannot cast them away.[71]

'Holding views derived from oneself without reliance on the ancients,' to paraphrase the above, is the central theme in Yüan Hung-tao's literary theory, and uniqueness consequently becomes the essence of literature. In a response to Li Yüan-shan's letter Yüan Hung-tao reiterated this theme in a different way:

> The [essence] of literary works is freshness, non-conformity and an absence of fixed forms. One need only find expressions that others cannot express, and when the rules governing sentence patterns, diction and prosodic modes all just spring forth from one's own bosom, this is true freshness and non-conformity.[72]

Yüan Hung-tao regarded versification and metrical rules as fetters because he felt they hindered the poet's free self-expression. However, the existence of rules is a reality, and a spontaneous utterance after all is not necessarily poetry. How to maneuver in this dilemma without losing one's uniqueness as an individual, and at the same time to comply with metrical models as a poet, is the major concern voiced by Yüan Hung-tao in the above quotation. That the norms and patterns should 'spring from one's bosom' is the solution suggested by him. In other words, the rules are not considered fixed and rigid; they have great flexibility. Most important of all is that the poet should find his personal freedom within the larger patterns and norms, and not let those stifle the personal expression of his own spirit – even if that means startlingly transcending the expected adherence to rules.

Substance (chih) and ornament (wen). The relative importance of substance and ornament has been debated ever since the time of Confucius,[73] and a conclusion has never been reached on this polemical issue. Yüan Hung-tao's views on this matter were rather extreme. In his work ornament was often derogatorily interpreted as artificiality or affectation; and substance was regarded as an unadorned quality, the opposite of ornament. What makes a literary work great and imperishable, as far as Yüan Hung-tao is concerned, is the significance of its content, not the embellishment of its diction. He believed that ornament was not an aid to substance and that, on the contrary, it detracted from substance.

Chih is different from the *Tao* of *wen i tsai-Tao* (literature is the vehicle of the *Tao*);[74] *Tao* in this context means to a great extent Confucius' moral teachings. While *chih* in Yüan Hung-tao's literary theory means the true emotion and insights of an individual, it has very little to do with Confucius' teachings.

Yüan Hung-tao's aversion to literary ornamentation somewhat echoes Lao-tzu's idea that 'Truthful words are not beautiful; beautiful words are not truthful' (*Hsin-yen pu-mei; mei-yen pu-hsin*).[75] In other words, substance and ornament are held to be incompatible. Yüan Hung-tao shared this idea and drew an analogy between literary ornament and a woman's make-up: '*Chih* is like [a woman's] face. If she feels that her face is not pretty and tries to make it up with rouge and powder, she will inevitably diminish her prettiness and magnify her ugliness.'[76] Therefore, in order to retain substance, one must cast away ornament. In the preface to the *Remaining Manuscripts from the Garden of Hsing-su* (*Hsing-su Yüan ts'un-kao*), Yüan Hung-tao elaborates on this point: 'When something is transmitted [to later generations] it is certainly because of its substance. When writings are not transmitted, it is not because of faulty craftsmanship. It is due to a lack of substance.'[77]

Yüan Hung-tao had a very strong desire to be a 'true man' (*chen-jen*) and to write 'true poetry' (*chen-shih*),[78] his idea of *chih* thus being closely related to the concept of *chen* (genuineness). In the preface to T'ao Hsiao-jo's *Collection Written While Sick in Bed* (*Chen-chung i*) Yüan Hung-tao pointed out the importance of genuine emotion and dismissed the significance of literary techniques and craftsmanship:

> Most folk poems of antiquity were written by grieving men and forlorn wives. It is not that [the works of] grieving men and forlorn wives are more embellished than those of scholars and literati. [The latter] have never truly experienced sorrow though they do have ornate diction. Thus they are not sincere in what they put forth, and their readers are not moved ... Most important is genuine emotion and straightforward diction. Thus at times the poetry of grieving men and forlorn wives is superior to that of scholars and literati.[79]

'Genuine emotion and straightforward diction' (*ch'ing-chen erh yü-chih*) are essential criteria for judging the quality of literary works: those that meet this standard will last; others will perish. Basing his argument on this belief, Yüan Hung-tao predicts that 'the poetry and prose of today will not survive, and the works which will by chance be passed down to later generations will be such songs as 'Po p'o yü' and 'Ta-ts'ao kan,' which are sung by   ₂nd children of the by-lanes and hamlets.'[80] The reason is that these women and children are 'ignorant and un-affected.' Generally speaking, the poetry of the 'true people' (*chen-jen*)[81] possesses the 'true sound' (*chen-sheng*).[82] When these people express themselves, says Yüan Hung-tao, 'they express freely according to their disposition' (*jen-hsing erh fa*),[83] and thus 'their happiness and sorrow, anger and joy, wishes and desires can still be perceived.'[84]

Chih, on the one hand, is the revelation of one's true emotion; on the other hand, it is the reflection of one's knowledge. Knowledge, as Li Chih indicated, could be detrimental to one's 'childlike mind' and thus hinder

one from producing truly great literary works.[85] Although Yüan Hung-
tao was deeply influenced by Li Chih, his attitude regarding the inter-
relationship between book-learning and literary creation was quite
different from Li Chih's. To accumulate knowledge from book-learning,
in Yüan Hung-tao's opinion, would not directly help one's writing.
However, the knowledge that one amassed could serve as a reservoir of
inspiration for later days. He describes this process in these terms:

> If a man has broad learning, he could be said to have amassed a
> great deal of knowledge. Still, it may not have been totally ex-
> perienced and understood in his mind. Only after a long while does
> it suddenly become clear to him. It is like someone who is drunk
> suddenly becoming sober, like swelling water about to burst
> through a dam . . . Once his mind is touched by the scene, he writes
> spontaneously . . . and that is the ultimate manifestation of *chih*,
> substance.[86]

Yüan Hung-tao realized that revelation of one's emotions alone would
not produce the literary works of the highest quality. In other words, a
great poetic idea was for him not merely emotional, but intellectual as
well. It was an amalgamation of personality, emotion and learning.

The Kung-an school has often been criticized as a school without
scholarship, and Yüan Hung-tao was the target of this criticism. However, if we read his works carefully enough, we find that Yüan Hung-tao
did not ignore the importance of scholarship. In his preface to the
Collection of the Shensi Provincial Examination Papers (*Shan-hsi hsiang-
shih lu*) he compared the scholar of the past with the scholar of the
present:

> I privately bemoan the fact that while scholars of the past wrote
> literature on the basis of scholarship, scholars of today build their
> scholarship on the basis of literature. As for those who wrote
> literature on the basis of their scholarship, their words came from
> what they understood, and their sounds echoed what was ac-
> cumulated [in their minds]. This was as though the clouds rolled up
> and the rain started pouring; a spring gushed forth and the water
> ran into a river. Therefore it was difficult [for them] to write, but it
> is easy [for us] to understand. Those who built their scholarship on
> the basis of literature picked up the spittle of others and sketched in
> empty works on the paper. This was like a poor boy who borrowed
> clothes from others or a woman who dyed her eyebrows. Therefore
> nowadays it is easy [for them] to write, but it is difficult [for others]
> to understand.[87]

The importance of scholarship in writing is clearly expressed in this quotation. In the preface to *Ssu-tzu kao*, Yüan Hung-tao wrote that currently there were three 'defects' (*ping*) in the field of literature: profusion (*hsien*), superficiality (*piao*) and plagiarism (*tai*); and these three 'defects' were all caused by nothing but the lack of scholarship in writing. He appealed to men of letters to pay attention to book-learning, for that was in his opinion the only remedy for the 'three defects.'[88]

The problem with Yüan Hung-tao's views on *wen* and *chih* lies not in his emphasis on substance and scholarship, but in the degree to which he ignored the significance of ornamentation and literary technique. Yüan Hung-tao's aesthetic standards are based on his fondness for naturalism. He contends that true beauty comes from a plain and unadorned quality and that any conscious effort to strive for refinement or craftsmanship will not only end in futility, but also ruin the beauty of nature. No matter how superior one's artistic technique may be, it can never compare with nature's skill. The following passage illustrates this idea: 'When the wind blows on the water, ripples form. When the sunlight comes to the mountains, mists arise. Even Ku [K'ai-chih] [*c* 345–406] and Wu [Tao-tzu] [*c*. 750] were not able to add any color to such scenes.'[89] The superiority of nature's beauty is beyond description, and unattainable. However, in setting this standard as an ultimate goal, he actually raised a paradox, for artistic activities, to a certain extent, must all be artificial. As soon as the activity of painting and writing takes place, so-called pure and absolute natural elements can no longer be preserved intact. To insist on an absolutely natural quality in a literary work is actually contrary to the activity of writing itself.

It is true that no artist can ever capture the image of 'real' nature and present it on a piece of paper; however, this should not lead to the conclusion that art is inferior to nature. In Yüan Hung-tao's literary criticism the barrier between nature and art is rather blurred, and the difference between genuineness and beauty is non-existent. With such a mixed concept of nature and art, and genuineness and beauty, Yüan Hung-tao often regarded emotion itself as poetry, without realizing that emotion is only the raw material for poetry and not poetry itself. Ch'ien Chung-shu quotes a certain Wang Chi, in his *T'an-i lu*, who speaks precisely about this problem of mixing emotion and poetry: 'Literature grows out of emotion, yet emotion itself is not literature; poetry is derived from one's personality, and yet personality itself is not poetry.'[90]

Doubtless, substance is essential to literary works. However, substance and ornament are neither mutually exclusive nor necessarily incompatible. In fact, the greatness of works passed on derives not merely from the quality of their content, but also from the beauty and refinement of their language. Without a certain degree of ornamentation, literature becomes dry and insipid. Therefore techniques and ornamentation should not be regarded as harmful to literary creation, but rather as aids that ensure the durability of certain literary works. This mutual dependence of substance and ornament was explained by Liu Hsieh:

> Water by nature is plastic, allowing the formation of ripples; and it is of the essential nature of trees to be solid, supporting flowers on their calyxes. The ornamental pattern of a thing is of necessity conditioned by its essential nature. On the other hand, tigers and leopards, deprived of their patterns, would have the same kind of hide as dogs and sheep; and rhinoceros skins require red varnish [when they are made into armor]. The essential nature of a thing also depends on its ornamental patterns.[91]

The importance of either substance or ornament should not be totally ignored. An unbalanced view of the two keeps a writer from achieving superiority and perfection in literary writing. The difficulty of stressing the need for naturalness and genuineness while preserving a balance is considerable. Even Yüan Hung-tao himself realized, in his later years, that he had gone too far in this issue and tried to correct some of his earlier mistakes. Since his reputation as an uninhibited and unconventional poet was already established by that time, his efforts attracted little attention from scholars.

Ch'ü and yün. Even though Yüan Hung-tao discounted the importance of literary ornament and technique, he called attention to a more subtle and intangible quality of literature. This quality he designated *Ch'ü,* which has been translated as 'zest' by Lin Yutang,[92] as 'gusto' by James J. Y. Liu,[93] and as 'flair' by David Pollard.[94] In the preface to Ch'en Cheng-fu's *Collection of Intuitions (Hui-hsin chi)* Yüan Hung-tao defined *ch'ü* as 'the color of mountains, taste in water, light in a flower, and charm in a woman.' Since it was so subtle, as Yüan put it, 'even the most eloquent person cannot describe it. Only the one who feels it intuitively knows it.' According to him *ch'ü* is a quality that a child possesses, and it diminishes with the increase of age. Furthermore, official titles and high position were, in his view, like bonds which tie *ch'ü* down. The study of reason (*li*) did not help the cultivation of *ch'ü*; on the contrary, it was harmful to its growth. Yüan Hung-tao wrote: 'The deeper one studies reason, the further one is away from *ch'ü.*'[95] Here we sense an anti-intellectual overtone in Yüan Hung-tao's definition of *ch'ü,* which seems inconsistent with his emphasis on scholarship. What should be distinguished is the difference between *hsüeh* and *li* in Yüan Hung-tao's literary theory. *Hsüeh* refers to scholarship and knowledge in general, while *li* specifically refers to Neo-Confucianism. Yüan Hung-tao was not anti-intellectual; he was just opposed to the study of Neo-Confucianism as a means of enhancing the quality of literary writing.

If *chih* is the substance of a literary work, then *ch'ü* is the flavor of the work. Substance can be sought after and cultivated partly through study and partly by maintaining a sincerity of emotion and expression. *Ch'ü* is something that cannot be attained through study or cultivation. As James J. Y. Liu interprets it, '"gusto" appears to mean both an ineffable air or flavor in a person's nature (and hence in his writings), and an instinctive joy commonly seen in children but rarely kept by adults.'[96] At this point we may ask a further question: What is the relationship between innate sensibility (*hsing-ling*) and *ch'ü*? *Hsing-ling*, as I understand it, is an innate quality possessed intrinsically, while *ch'ü* is what emanates from this innate quality. Therefore *hsing-ling* itself is beyond perception, and what makes it perceptible is *ch'ü*.

In Yüan Hung-tao's literary theory another term used synonymously with *ch'ü* is *yün*. He describes the functions of *yün* as follows: 'Mountains have luster, that is vapor; water has patterns, that is ripples; and those who study the *Tao* [the way of life] have flavor, that is *yün*. When the mountains have no vapor, they become withered; when water has no ripples, it spoils; and when those who study the *Tao* have no *yün*, they are merely pedants.'[97] Even though *ch'ü* and *yün* are intangible, they determine the impression a person receives from another person or from a work. In the same essay Yüan Hung-tao indicates that it is extremely important to keep one's mind unoccupied. It is the emptiness of one's mind that allows one to be sensitive, and thus makes one capable of creating great literature. Yüan Hung-tao's idea of *ch'ü* and *yün* was greatly influenced by Taoism in general, and by Li Chih's 'childlike mind' in particular.

Ch'ü and *yün* are not imperceptible, but to what degree should they become perceptible? In answering this question, Yüan Hung-tao used the term 'mild' (*tan*) as the ideal degree for perceptibility. If *ch'ü* and *yün* are 'flavor beyond flavor' (*wei wai wei*),[98] then 'mildness' is an absence of flavor. The reason that mildness is so valuable, as Yüan Hung-tao explains, is that it possesses flexibility. The flavor of *tan* is so light and mild that it permits no excess of any kind to build up. In other words, the value of *tan* lies in its special quality of 'tastelessness.' Yüan Hung-tao describes the quality of *tan* in the preface to *Kuo-shih chia-sheng chi*:

Su Tzu-chan [Su Shih] was extremely fond of T'ao Yüan-ming's [365/372/376–427] poetry, valuing its mildness (*tan*) and relaxed manner (*shih*). As for things, fermentation produces sweetness, and roasting produces bitterness; only [the taste of] mildness (*tan*) cannot be created. The fact that it cannot be created is the true essence of literature.[99]

This quality of mildness comes naturally and effortlessly; it cannot be brought into being by conscious efforts.

In Yüan Hung-tao's literary theory *ch'ü* and *yün* somewhat balance his emphasis on *chih* (substance), and *chen* (genuineness). It is this balance that prevents his writing from becoming insipid, and that suffuses his works with a certain charm.

His interest in novels

The rise and flourishing of fiction was one of the most significant events to take place in late Ming literary world. Even though the origin of fiction can be traced back to the Sung, T'ang or even earlier dynasties, it was not until the late Ming that this new genre attracted favorable attention from learned scholars and men of letters. Li Chih was the pioneer of this trend, and his critical acclaim of *Shui-hu chuan* was unprecedented in the history of Chinese literature. Since Yüan Hung-tao was an enthusiastic follower of Li Chih, it is not surprising to find that Yüan also commented favorably about novels. However, Yüan Hung-tao's reasons for praising novels were, in my opinion, quite different from his reasons for appreciating and adopting the language of folk songs, even though folk songs and novels were usually classified under the same category, that of folk literature.

Yüan Hung-tao praised folk songs because they were free in form and genuine in emotion; they exemplified the two most essential features of his poetic criticism. Folk songs, moreover, provided him with new inspiration and terminology: 'I casually pick up slang and street talk, and I have no inclination to copy from the pre-Ch'in [literature].'[100] Folk songs and street talk actually served as sources for Yüan Hung-tao's poetic writing. Was his acclaim of novels based on the same criteria? After a careful study of the limited materials that are available I have found that his motives for speaking highly of novels were based more on didacticism and a certain kind of sensualism and curiosity, rather than on any appreciation of their literary excellence.

Yüan Hung-tao wrote commentaries on only two novels: the *Chin P'ing Mei* and *Shui-hu chuan*. Since his commentary on *Shui-hu chuan* is too limited to warrant a detailed discussion, only the *Chin P'ing Mei* will be dealt with below.

Yüan Hung-tao was the first scholar to comment on the *Chin P'ing Mei*.[101] In 1596, while serving as the magistrate of Wu-hsien, he wrote a letter to Tung Ch'i-ch'ang (1556–1636) in which he mentioned this novel:

> Where did you find the *Chin P'ing Mei*? I skimmed through it while lying in bed. [This novel] is filled with eroticism and is far superior to Mei Sheng's 'Ch'i-fa.' Where is the latter part? Please let me know where I can return it to you, once it has been copied, and exchange it for the other part.[102]

The tone of this letter is very casual. After having read the first part of the *Chin P'ing Mei*, Yüan Hung-tao found the novel very enjoyable, and as his curiosity was aroused by the incomplete story he very much wanted to obtain the latter half of the novel. There is nothing unusual about his reaction. What deserves attention in this letter is his comparison between the *Chin P'ing Mei* and Mei Sheng's (?–140 BC) 'Ch'i-fa.' Mei Sheng lived during the reigns of the Emperors Ching (156–141 BC) and Wu (140–87 BC) in the Han dynasty and was one of the greatest *fu* writers of the period. 'Ch'i-fa' was written in the mid-second century BC and was preserved in the *Wen-hsüan*, an anthology compiled in the sixth century by Prince Chao-ming (Chao-ming t'ai-tzu, Hsiao T'ung (501–31)).

There is literally nothing in common between 'Ch'i-fa' and the *Chin P'ing Mei*. Not only do they belong to different genres, but they are also addressed to completely different audiences. 'Ch'i-fa' was addressed to the Prince of Ch'u, or to rulers in general, while the *Chin P'ing Mei* was addressed to the general reading public. The overriding characteristic of the *fu* genre is its abstruseness and highly ornate language, while that of the novel is its use of plain and colloquial language. Moreover, about 1,600 years separates these two works. Therefore the comparison made by Yüan Hung-tao was by no means based on their form, structure, or even literary excellence. On what basis, then, would Yüan Hung-tao say that 'the *Chin P'ing Mei* . . . is far superior to . . . "Ch'i-fa"?'

A clue to the answer lies in the theme of these two works. 'Ch'i-fa' has been regarded by scholars as a typical example of *feng-chien* (to remonstrate to a ruler in an indirect way) in *fu* writing.[103] The composition begins with a dialogue between the Prince of Ch'u and the Wu k'o, a certain visitor from Wu. The Prince was ill, and the visitor from Wu diagnosed the causes of his illness and prescribed a cure:

> He who gives in to the desires of ear and eye, who indulges in the comforts of body and limbs, will hurt the harmony of blood and

vessels. Indeed, going by sedan chair has been called 'an omen of paralysis.' Secluded apartments and cool palaces have been called 'go between of chills and fever.' Gleaming teeth and moth-like eyebrows have been called 'axes that cut vitality.' Sweet, crisp, fat, strong food and wine have been called 'drugs that rot the intestines.' At present Your Royal Highness's complexion is pale, your four limbs are numb, your vessels are enlarged, your hands and feet inert. Girls from Yüeh serve you in front, beauties from Ch'i wait on you in back. Always coming and going from one amusement and feast to another, yielding to pleasures in secluded rooms and private apartments – this is swallowing poison voluntarily, and playing with the claws and teeth of wild beasts. By now this has gone quite far. There is a chronic congestion which does not come out into the open. Even if you had Pien Ch'üeh as a physician and Wu Hsien as a shaman, nothing could be accomplished. Now in the case of an illness like Your Royal Highness's, the only proper thing to do is to have gentlemen outstanding in this age for their broad experience and retentive memory seize the opportune moment to speak to you of the things they know, to reform your thoughts and change your view, constantly at your side, like the wings that lift a bird.[104]

The dialogue goes on with various descriptions of such sensual pleasures as music, food, charioteering, traveling and hunting, and the Prince of Ch'u was not able to enjoy any of them owing to his illness. Finally, the Prince of Ch'u was enlightened and mysteriously cured by listening to a description of the last pleasure, in which the visitor from Wu mentioned the 'marvelous doctrines,' and 'the most essential words' from the *Tao* of Confucius, Mencius, and some other pre-Ch'in philosophers.[105] The whole story is thus strongly tinged with moral and didactic overtones.

Yüan Hung-tao's comparison between the *Chin P'ing Mei* and 'Ch'i-fa' makes sense only if his comparison is based on thematic grounds and refers to the didactic purposes of these two works. In other words, Yüan Hung-tao believed that the *Chin P'ing Mei* was not merely an erotic novel, but a book containing moral teachings, and that there were serious meanings hidden behind the vivid descriptions of love-making.

In a preface to the *Chin P'ing Mei*, a certain Nung-chu k'o from Tung-wu explained Yüan Hung-tao's reasons for praising the *Chin P'ing Mei*:

> The *Chin P'ing Mei* is an obscene book. Yüan Shih-kung [Hung-tao] speaks extremely highly of it, for he wants to express his grievances through this book. It is not because of his consideration

of its worthiness. The author's intention was to use this book as a warning to the world, not as an encouragement.[106]

According to this preface, it is quite clear that Yüan Hung-tao's praise of the *Chin P'ing Mei* was based on something other than its literary qualities. In another preface to the *Chin P'ing Mei*, written by Hsin-hsin tzu,[107] he repeatedly pointed out: 'It is my personal opinion that Hsiao-hsiao Sheng of Lan-ling [the pseudonym of the *Chin P'ing Mei*'s author] has written the *Chin P'ing Mei* to express his view of contemporary morals.'[108] What he wanted to express is hidden behind the 'common talk of the streets and the trivial words of the bedroom.'[109] Hsin-hsin tzu also contended that this novel would help to enhance 'social morality' (*shih-tao feng-hua*). This idea was shared by Nien Kung, the author of a postscript to the *Chin P'ing Mei*:

> It is said that the *Chin P'ing Mei* was written by a great scholar in the reign of Shih-tsung [1522–66]. It contains satires and exposes the dark side of society. [The author's motive for writing this novel] is similar to that of Confucius' editing of the *Book of Poetry* in which he did not delete the poetry of Cheng and Wei.[110] Retribution is embedded in the story, and circulation of this book would benefit the world tremendously. Those who are not aware of [the book's benefits] regard this book as pornography. They not only miss the author's purpose [in writing this novel], but also treat unjustly those who made this novel known to the world.[111]

Although it has been suggested that Nien Kung was actually one of Yüan Hung-tao's pseudonyms,[112] convincing evidence does not exist to prove the case, and solving this mystery is not my major concern here. What this postscript demonstrates is that during the late Ming period, didacticism seemed to have provided men of letters with a convenient justification for any writing that deviated from what was deemed orthodox literature. And many liberal intellectuals had become aware of the educational function of novels. They realized that if novels were properly used, moral teaching could be instilled in an unobtrusive and imperceptible way. The didactic function of novels was more subtle, but no less effective, than that of the Confucian Classics.[113]

Feng Meng-lung (1574–1646),[114] a contemporary of Yüan Hung-tao, and the compiler of the famous *San-yen* collections, was an exemplary critic who held this opinion. His original intention in collecting and compiling stories, as the preface to his collection, *Hsing-shih heng-yen*, makes clear, was educational rather than literary:

Aside from the *Six Classics* and *Dynastic Histories*, no other works were able to stimulate and enlighten common people. This is why the forty chapters of *Hsing-shih heng-yen*, following the collections *Ming-yen* and *T'ung-yen*, were published. *Ming* means to guide the foolish. *T'ung* means to cater to popular tastes, and *heng* means to keep on learning without tiring and to pass [these stories] to posterity. Although the titles of the three collections are different, their purposes are the same.[115]

In the preface to another collection, *Ching-shih t'ung-yen*, Feng Meng-lung illustrated how effectively a novel could change and influence a person's belief and behavior:

There was a child living in the neighborhood whose fingers were injured while he was cooking, yet he did not cry out. I was curious and asked him [about it]. He answered: 'I just listened to the storyteller relating *San-kuo chih* at Hsüan-miao kuan. When Kuan Yün-ch'ang was undergoing bone surgery in order to cure a tumor, he was talking and smiling as though nothing were happening to him. How could I cry out for such a little pain?' Since a story can make a neighborhood child so brave, with the same method we can easily teach filial piety, loyalty, chastity and righteousness to the readers.[116]

No known evidence exists that Yüan Hung-tao ever met Feng Meng-lung or that they influenced each other. What we do know is that both men condemned the imitative approach to literary writing, and both held high opinions of folk songs and novels. In general, literati of the late Ming period believed that novels served a didactic purpose.

In 1609 Feng Meng-lung had the opportunity to read the *Chin P'ing Mei* and urged Shen Te-fu (1578–1624) to print it. The suggestion was rejected by Shen on moral grounds. Shen replied:

Although eventually someone was bound to publish the book [*Chin P'ing Mei*], once published it would circulate from person to person and from household to household, corrupting men's minds. And if one day Yama were to tax me with setting off this catastrophe, what excuse should I be able to offer? How could I possibly risk all the torments of Niraya for the hope of a paltry profit?[117]

The moral issue was a two-edged knife which cut both ways: for such conservatives as Shen Te-fu, to protect the traditional code of ethics was the very reason for banning the publication of novels like the *Chin P'ing Mei*. However, for such liberal spirits as Yüan Hung-tao and Feng Meng-lung it remained a moral issue to contend that novels had a didactic function in society. They believed that moral lessons in an erotic novel were like 'the bitter olive of morality embedded in the sweet flesh of dates.'[118] Their arguments, then, were actually two sides of the same coin. The disagreement was not whether literature should serve as a vehicle for moral edification, but whether or not the novel could serve this purpose effectively. Both sides used the same rationale to justify their arguments. The idea that fiction has an independent domain of its own and need not necessarily be a vehicle for morality or social education may never have occurred to them.

The other well-known comment Yüan Hung-tao made about the *Chin P'ing Mei* is found in his 'Shang-cheng,' or 'Rules of Drinking,' a small pamphlet written in 1607.[119] In entry 10, entitled 'Chang-ku,' or 'Anti-quarian Anecdotes,' Yüan Hung-tao listed scores of books as the indis-pensable sources of joy for those who truly enjoy drinking. The list starts with the *Six Classics* and ends with *Shui-hu chuan* and the *Chin P'ing Mei* as *I-tien* (unofficial classics).[120] 'Those who are not familiar with these books,' says Yüan Hung-tao, 'would become abominable in looks and dull in conversation, and should not be considered as true drinkers.'[121] This entry in 'Shang-cheng' has been widely quoted by modern scholars as evidence that Yüan Hung-tao greatly elevated the position of the novels by juxtaposing *Shui-hu chuan* and the *Chin P'ing Mei* with the *Six Classics* and some other works by Confucius and Mencius.[122] However, before this conclusion can be reached, two questions have to be answered. First, how serious was Yüan Hung-tao when he made this comment? And second, does this remark deserve such attention from modern scholars? In order to answer these questions, the circumstances surrounding the composition of this essay must first be examined.

In his short preface to 'Shang-cheng,' Yüan Hung-tao explains why this pamphlet was written:

> I could not even drink a small cup of wine. However, I became excited whenever I heard the clapping sounds of wine jars . . . Recently, quite a few drinkers joined our [Grape] Society. Because of their poor drinking manners, I felt pretty uncomfortable about it. It was my responsibility to set up some rules. Thus I adopted some simple and sound old regulations, added some new items, and called it 'Rules of Drinking.' Those who enjoy drinking should have a copy of it.[123]

If this preface is read alone, 'Rules of Drinking' seems to be a pamphlet containing drinking regulations. Actually it is a collection of anecdotes about the quality of wines, the history of goblets, and some suggestions on how to enjoy drinking. The purpose of writing 'Rules of Drinking' was not to discuss literature, but to provide some interesting and humorous topics for conversation while drinking. Since the 'Rules of Drinking' was meant to entertain, Yüan Hung-tao's remark on the *Chin P'ing Mei* should not be taken to mean that it merits being treated as a scholarly work. The furthest we may go based on this remark is that Yüan Hung-tao took great delight in reading the *Chin P'ing Mei*, and he believed that by encouraging his drinking friends to read the novel he would enhance the atmosphere of their drinking parties. As far as this is concerned, it would appear that Yüan Hung-tao's major concern in the passage in question is the art of drinking rather than an appreciation of literary works. It seems clear from the context that it cannot be read as a critical judgement about the literary value of a piece of contemporary fiction.

To praise the value of novels was quite in vogue among the progressive writers of the late Ming. Li Chih, Yüan Hung-tao and Feng Meng-lung were the most eminent representatives of this vogue. Modern scholars have regarded their favorable attitude toward vernacular fiction as a sign of great insight and considered it a breakthrough in the conception of literature during that period. What they have overlooked, however, were the motives behind this praise. What was the theoretical basis for their appreciation of novels?

The 'historical view' of Li Chih and the Yüan brothers did not enable them to realize that the vernacular novel was the most innovative literary form in the late Ming. When they praised novels, they never argued on the basis of literary development, but rather in support of the didactic function of novels. They failed to realize that this very argument could inadvertently put novels in a secondary position, making novels supplementary to the *Classics* as works which only catered to the needs and tastes of those who were not well educated.

It must be remembered that whereas didacticism can serve as a pretext to justify the publication of a novel like the *Chin P'ing Mei*, this very practice precludes such literary works from being judged in their own right. In the long run, didacticism could prove detrimental to the development of literature in general, and fiction in particular. Thus, while one may applaud Yüan Hung-tao as a pioneer who elevated the position of fiction, the fact remains that his insights were not without conceptual limitations.

Yüan Chung-tao: the reformer of the Kung-an school

Yüan Chung-tao, the youngest of the three Yüan brothers, outlived his two elder brothers. He died in 1624, fourteen years after Hung-tao's death. He shared the closest relationship with Hung-tao and defended him most earnestly and faithfully. He lived to witness the decline of the Kung-an school and to see Yüan Hung-tao's theories misinterpreted and abused. His works not only preserve the most reliable biographical material on the Yüan family, but also present the Kung-an theory in its later stages.

Even though Yüan Chung-tao's views on literature were basically a modification of his brother's ideas, we should not allow his achievements and views to be overshadowed by those of Hung-tao. While defending and interpreting Hung-tao's arguments, he actually established a theoretical framework of his own which, albeit less distinctive, was nevertheless more balanced than Hung-tao's. The role that Chung-tao played in the development of the Kung-an school was not merely that of the last survivor of the three Yüan brothers, but also that of a reformer of Kung-an literary theory. His views on literature may not yet have received the critical attention they deserve; nevertheless, they provide us with an essential key to understanding the shortcomings of Yüan Hung-tao's literary theories.

In the early stage of the Kung-an school clarity and comprehensibility of language was stressed. Yüan Tsung-tao quoted Confucius' dictum 'Words communicate, and that is all' (*Tz'u ta erh i i*) as the ultimate doctrine a writer should follow.[124] In Tsung-tao's 'Lun-wen' ('On Prose'), the degree of clarity is held to be almost the only criterion in judging the quality of literature. He unequivocally stated that 'the degree of comprehensibility is the criterion which determines whether a work is well-written or not.'[125] Later Yüan Hung-tao also stressed the importance of spontaneity and straightforwardness of expression. To a certain extent, he believed that the more straightforward the expression is, the better the poem becomes. He wrote in the preface to Chung-tao's poetry: 'Some critics criticized [Chung-tao's poetry] as being too straightforward. What they did not realize was that the emotion changes with the scene, and words are generated from emotion. I only worry that an idea will not be fully conveyed. How can [the poetry] be too straightforward?'[126] Indeed, this concept of poetry can be used as a very effective means to oppose the imitative approach advocated by the Archaist school and to prevent poetry from becoming merely a way to show off one's erudition. However, when these ideas are carried too far, poetry can become shallow and tasteless. It was with this realization in mind that Yüan Chung-tao presented his own interpretation of literature.

Meaning beyond words (yen wai chih i)

Yüan Chung-tao observed the danger of overemphasizing clarity and straightforwardness in literary writing: 'The greatness of literature lies in reserving and enfolding, not in stripping and exposing.'[127] He contended that good literature is not exhaustible in meaning, but contains limitless implication, connotation and suggestion. He elaborated upon this idea in the preface to the *Tan-ch'eng Collection* (*Tan-ch'eng chi*):

> With all literature there is nothing more wonderful than that in which, when the words come to an end, the meaning is without bounds; second to that would be those writings that succeed in saying exactly what they mean. Reading *Tso-chuan*, 'T'an-kung' [a chapter of *Li-chi*] or *Shih-chi*, it is as though 'one chants it once and then sighs three times' (*i-ch'ang san-t'an*), the meaning lying beyond the words.[128] With Pan Meng-chien [Pan Ku 32–92] and his contemporaries, the stripping-bare in their works became more pronounced. The talent of Su Shih is surely superior to that of Han [Yü] and Liu [Tsung-Yü]. He is inferior to Han and Liu in that he revealed himself too much. Poetry is like this as well.[129]

Thus an ideal literary work to Chung-tao is a work with suggestive or associative implications conveying rich meanings beyond its literal and explicit sense. This idea echoes Yen Yü's criterion for judging the quality of poetry. Yen Yü commented on High T'ang poetry: 'It is like sound in the air, color in appearances, the moon in the water, or an image in the mirror, the words come to an end and the meaning is without bounds.'[130] Yüan Chung-tao used this very line – 'the words come to an end and the meaning is without bounds' (*yen yu chin erh i wu-ch'iung*) – to describe the highest quality of literature. Moreover, the expression *i-ch'ang san-t'an* is also found in the passage quoted from *Ts'ang-lang shih-hua*. Chung-tao's idea of 'meaning beyond words,' therefore, was apparently derived from Yen Yü.

Yen Yü's *Ts'ang-lang shih-hua* has been regarded by Kuo Shao-yü and many other scholars as the theoretical foundation for the Archaist school in the Ming period.[131] As Richard Lynn states in 'Orthodoxy and Enlightenment': 'Much of Ming and Ch'ing poetry is characterized by excessive formalism and slavish imitation, and the blame for this can be laid ultimately at Yen Yü's door.'[132] The close relationship between the

Archaist school and Yen Yü's *Ts'ang-lang shih-hua* is beyond doubt. However, surprisingly enough, the influence that Chung-tao received from the *Ts'ang-lang shih-hua* is rather obvious and is of quite another kind. Here we see the anomaly of the same Sung dynasty critical work being used to fuel both sides of a late Ming debate on literary values.

The idea of 'meaning beyond words' is literally incompatible with Tsung-tao's principles of clarity and straightforwardness in literary writing. This change in Chung-tao's views on literature, however, should not be taken as a deviation from, or a rebellion against, the Kung-an tradition, but should be seen instead as a corrective for the deterioration of the Kung-an style in its latter period. This deterioration was described by Chung-tao as follows:

> Later [those who followed Hung-tao] slightly turned to vulgarity and simplicity. There was no scene they would not use, and there was no emotion they would not depict. Words simply burst out from their mouths without any contemplation and therefore poetry became defective (*ping*) again . . . Nowadays those who try to render homage to Chung-lang [Hung-tao] should learn how to express their innate sensibility and should stop this later practice of vulgarity and simplicity.[133]

This quotation explains Chung-tao's purpose in saying that limited words containing unlimited meaning is the highest standard of literature. His intention is not to make literary works obscure or incomprehensible, but to save them from degenerating into vulgarity, simplicity and shallowness. Because of this concern, Chung-tao's attitude towards poetry became more selective. He repeatedly pointed out that a writer had to discriminate between what is worth depicting and what is not. Only works delineating worthwhile emotions and scenes could add profundity to poetry. It was this discriminating attitude that distinguished him from Hung-tao.

Selectiveness: his attitude toward T'ang and Sung poetry

One of Yüan Hung-tao's strategies in attacking the Archaist school was to downgrade the veneration of T'ang poetry and Ch'in and Han prose by upgrading the merit of Sung poetry and Yüan drama. He boldly wrote, in a letter to Chang Yu-yü, that 'the T'ang has no poetry . . . the Ch'in and Han have no prose.'[134] Such radical opinions as this cannot be found in Chung-tao's works. Chung-tao in fact recognizes the superiority of the T'ang in the achievement of *shih* poetry and frequently indicates that T'ang poetry is the supreme model for those who write poetry:

'Those who disregard T'ang poetry and try to learn from other sources have all deviated from the right path.'[135] However, he still gave credit to the literary achievements of the Sung and Yüan dynasties. In the preface to the *Collection of Sung and Yüan Poetry* (*Sung Yüan shih*), he wrote:

As for poetry, no dynasty has flourished more than the T'ang. As long as a poem was written by the hand of a T'ang poet, if one looked at it, its luster could be seen; if one knocked on it, its sound could be heard; and if one smelled it, its fragrance could seemingly be sensed. Even though they were written more than a thousand years ago, they resemble newly sharpened knives and newly plucked flowers. Later, gentlemen of the Sung and Yüan periods concentrated their talents and emotions on the composition of *tz'u* and *ch'ü*. Even if T'ang poets had been willing to debase themselves to write *tz'u* and *ch'ü*, their achievement would not have surpassed [those of gentlemen in the Sung and Yüan]. Nevertheless, in *shih* poetry, the Sung and Yüan must give ground to the T'ang.[136]

In many cases Chung-tao's arguments comprised merely a revision or a modification of Hung-tao's theories. However, on the issue of T'ang poetry there were some sharp disagreements. Yüan Hung-tao downgraded the supremacy of T'ang poetry very much as an emotional response to the prevailing influence of the Archaist school of his time. He was so anxious to discredit the authoritative stance that 'prose must be Ch'in and Han, and poetry must be High T'ang' that he became personally involved in the argument. For Chung-tao the distance of time had diluted the intensity of his personal involvement in the issue, and he was able to reconsider calmly whether Yüan Hung-tao had adopted an extreme position.

Yüan Chung-tao gave some thoughtful advice to his nephews about writing poetry:

Recently my nephews Ch'i-nien and P'eng-nien [Hung-tao's sons] wanted to study poetry. I told them: 'You should thoroughly study the poetry of Han, Wei and the three periods of T'ang; only then can you start writing. You must not take a casual and conceited attitude and assume that you are free from the metrical regulations and will become famous in this way. Indeed, although we should not restrain ourselves from depicting any emotions, there are still emotions not worth depicting. Likewise, we should not restrain ourselves from using any scenes, but even so there are scenes not worth using. Only after you know this can we talk about poetry.'[137]

Compared with what Hung-tao had said in the letter to Chang Yu-yü (i.e. that the T'ang has no poetry), Chung-tao's advice here is not merely a revision of Hung-tao's view, but almost a complete reversal. Casualness and spontaneity are no longer advised in writing poetry; selectiveness is again emphasized. Unfortunately, Yüan Chung-tao did not draw a clear line between what is worth depicting and what is not. However, his message is still clear: in writing poetry, the T'ang is a period that has to be studied seriously, and there are rules that cannot be ignored. This advice reveals, on the one hand, how anxiously Chung-tao desired to change the direction of the development of the Kung-an school; on the other hand, however, it also tells us how badly Hung-tao's theories were abused and misunderstood. Even his own sons had to be instructed on the right path to take. Similar advice was given in a letter to his friend Ch'iu T'an:

> The *Tu-liao Collection* contains a great deal of surprising gusto (*ch'i-ch'ü*). However, there are a couple of casual and simple expressions that need to be deleted. Only then can this collection be published. I am hoping that you will select some succinct, condensed, unique and classical works from your *Complete Works* and collect them into two volumes, so that these works will demonstrate some degree of painstaking effort, not just shallowness.[138]

The real problem of the Kung-an school in its latter days, as Yüan Chung-tao observed, lay in its lack of selectiveness in poetic writing. Selectiveness was hardly a concern in Hung-tao's theories; but for Chung-tao, it became a major issue in literary writing. Basically, Chung-tao still believed that poetry was a form of self-expression, but in regard to what it should express his attitude was more critical than Hung-tao's. Genuineness of emotions was no longer the sole criterion for determining the quality of poetry; the substance or basis of emotion became equally important. Chung-tao criticized Sung poetry from this perspective:

> They [the Sung poets] never were willing to conform to each other and to plagiarize, to lick up the spittle left behind by others, to perish beneath what people of the past had already said. In this way they let their *ch'ing* [emotions] fully run their courses so there was nothing they did not express. They let the *ching* [scene] develop in every way possible so there was nothing they did not cover. However, since they covered everything, they covered scenes that need not be covered – this to the extreme that some became bombastic and clumsy, crude and rash, as if they expected to produce poetry in

the same manner as dumping grain out of a granary or tipping something out of a sack.[139]

Even though Chung-tao criticized Sung poetry, the shortcomings of the Kung-an school were quite similar to those he criticized in this passage. One may even say that Chung-tao used Sung poetry to illustrate the undesirable consequences attendant upon the failure to exercise selectiveness and restraint in writing poetry.

Yüan Hung-tao succeeded in ranking Sung poetry above that of the T'ang, or at least in presenting the poetry of the two eras as equal in merit. Chung-tao entertained little doubt about the supremacy of T'ang poetry. The difference between their attitudes towards T'ang and Sung poetry not only reflects different points of view, but it also suggests that the gap between the Kung-an and Archaist schools was no longer unbridgeable.

His attitude toward the Masters of the Archaist school

In assessing the literature of the Ming dynasty, Yüan Chung-tao showed more understanding, sympathy, and even respect, toward the Masters of the Archaist school than did Hung-tao. Chung-tao may not have agreed with their points of view, but he recognized their contribution to Ming literature and the quality of their works. He seems to have been more open-minded than Hung-tao in examining the real significance of Archaist theories. He rarely criticized the idea of *fu-ku* (restoring antiquity); in fact, he felt that it was the right measure to take in order to revive the vitality of Ming poetry. What he did oppose was the slavish emulation of past writers espoused by the followers of the Former Seven Masters. In the preface to the *Freedom Collection* (*Chieh-t'o chi*), he comments on the Former and Latter Seven Masters:

> From the T'ang and Sung down to the present time there have been masters in every dynasty. During the period of Hung[-chih] [1488–1505] and Chia[-ching] [1522–66] some scholars [i.e. the Former Seven Masters] promoted the idea of restoring antiquity (*fu-ku*) as a remedy to save literature from the shallow and vulgar practice of the time. This idea was not inadequate. However, it later deteriorated into plagiarism and the use of hackneyed expressions. Moreover, in the latter time [i.e. during the Chia-ching period] there were certain scholars [i.e. the Latter Seven Masters] who adopted this idea as a dogmatic principle. They stopped searching for the spirit and meaning of literature and merely imitated words and sentences. Their arguments were narrow-minded and conceited.

Their followers, with little knowledge about literature, compounded the deteriorating situation.[140]

Even though the Former and Latter Masters shared many basic views on literature and are often regarded as one group by modern Chinese literary historians, Yüan Chung-tao treated them very differently. He held that the ideas advocated by the Former Seven Masters contributed to Ming literature, and hence he did not condemn this group. His attitude toward the Latter Seven Masters was more critical. He believed the degeneration of Ming literature was brought about by the Latter Seven Masters because of their blind and exclusive admiration for High T'ang poetry. In the preface to *Yüan Hung-tao's Complete Works* (*Chung-lang hsien-sheng ch'üan-chi*), he applauded the Former Seven Masters:

> Beginning with the Sung and Yüan dynasties, poetry and prose were filled with conventional and coarse expressions. This malpractice was not corrected until the rise of the scholars [i.e. the Former Seven Masters] in this dynasty. As for prose, they modeled themselves after the Ch'in and Han; for poetry, they followed the work of the High T'ang. Only then did people become aware of the classical style in literature. But after them plagiarism prevailed and literature became similar to sham antiques.[141]

Yüan Chung-tao further indicated that there was nothing wrong in learning from High T'ang poetry, but it was not right in his opinion to exclude other periods of T'ang poetry and only cling to one or two poets of the High T'ang. It was this limited approach to T'ang poetry that disturbed Yüan Chung-tao. He criticized the Latter Seven Masters on this point:

> The Seven Masters of the Lung [-ch'ing] [1567–72] and Wan [-li] [1573–1619] periods [i.e. the Latter Seven Masters] also advocated learning from the T'ang dynasty. However, they did not learn from all the Masters of the T'ang, but merely modeled themselves on one or two of the High T'ang . . . Later, this became a doctrinal creed from which no one was allowed to deviate. And it gradually developed into a convention which was extremely disgusting.[142]

The three Yüan brothers were often portrayed by Ch'ing critics as hostile rebels who opposed the Former and Latter Seven Masters. This inaccurate assessment led many to believe there was nothing in common between these two groups of Ming writers. However, as we have seen, the three Yüan brothers, especially Chung-tao, were all quite capable of making independent judgements without regard to an author's literary affiliation.

His comments on the Chin P'ing Mei and Shui-hu chuan

Yüan Hung-tao spoke highly of folk literature in general, and of the *Chin P'ing Mei* and *Shui-hu chuan* in particular, and viewed them all as works of great value. Chung-tao's attitude toward these two novels was more cautious and less enthusiastic. He did not deny that a novel possesses didactic potential. However, he warned that there was some danger in overpraising these novels. In a diary entry dated 1614 he illustrated how much influence *Shui-hu chuan* could exert on a person. A monk named Ch'ang-chih copied *Shui-hu chuan* for Li Chih. Since he often heard Li Chih praising the characters in the novel as heroes, he greatly admired their brave and heroic deeds. Later, he imagined himself to be one of the heroes in the novel and almost committed murder and arson. Even Li Chih could no longer tolerate him and so expelled him.[143] Regarding this story, Yüan Chung-tao commented:

> Yüan Wu-ya came to see me and brought me a newly printed *Shui-hu chuan* with Li Chih's commentary and punctuation ... Generally speaking, this kind of book is like wild flowers and weeds in the world. There is no way to eliminate them; however, there is also no need to overpraise them. Sometime ago, I visited Tung Ssu-pai [Tung Ch'i-ch'ang] and with him discussed good novels. Ssu-pai told me: 'Recently a novel entitled *Chin P'ing Mei* has come out and is extremely good.' Later, I followed Chung-lang [Hung-tao] to Chen-chou and read half of this novel. It describes erotic affairs in great detail. The story is derived from P'an Chin-lien in *Shui-hu chuan*. 'Chin' refers to P'an Chin-lien, 'P'ing' refers to P'ing-erh, and 'Mei' refers to Ch'un-mei, the maid ... I recalled when Ssu-pai talked about this novel, he said: 'This book has to be burned.' It is my opinion that it need not be burned, and it need not be praised either. We can simply let it be. If we burn it, someone would still preserve it, and there is no way to obliterate this book completely. However, if *Shui-hu chuan* is praised, violence will be propagated; and if *Chin P'ing Mei* is praised, lasciviousness will be propagated. Why should those who believe in Confucian ethics astound the world by surprising the fool and poisoning the people?[144]

If this statement is juxtaposed with Li Chih's 'Preface to the Water Margin of Loyalty and Righteousness' ('Chung-i Shui-hu chuan hsü') and Yüan Hung-tao's comments on the *Chin P'ing Mei*, the difference in perspective is readily apparent. Even though Yüan Chung-tao did not mention Li Chih and Hung-tao by name, his disagreement and dissatisfaction with his teacher's and brother's views can easily be sensed here.

Yüan Chung-tao tried to defend the Kung-an theories against criticism, and his tempered, passive reactions shaped the transition from the Kung-an to the Ching-ling school. Yüan Chung-tao's transitional role in these two schools will be discussed further in the epilogue.

3

THE POETRY OF YÜAN HUNG-TAO

Yüan Hung-tao was not the most influential poet in the late Ming, but he certainly was one of the most controversial literary figures of the period. His works were banned in the Ch'ing dynasty and were considered heterodox and unconventional. He was held responsible for bringing about the decline of Ming poetry. This traditional criticism of Yüan Hung-tao was summed up by the editors of the *Ssu-k'u ch'üan-shu tsung-mu t'i-yao*:

> The poetry and prose [of the three Yüan brothers] redirected late Ming literature from the rigid and heavy (*pan-chung*) to the light and frivolous (*ch'ing -ch'iao*), from affectation (*fen-shih*) to originality (*pen-se*). They opened a new vista to the world, and they were in turn impetuously followed. The Seven Masters still rooted themselves in scholarship, while the three Yüan [brothers] relied totally on their wits. Those who followed the Seven Masters [committed the mistake of] merely imitating antiquity, and those who followed the three Yüan [brothers] reached the point of taking pride in their cleverness, violated the prosodic regulations, and ruined versification. In the name of correcting the errors of the Seven Masters, they committed even more serious errors.[1]

Another grave accusation was lodged by Shen Te-ch'ien (1673–1769). He charged, in his *Ming-shih pieh-ts'ai*, that the three Yüan brothers were responsible for the deterioration of 'moral education through poetry' (*shih-chiao*) and had jeopardized the continuation of the Ming dynasty.[2] Throughout the Ch'ing dynasty Yüan Hung-tao's poetry was regarded as 'the sound of decadence' (*wang-kuo chih-yin*; literally 'the sound of the collapse of the state')[3] and as having presaged the ruin of the Ming. This kind of accusation now seems rather far-fetched and irrelevant. However, in Ch'ing times, it sufficed to have a writer's work banned.

The two poems most often quoted to demonstrate the shallowness and eccentricity of Yüan Hung-tao's verse are 'West Lake' ('Hsi-hu') and 'Seeing Some White Hair by Chance' ('Ou-chien pai-fa'):

West Lake
One day I walk beside the lake.
One day I sit beside the lake.
One day I stand beside the lake.
One day I lie beside the lake.[4]

Seeing Some White Hair by Chance
For no reason [a gust of wind] reveals my white hairs;
I wanted to cry but laughed instead.
Since I like the idea behind a laugh,
I let out a laugh and jumped [for joy].[5]

These two poems were first quoted by Chu I-tsun (1629–1709) in *Ching-chih chü shih-hua* (*Notes on Poetry from the Studio of Ching-chih*),[6] and later quoted by Tseng I in *Chung-kuo wen-hsüeh shih* (*A History of Chinese Literature*),[7] Hsieh Wu-liang in *Chung-kuo ta wen-hsüeh shih* (*A Comprehensive History of Chinese Literature*),[8] Ch'ien Chi-po in *Ming-tai wen-hsüeh* (*The Literature of the Ming Dynasty*)[9] and Sung P'ei-wei in *Ming wen-hsüeh shih* (*A History of Ming Literature*).[10] Very recently 'West Lake' was also included in *Pilgrim of the Clouds*, Jonathan Chaves' translation of a selection of poetry and prose from the writings of the three Yüan brothers.[11] These two rather eccentric poems were taken as the hallmarks of Yüan Hung-tao's poetry. However, Jonathan Chaves did state in the introduction to his book: 'Frequently, Yüan Hung-tao's admittedly bizarre poem "West Lake" is the sole example quoted, and is used to demonstrate the sheer weirdness of Kung-an poetry. This is unfair, as virtually no other poem of Yüan's can be called weird, at least in the same sense as this one.'[12] Nevertheless, he assumed that the poem 'West Lake' was written by Yüan Hung-tao.

The authenticity of 'West Lake' is open to question. 'West Lake' and 'Seeing Some White Hair by Chance' appear in *K'uang-yen* and *K'uang-yen pieh-chi*, two short miscellaneous collections containing poetry, prose, correspondence and notes. These two collections first appeared in *Yüan Chung-lang shih-chi*, a fourteen-*chüan* collection of Yüan Hung-tao's work, compiled by Chou Ying-lin, from Hsiu-shui (Chia-hsing), Chekiang province, and published shortly after Yüan Hung-tao's death. In his 1615 diary Yüan Chung-tao mentioned this collection and indicated that *K'uang-yen* and *K'uang-yen pieh-chi* were forgeries per-

petrated by a certain 'vulgar person' (*ts'ang-fu*).[13] Chung-tao repeatedly
expressed his indignation about this matter, and intended to correct it.[14]
His efforts, however, later proved futile, for the circulation of *K'ung-yen*
not only continued, but the volume became more and more popular.[15]

Modern scholars are in general agreement that *K'uang-yen* and *K'uang-
yen pieh-chi* are forgeries. Iriya Yoshitaka, a Japanese authority on Yüan
Hung-tao and the Kung-an school, stated in his meticulously researched
paper, 'A List of the Works of the Three Yüan from Kung-an' ('Kōan san
En chosakuhyō'), that *K'uang-yen* and *K'uang-yen pieh-chi* were not
written by Yüan Hung-tao.[16] Recently, these two collections were
excluded from *Yüan Hung-tao chi chien-chiao* (*The Annotated Complete
Works of Yüan Hung-tao*), edited by Ch'ien Po-ch'eng. This is by far the
best edition of Yüan Hung-tao's works that has been published to date.
In the 'guidelines' (*fan-li*) to this three-volume collection the editor stated
without any doubt that *K'uang-yen* and *K'uang-yen pieh-chi* were
forgeries.[17]

Yüan Hung-tao's collected works, except for *K'uang-yen* and *K'uang-
yen pieh-chi*, are all arranged in three sections: poetry, prose and correspondence. Yet the same works in these three categories are randomly
arranged in *K'uang-yen* and *K'uang-yen pieh-chi*. This poor editing style
reveals an inconsistency in compilation which may also be regarded as
evidence of forgery.

The criticism that has so far been lodged against Yüan Hung-tao's
poetry has been based in part on some spurious works. Therefore the first
thing we must do to evaluate properly Yüan Hung-tao's achievements in
poetry is to establish the authenticity of the poems in his collected works.
Then, and only then, will we be able to assess his place in the development
of Ming poetry.

The most commonplace criticism of Yüan Hung-tao's poetry holds
that while his poetry was rich, original, and truly reflected his *hsing-ling*,
or innate sensibility,' it was nevertheless flawed by shallowness and
vulgarity of expression. To a certain extent, this criticism is valid. Yüan
Hung-tao's poetry does contain these merits and flaws. However, such
traditional critics as Shen Te-ch'ien and Chu I-tsun failed to point out
that Yüan Hung-tao's poetry passed through many stages, and the poems
of each stage had their peculiar characteristics, strengths and weaknesses.
This gradual development and divergence of his poetic style is especially
significant because he was very consciously establishing a new style at
each stage. In this chapter Yüan Hung-tao's poetry will be discussed in
three phases: the formative period, the creative period and the period of
moderation.

The formative period

Since no writer can completely escape the impact of the age in which he lives, it is no surprise to find that, in his early years, Yüan Hung-tao was not altogether free from the influence of the Former and Latter Seven Masters. Under the prevailing vogue of imitating T'ang poetry, Yüan Hung-tao as a young poet quite naturally flowed with the current. Even though his early works are no longer extant, from the materials that survive we can surmise something about the poetry Yüan Hung-tao composed in his youth. Chiang Ying-k'o (1556–1605),[18] one of Yüan Hung-tao's best friends and the most faithful adherent of the Kung-an school, gives us some clues about how closely Hung-tao modeled his works on T'ang poetry. In the preface to Yüan's *Pi-ch'ieh chi* (*A Collection of Broken Bookcases*) Chiang states: '[Yüan Hung-tao] was able to write poems when he was a child, and none of his many poems [in the early period] failed to resemble the works of the T'ang. But later he derided himself and said: "Why do I have to follow the works of T'ang; why not write my own poetry?"'[19] Chiang Ying-k'o did not indicate the year in which Yüan Hung-tao came to the above realization. However, it is clear that Yüan Hung-tao did go through an imitative period during which he was conscious of this practice, and that he later desired to change it.

While Yüan Hung-tao was still alive his poetry had already won a reputation for unconventionality, and his contemporaries mocked his poetry for being unlike T'ang poetry. Was Yüan Hung-tao's poetry indeed so unique and unconventional? In the preface to *Wang T'ien-ken's Prose Collection* (*Wang T'ien-ken wen*), Yüan Chung-tao said that this was only a stereotyped reaction to his brother's poetry. As a matter of fact, there are quite a few poems modeled on the T'ang tradition in Hung-tao's works:

T'ien-ken got along with us brothers very well, and he was extremely fond of Chung-lang's [Yüan Hung-tao's] poetry and prose . . . Last year T'ien-ken went to the provincial capital to take the examination. There were a few poets who ridiculed Chung-lang's poetry for not being T'ang-like. T'ien-ken remained quiet. Later he selected some of the most T'ang-like poems in Chung-lang's collection, made a copy of them and wrote them on a fan. T'ien-ken showed this copy to the poets and asked: 'Which dynasty do these poems seem to be from?' All the poets responded unanimously: 'The best ones seem to be from the High T'ang and the less good ones from the Middle and Late T'ang.' T'ien-ken laughed loudly and said: 'These are Yüan Chung-lang's poems, which you gentlemen thought were unlike those of the T'ang.'[20]

In a letter to Chang Hsien-i, Yüan Hung-tao confessed that he modeled his works on T'ang poetry: 'You [Chang Hsien-i] said that my poetry looks like T'ang poetry, and you were absolutely right. However, what you liked were those poems which resembled T'ang poems, not the ones that I was most pleased with.'[21] This passage indicates the difference between the quality of Yüan Hung-tao's imitation and that of the Seven Masters, for Yüan Hung-tao was never satisfied by merely imitating the T'ang poets. His ultimate goal was to create his own style and to write his own poetry. In the preface to *P'ing-hua chai chi*, Tseng K'o-ch'ien commented on Yüan Hung-tao's works and pointed out that 'Shih-kung's [Yüan Hung-tao's] prose was derived from the work of the Ch'in and Han, and Shih-kung's poetry was learned from Lao Tu [Tu Fu].'[22] Later, Yüan Hung-tao wrote a letter to Tseng K'o-ch'ien expressing his appreciation for this preface: 'Your preface to [my] *P'ing-hua chai chi* is excellent! You have indicated something [i.e. the origin of my poetry and prose] that no one has ever said before.'[23] These quotations lead us to believe that in the formative period of Yüan Hung-tao's literary career his poetry was not unconventional or rebellious in tone. Quite the contrary, his early works closely complied with the imitative theory proposed by the Archaist school. This practice provided Yüan Hung-tao with some firsthand experience of imitative approaches to composition, and that is precisely why he was able to launch powerful and sharp attacks against the Seven Masters. Yüan Hung-tao's reaction against the orthodox tradition certainly reflects his independent thought and his rebellious character. However, the extent of this reaction also demonstrates how much he had already been influenced by the Archaist school.

The creative period

The transformation of a writer's poetic style usually takes place gradually and imperceptibly. It is not possible to single out one year to mark the point where Yüan Hung-tao discarded the imitative approach to composition and began his more creative period. Nevertheless, we know that this transition took place during his early twenties. By 1591, when he first visited Li Chih at Lung-hu, in Ma-ch'eng, Hupeh province, Yüan Hung-tao had already been recognized as a brilliant scholar.[24] Li Chih was extremely impressed by this young man, and he remarked that

Yüan Hung-tao was 'prominent and outstanding' (*ying-t'e*).[25] During this visit Li Chih read one of Yüan Hung-tao's works entitled *Chin-hsieh* and wrote a preface to it.[26] In a poem, Li Chih states:

Having read your *Chin-hsieh*,
Even to be your driver is my deep pleasure.
Had I followed your words earlier,
I would not have suffered in the twilight of my life.[27]

According to 'Li-pu yen-feng ssu lang-chung Chung-lang hsien-sheng hsing-chuang,' a biography of Yüan Hung-tao written by Chung-tao, *Chin-hsieh* seems to have been a philosophical work rather than a collection of poetry.[28]

Li Chih was deeply impressed by Yüan Hung-tao's philosophical insights, but Yüan was no less impressed by Li's liberal and individualistic views on literature. After this visit, Yüan Hung-tao had a dramatic change in his attitude toward literature. Chung-tao recorded this change as follows:

Only when [Hung-tao] met Lung-hu [Li Chih] did he realize that until then he had been culling worn-out phrases and had thoughtlessly stuck to conventional opinions, as if he were crushed under the language of the ancients and a vital spark was completely covered up. But then the floodgates opened, and like a down feather carried along by a favorable wind, like a giant fish sporting in a huge waterway, he was able to be the master of his thoughts, not mastered by them, was able to manipulate the ancients, not be manipulated by them; when he spoke forth, each word flowed out from his innermost being.[29]

It would not be appropriate to say that Li Chih alone accounts for the change in Yüan Hung-tao's literary view. However, Li Chih's influence was a decisive element in Yüan Hung-tao's transformation from a classical imitator to a liberal and individualistic writer. Yüan Hung-tao's meetings with Li Chih at Lung-hu were a milestone in the development of his poetry as well as of his philosophy of life. Not only did his style of writing change drastically in the early 1590s, but his philosophy of life also underwent a transformation from an orthodox Confucian approach to a more Taoist and Buddhist view of the world. Thus the early 1590s should be regarded as the beginning of Yüan Hung-tao's creative period, which lasted for more than a decade until about 1606, the last year of his seclusion in Liu-lang. Then his writing style entered another stage – a period of moderation.

The period from 1590 to 1606 comprised Yüan Hung-tao's most creative and productive years. During these fifteen years he wrote his major works: the *Chin-fan chi* (*The Embroidered Sails Collections*) and *Chieh-t'o chi* (*The Freedom Collection*), each in four *chüan*, *P'ing-hua chai chi* (*The Vase-Flower Studio Collection*) in ten *chüan*, *Kuang-ling chi* (*The Kuang-ling Collection*) and *T'ao-yüan yung* (*The T'ao-yüan Poetry Collection*), each in one *chüan*, and *Hsiao-pi t'ang chi* (*The Hsiao-pi Hall Collection*) in twenty *chüan*.[30] About half of this large body of writings is poetry.

Yüan Hung-tao had always esteemed freedom, but his desire for freedom was never stronger than after he had served for two years as the magistrate of Wu-hsien, Kiangsu province. These two years of bureaucratic life were a disillusioning nightmare. He never again became enthusiastic about politics. After a great deal of difficulty he finally resigned from the post and left office in 1597. He traveled with T'ao Wang-ling and some other friends to Hangchow, where he visited the mountains in Chekiang province for three months.[31] During this time he put together a collection of poetry and prose entitled *Chieh-t'o chi*. *Chieh-t'o* means 'to free oneself from worldly worries' or 'to be released from shackles.' The title reflects not only his feelings at that time, but also his attitude toward poetic composition.

In the preface to Yüan Hung-tao's complete works, his brother Yüan Chung-tao commented on two collections, *Chin-fan chi* and *Chieh-t'o chi*, written in 1596 and 1597 respectively, during Hung-tao's twenty-ninth and thirtieth years:

> With his poetry and prose in the *Chin-fan* and *Chieh-t'o* collections [Yüan Hung-tao] intended to free himself from bonds and fetters; therefore he often used playful expressions. This attitude stemmed from his outstanding talent and courage, and his dispassionate regard for worldly praise and disparagement. He merely utters whatever his mind wants to say.[32]

However, this approach was not without fault. Later in the same preface Chung-tao indicated the shortcomings of Hung-tao's poetry composed in this period. 'The works written in his early years,' he wrote, 'are extremely straightforward and candid, spontaneous [and produced] without much contemplation. The emotions and scenes are too realistic in these works; they are too familiar and not imaginative enough. Nevertheless, they are all derived from his own sensitive mind, and spoken with his voice of wisdom.'[33] The unfavorable criticism Hung-tao received in his later years for his shallowness and colloquialism was mostly based on the works that

he composed in this period. But at the same time such works also won
him a reputation for unconventionality. In the preface to *Hsiao-pi t'ang
chi*, Lei Ssu-p'ei concluded his comments on Yüan Hung-tao's poetry
with the word 'genuineness' (*chen*) and stated that Yüan's works expressed 'what people wanted to say, what people could not say, and what
people dared not say.'[34] He called Yüan's poetry true 'Ming poetry.'[35]

At about the age of thirty Yüan Hung-tao took great pains to write
poems that accorded with his own literary theory. He was more successful
in adopting contemporary colloquialisms to poetic forms than in creating
a new form of poetry. Most of his poetry was still written in *lü-shih*
(regulated verse), or *chüeh-chü* (quatrain) styles, with five or seven
characters to each line. Even though he did compose some experimental
poems in a new form, the outcome was not very impressive either in
quality or in quantity.

The most distinct characteristic of Yüan Hung-tao's poetry during this
period was the adoption of the folk song. He claimed: 'At present, there is
no true literature; genuine poetry can only be found in the streets and
lanes.'[36] And in a letter to Yüan Tsung-tao, Hung-tao wrote:

> Recently I have made great progress in poetry; my poetry collection
> has been greatly enriched, my poetic mind and eyes broadened.
> Poeple in the world are writing poetry by imitating poetry, so
> inevitably they will be unhappy with the result. I am writing poetry
> by adopting [such folk songs as] 'Ta-ts'ao kan' and 'Po p'o yü.'
> Therefore I enjoy writing poetry a great deal.[37]

He also said: 'I would rather be modern and vulgar, and I refuse to pick
up a single word from others.'[38] Folk songs had become for him a source
of poetic inspiration. They not only provided him with fresh diction and
expressions, but also brought vitality to his poetry. His appreciation of
folk songs illustrates on the one hand his willingness to use current
vocabulary and diction, and on the other hand his independent personality. He wrote, in a letter to Ch'ien Yün-men: 'My poetry and prose are
simple and plain. They are like old farmers talking about farm work.'[39]
There can be no doubt about his intentions in writing colloquial and folk-
song poetry. What we should examine is how faithfully and seriously he
put his beliefs into practice. In Yüan Hung-tao's collections of poetry we
do find some poems deeply influenced by folk songs; however, they are
very few. This scarcity demonstrates that writing folk songs was by no
means his major interest, but was undertaken more as an occasional
experiment than as a constant and serious practice. Here I shall give two
examples to illustrate how far he did actually go in this direction.

Lotus-Picking Song
Picking lotus blossoms –
How fresh at blossom time!
Shining in the moonlight like a virgin,
Bending in the wind like a dancer.
Deep red and tender white, intermingled with autumn water.
Lady Ma[40] and Goddess of the Lo[41] would die of envy.

Picking lotus leaves –
The leaves wreathe fragrant oars.
Like an ancient jade plate with patterned green petals,
To be presented to Lady Ch'in and Consort Yen.

Picking lotus seeds –
Break open the pods, all sweetness and beauty.
Delicate hands sort out seeds, every one perfect.

'Why stay submerged in water all year long?
If the water were deep, it might be bearable;
But, if it were turbid, how could you stand it?'
'Please ask the spring mud in South Creek,
If it knows the bitterness of a heart like mine?'[42]

At the Ferry Crossing on Heng Pond
At the ferry crossing on Heng Pond,
Walking along the river,
You, a young man, come from the west,
While I, this humble maiden, go toward the east.
I am not a sing-song girl,
But live in the red pavilion of a fine family.
While blowing on a flower, I mistakenly spit on you;
How much I cherish your treasured glance!
My home is at Rainbow Bridge,
With a red gate at the intersection.
If you come, look for the magnolia,
But do not go past the plum tree.[43]

'Picking lotus flowers' (*ts'ai-lien*) was a popular theme for folk songs in the area to the south-east of the Yangtze river. Since *lien* is a homonym for other words meaning either 'to feel tender regard for someone' or 'pitiful,' lotus-picking thus became a common metaphor used by women to express their affection and their bitterness.[44] 'At the Ferry Crossing on Heng Pond' is a love poem that describes a girl who is pointing out the location of her home to a man in order to rendezvous with him at a later date. It is interesting to note that Yüan Hung-tao often adopted the voice of a female in his folk-song poetry. However, I would not interpret this as a sign of his sympathy toward women. In these two poems, except for the names of a few legendary beauties in the 'Lotus-Picking Song,' we find no metaphors or allusions, devices which are unavoidable in the poetry of the literati. The diction of these two poems is simple, and the ideas are clear.

During this period Yüan Hung-tao was particularly fond of using the mode of *yüeh-fu* poetry. *Yüeh-fu* originally meant 'the Music Bureau,' a government institution established by Emperor Wu of the Han dynasty (r. 140–87 BC). The function of this organization was to collect folk songs from the countryside because the government believed that folk songs reflected the mood of the people and hence had political value. *Yüeh-fu* poetry therefore has deep folk roots in Chinese literature.[45] There is a section consisting of seventeen poems entitled 'Imitating the Ancient *Yüeh-fu*' ('Ni ku yüeh-fu') in the first chapter of *P'ing-hua chai chi*, a collection written between 1598 and 1600. Yüan's fondness for the *yüeh-fu* style is further evidence of his general interest in folk or popular songs. The following example is selected from 'Imitating the Ancient *Yüeh-fu*':

> *Song of an Ill-Fated Wife*
> Falling petals that depart old branches,
> Still have roots upon which to rest.
> But when a woman loses her husband's heart,
> To whom can she turn and tell her feelings?
> A lamp's glow never lasts till dawn,
> A man's love never remains unchanged.
> I have only these two moth-eyebrows,
> How many times can I afford to let you look?
> If you look too often I will become familiar,
> Without really ever being old at all.
> A flower that has bloomed many times,
> Is not as good as a blade of new-grown grass.
> I could weave you a cloak with strands of my hair,
> But you would spurn it as inferior to a piece of paper.
> I would cut my belly to make you food,
> But you would swallow it and say that water is better.
> An old lover's total obedience,
> Is not as favored as the curses of new love.
> If with my death I could turn back your lost heart,
> I would wait for you through the eternal night.[46]

Yüan Hung-tao stated in his short preface to the section entitled
'Imitating the Ancient *Yüeh-fu*' that 'While I was resting on a boat trip, I
casually wrote these few poems. Although they are not highly refined in
language, they do convey my ideas.'[47] His purpose in writing poems in
the *yüeh-fu* style was to establish a model for colloquialism in poetry.

The influence of folk songs is no longer so apparent in the works
written after Yüan Hung-tao passed the age of thirty-three, in 1600, but
the simplicity and plainness of language still remained characteristic of his
poetry. He used very colloquial words not only in folk songs and *yüeh-fu*
ballads, but also in traditional poetry. The following two poems illustrate
this:

Random Lines in Imitation of Yüan [Chen's] Style
Gaining and losing in the world are simply like this:
To gain, always a delight, but can one be aware of loss?
I pass long days in idle talk,
For peace of mind, I learn to endure a losing chess game.
I sent a letter home asking for a smoked goose,
A guest newly arrived from Fukien brought me some lichees.
The ups and downs of past and present are but a dream.
Who cares about sincerity or frivolity.[48]

In a Boat Travelling through Huai-an
A road of one thousand *li* along the canal;
Willow catkins – myriad broken hearts.
Being a sojourner – the stem of clinging sorrow;
Meditation – a prescription for pain.
My yearning for home – longing for a bowl of roe-flavored rice;
My drunken dream – a cup of clam soup.
Gradually, I grow tired of studying;
A wandering spider weaves a web over my brush tray.[49]

The names of such common foods as smoked goose, lichees, roe-
flavored rice and clam soup can hardly be found in traditional poetry
because they were not considered poetic. However, it is not unusual for
Yüan Hung-tao to use the language of daily life in his writing. If we look
at the diction alone, the gap between Yüan Hung-tao's poetry and prose
is rather insignificant. No expressions that can be used in prose are
considered taboo in poetry. Indeed, the disappearing barrier between the
language of poetry and of daily life is one of the distinctive characteristics
of Sung poetry.[50] Su Shih, the Sung poet Yüan Hung-tao most admired,

said: 'Everyday words, the language of the streets – all can be used in poetry. The only thing that is required is skill in using them.'[51] We can see reflected in his poetic practice elements of Yüan Hung-tao's praise of Sung poetry and his close identification with Su Shih, for the development of Yüan Hung-tao's poetry from the formative to the creative period is analogous to the general stylistic transformation of poetry that occurred from the T'ang to the Sung period, or roughly between the seventh and twelfth centuries.[52]

Yüan Hung-tao's poetry covers a wide range of topics: from social intercourse to personal contemplation, from the description of natural scenery to historical nostalgia. It is literally impossible to establish a neat set of categories which would systematically comprise all his poetry. Here, then, I will give a few examples of some of the major poetic themes that often appear in his poetry from this period.

Even though Yüan Hung-tao was not very active politically throughout his life there is no dearth of political poetry in his work. The following two poems exhibit his two different approaches to political poems – sarcasm and serious concern:

> *A Jocular Song about the Land of the Happy Drunks*
> Wine in heaven makes it stand upright,
> Wine in a nation stops all strife.
> When a true king appears,
> Benevolence comes only after generations.
> Why must virtue be used to govern?
> Punishment to bring order?
> Just make a river of wine,
> And pile up yeast as high as a wall.
> Wherever the sun and moon shall shine,
> Wherever the frost and dew fall,
> Of those who have blood and breath,
> None are not drowsy with wine,
> The dead do not know they are dead,
> The living do not know they are alive.
> Only when thoroughly soused can the crafty devil be known.
> Why worry about the world not being at peace?[53]

This poem appears in *Chieh-t'o chi, chüan* 1, and was written shortly after Yüan Hung-tao had resigned as the magistrate of Wu-hsien in 1597. His resignation was intended as a protest against the government of the time. Two years in government service made clear to him the price of political involvement. However, his interest in politics did not disappear. In the poetry composed during this period we can still see his concern for government and his sympathy toward the people. While he was still the magistrate of Wu-hsien, he wrote in a poem: 'My concern for the people makes me ill in my heart. My feelings for the world bring tears that turn into poems.'[54] After he left Wu-hsien, his attitude became more sarcastic and cynical; his criticism was no longer direct, but the message carried in the poetry was no less clear. 'The Jocular Song about the Land of the Happy Drunks' affords a good example of his political sarcasm. This frivolous attitude changed again while he was serving as an instructor in the Imperial University in 1598. He could no longer hide his emotion and indignation at the deteriorating condition of the Ming government, composing at this time several poems on such topics as 'A Song of Evading Taxes' ('Pu-fu yao') and ' A Song of a Ferocious Tiger' ('Meng-hu hsing'),[55] which directly criticized heavy taxes and the savagery of government officials.

In Yüan Hung-tao's complete works there is no dearth of criticism and pessimistic comment about late Ming China; what we do not find in his life is action. His dissatisfaction about the political situation led him to withdraw from his post, but never led him to take positive action. The following poem, written in 1599, perfectly illustrates his feeling of help-lessness about late Ming politics:

> *Gathering Friends at the Hsien-ling Temple to Write Poems on*
> *Rhymes with* Ch'eng [*city*], Shih [*market*], Shan [*mountain*]
> *and* Lin [*forest*]
> Wild flowers block my view, tears flow into wine,
> I plug my ears as it saddens me to hear the latest court news.
> I gather the capital gazettes into a pile and burn them to ashes,
> I pawn my court robe in the flower market.
> Every day I write over a thousand words of new verse,
> Among them not a single word laments the fate of the people.
> Bystanders say I am just a muddled fool;
> I cannot reply but only point my finger at green hills.
> Ever since Tu Fu achieved fame as a poet,
> The phrases 'worry for your lord' and 'love your country' have
>   become a joke.
> Since my words are useless, and I cannot keep silent,
> How could Juan Chi not get himself dead drunk?
> Before my eyes, a cup of rich, spring wine;
> I weep and feel sadder than a youth from Lo-yang.[56]

Philosophical reflection is another important theme in Yüan Hung-
tao's poetry. His political poems often reveal the Confucian aspects of his
thought: his sense of responsibility to the country and people, and his
anger and frustration toward the current government. But his philosophical poems reflect more a Buddhist and Taoist influence and present
the somewhat skeptical and passive side of his mind. The transience of
human life and the unreliability of fame and wealth were the topics that
he often treated. The following example is selected from *Pi-ch'ieh chi*. The
idea that Yüan Hung-tao tries to express in this poem might not be new,
but the form that he uses is unique. The poem contains twenty-two lines.
Except for the last two lines, which have seven characters each, there are
three characters in each line. This poem is found in the section of his
poetic works entitled 'Miscellaneous Style' ('Tsa-t'i'). A handful of poems
included in this section can be regarded as Yüan Hung-tao's experiments
with new poetic forms.

> *A Deep Sigh*
> When clouds turn into rain,
> They cannot change back.
> When arrows leave a bow,
> They can never return.
> Yesterday, a dog,
> The day before, a lion.
> For awhile, a flower,
> For awhile, turned into mud.
> Flowers look beautiful;
> Fences guard them.
> Those with handsome faces,
> Mirrors reflect their looks.
> The mirrors stay new,
> But the faces do not.
> Before the fences decay,
> Flowers have all vanished.
> The short can be lengthened,
> But by what means?
> One stanza of a song,
> And three cups of wine.
> To wish a long life for everyone in the world, I would pull up my
> sword to lop off the feet of the golden crow [i.e. the sun].[57]

Yüan Hung-tao's poetry reveals his personality. In his poetry he
expressed every aspect of his persona: his happiness and sadness, his likes

and dislikes, his personal idiosyncrasies and eccentricities – all are presented in his poetry without any reservation. Poetry was for him not merely an emotional outlet or a form of social communication; writing poetry was simply a part of his daily life, an essential means of expressing his feelings and thoughts.

Yüan Hung-tao's reputation as a poet has largely been based on the works composed during the period from 1590 to 1605. During these fifteen years, he established himself as a liberal, individualistic and expressive poet with little concern for literary techniques. His poetic diction does strike us with the power of its clarity and freshness. However, when the poetry composed in this period is examined as a whole, an unbridgeable gap appears between his theory and practice, both in form and in content. His poetry was never as extreme as he claimed it would be, or should be, in his theories. Except for a handful of poems, all his poetic work was composed in one traditional form or another.

He valued folk songs and regarded them as a source of his poetic inspiration, yet he never seriously committed himself to the composition of folk songs, or made any effort to preserve folk songs, as his contemporary, Feng Meng-lung (1574–1646), did.[58] Unlike many other contemporary dramatists and novelists Yüan Hung-tao remained after all a traditional scholar and a man of letters.

The period of moderation

The poetry written between 1605 and his death, in 1610, was more moderate in form and style than what had preceded it. The significance of these five years does not reside in how much he wrote, but in how much he changed as a poet and in how much more aware he became of the shortcomings in his own approach to poetic writing. Yüan Hung-tao's attempts to turn his writing toward a more conventional style were largely ignored by Ch'ing critics as well as by twentieth-century scholars. However, without a discussion of the works of his later years, the study of Yüan Hung-tao's poetry would be far from complete, and in fact can draw one to misleading conclusions about his poetry as a whole.

Chiang Ying-k'o, one of his best friends, died in 1605. Yüan Hung-tao was extremely saddened on learning of Chiang's death, and he wrote ten poems and a long preface in memory of his lost friend. *Ming-shih chi-shih* contains the following assessment of the two poets: 'Chin-chih [Chiang Ying-k'o] is not as talented as Chung-lang; however, his colloquial and frivolous style in poetry is similar to that of Chung-lang.'[59] In the preface to the mourning poems Yüan Hung-tao noted this similarity and commented on it:

Chin-chih was a man of superior talent and frank manner. In writing he strove for innovation. Even the best writers since the Chia [-ching] and Lung [-ch'ing] eras cannot be compared to him. However, in his writings, he went to excess in correcting previous errors, and his writings were criticized by mediocre scholars. In the past I had intended to tell Chin-chih [of his shortcomings], but I never had the chance. I was thus disloyal to him. My own shortcomings are the same as his. I did not expect that Chin-chih would die so soon. How sad! . . .

I asked you to write prefaces to my *Chin-fan* and *Chieh-t'o* collections, and I was really pleased with them. However, at the time, my poetry was not sturdy and my prose lacked organization. Now my *P'ing-hua* and *Hsiao-pi* collections have been published, but how can I ever ask you to write prefaces again?[60]

In this quotation two points are worth noting. First, Yüan Hung-tao confessed that both he and Chiang Ying-k'o went too far with poetic innovations. This suggests that he did feel some regret about his early works. It was in this state of mind that he entered his period of moderation. Second, even Yüan Hung-tao himself could not deny that the poetry and prose included in the two collections of *Chin-fan* and *Chieh-t'o* were 'not sturdy' and 'lacked organization.'

In Yüan Hung-tao's literary theory 'spontaneity' and 'writing in a casual manner' were the two essential points that he stressed in his early days. He later came to realize that spontaneous emotional outbursts alone would not make good poetry, and that in writing poetry certain basic rules had to be observed. Thus his casual and extemporaneous approach to poetry became over time more serious and concerned with aesthetics. In a letter to Huang Hui, Yüan Hung-tao expressed this idea: 'Poetry and prose are serious matters to us. Without them we could not live . . . Were Po [Chü-i] and Su [Shih] not great masters? Their techniques for writing poetry and prose cannot be learned through casual efforts. I hope you do not adopt a casual manner as a shortcut.'[61] What Yüan Hung-tao stressed in his letter was that casual efforts cannot lead a poet to supreme or sublime accomplishments, and thus a certain amount of discipline in poetic writing becomes necessary. This attitude represents a drastic and fundamental change from the slogan of his early days: 'Casually follow your wrist and mouth, and all the words will find their metrical rules' (*hsin-shou hsin-k'ou chieh ch'eng lü-tu*).[62]

Part of Yüan Hung-tao's poetry written from 1604 to 1605 was included in the *Hua-yüan* collection. His brother, Yüan Chung-tao, wrote a
colophon to this collection, in which he indicated how Hung-tao's poetic
style had changed:

> These are works written by my late brother Chung-lang during the
> years of *Chia-ch'en* and *I-ssu* [1604–5] . . . The poems written prior
> to the *Hua-yüan* collection are sometimes marred with vulgarity and
> crudeness. But those written after the *Hua-yüan* collection have
> both substance and refinement. This is also true of his prose. The
> extant draft [of the *Hua-yüan* collection] is now presented here. We
> can see that it has been revised many times. It was not an im-
> promptu composition, but rather the result of painstaking
> craftsmanship and contemplation, neither of which can be easily
> measured.[63]

In defending his late brother from the charge of vulgarity and shallowness, Yüan Chung-tao considered the change in Hung-tao's poetic style in
his later years to be the most direct and conclusive evidence in support of
his brother's ability to produce poetry of the highest caliber. Therefore he
repeatedly described how this transformation took place. From the
winter of 1609 until his brother's death in the autumn of 1610 Chung-tao
shared a very intimate relationship with him.[64] In an article written in
memory of his late brother Chung-tao recalled: 'When we discussed
poetry and prose, [Hung-tao] often said to me: "Only very recently have I
come to feel that I have made some progress. I had been too frank and
straightforward, and not reserved enough in writing."'[65] In this dialogue,
Yüan Hung-tao's regrets concerning his early works are obvious. Commenting on the works of Yüan Hung-tao's later years, Yüan Chung-tao
says: 'The travelogues and poetry were profound and refined. Compared
to the previous works, this is another style.'[66] He elaborated on the
significance of this new style as follows:

> [Yüan Hung-tao's] scholarship changed with the years, and his
> writing matured with age. After the *P'o-yen* collection [written in
> 1608], there was not a single sentence that was not alive, and there
> was not a single essay that was not sturdy. Each was as forceful as
> an arrow penetrating a stone, and as pretty as a flower growing out
> of water. In his writing we find the influence of Mo-chieh [Wang
> Wei], Tu-ling [Tu Fu], Ch'ang-li [Han Yü], Ch'ang-chi [Li Ho],
> Yüan [Chen] and Po [Chü-i]. And, of course, we can also find
> Chung-lang himself.[67]

The significance of this paragraph does not lie in the description of Yüan Hung-tao's writing style, but in the six names mentioned as the sources of influence that changed his style. All six are T'ang poets. Yüan Chung-tao deliberately and carefully ruled out the name of Su Shih, Yüan Hung-tao's most admired literary hero, and added Li Ho (791–817), a short-lived T'ang poet who was best known for the involution, obscurity and ornamentation of his poetic diction as well as for his fondness for technical dexterity.[68] He is often regarded as the forerunner of Late T'ang mannerism.[69] As far as literary theory is concerned, Yüan Hung-tao could least agree with Li Ho's poetic style. Yet, surprisingly enough, Chung-tao included Li Ho as one of the poets who influenced his brother in his later years. What Chung-tao intended to convey in this paragraph was that Hung-tao was a serious and eclectic poet who did not ignore the importance of literary technique.

Both Yüan Hung-tao and Chung-tao considered this modification of poetic style as a change for the better. On the one hand, this change surely represents a maturing of Yüan Hung-tao's literary abilities. On the other hand, the change can also be seen as a concession to current literary conventions. One may even say that the sophistication of his aesthetic techniques came at the expense of his own uniqueness as a poet. From this point of view, Hung-tao's change from being a 'radical' to being a 'revisionist' represented a loss rather than a gain in the overall development of the Kung-an school's literary theories. In order to facilitate the discussion that follows, some examples of the poetry composed during the last six years of his life are presented below:

> *Occasional Poem*
> My head is white but I've yet to achieve a single thing;
> When tired I throw away my books – when full I go for a stroll.
> Only as old age approaches do I realize I should thoroughly
>   study the *Pen-ts'ao*,[70]
> With added leisure, I have begun to enjoy the works of T'ao
>   Yüan-ming.
> I will buy my eastern neighbor's stream for the price of a whole
>   village,
> In the western quarter, thickets will grow all around my house.
> If only [Po] Le-t'ien were my neighbor,
> I could borrow his song clappers to accompany the oriole's
>   song.[71]

This seven-character regulated verse poem (*lü-shih*) is selected from *T'ao-yüan yung*, a one-*chüan* collection written in 1604. The next example is a

seven-character abbreviated regulated verse poem (*chüeh-chü*) written on
his thirty-eighth birthday:

> *The Year I-ssu (1605): My Birthday*
> A natural affinity I have with white boulders and green mountains.
> When the moon is high, I comb my hair;
> When the sun is high, I sleep.
> Nothing achieved, I feel ashamed in the eyes of Confucius.[72]
> For I am now two years short of forty.[73]

At about the age of thirty-eight not only did Yüan Hung-tao's literary
views undergo a transformation, his personal philosophy and personality
changed dramatically as well. He became humbler and less assertive.
When he was young he used to say: 'A phoenix should not stay with
common birds in one nest,'[74] or: 'Besides Yüan Chung-lang, all the world
is a butt for laughter.'[75] But now he wrote: 'Those who study the *Tao* [the
way of living] should conceal their talents and not show off their capa-
bilities.'[76] In the poetry composed in his early days, he often portrayed
himself as a fighter, a hero, or even a genius. Now, as a middle-aged man,
he seemed to realize the limits of his own abilities. His earlier confident
and euphoric tone is no longer found in the works written a few years
before his death. Instead, a certain gentle melancholy permeates his
poetry.

Leisure (*hsien*) tinged with sadness is the major theme of the poetry
composed in his last years. Yüan Hung-tao, once the active leader of the
Kung-an school and challenger of the prevailing orthodox trend, was no
longer fighting for any causes. If freedom was what Yüan Hung-tao
pursued in his early thirties, then in his later years a mind at peace was all
that he truly desired. The following two poems further evidence this
point:

> *In a Boat on the Lu River Responding to a Parting Poem by*
> *Hsiao-hsiu*
> I would like to find a hide-away place,
> But fear servant-boys will look for me on the road.
> Could a fish fear the watery expanse?
> Or a bird dread the mountain's depth?
> Autumn leaves redden the frost-covered temple,
> Spring shoots turn the bamboo grove purple.
> I feel like a released parrot,
> Harboring no longing for his cage.[77]

This five-character regulated verse poem (*lü-shih*) is one of a set of ten
poems written in 1608. The next example is selected from *Hua-sung yu-*

ts'ao, a two-*chüan* collection written one year before Yüan Hung-tao's death.

> *Improvised while on the Road*
> When I become bored with books,
> My mood always leads me to leisure.
> I wake from dreams with nothing to do,
> Except to gaze at West Mountain.[78]

Yüan Hung-tao considered *tan*, mildness of taste, to be a literary quality that could not be fabricated. Nevertheless, there does not seem to be much mildness in his poetry written before 1604; thereafter, however, mildness can not only be perceived in the language that he used, but also in the emotions that he expressed. His sentiments were no longer revealed as easily and as directly as they once were. His bold and uninhibited character gradually faded and the twilight of his life was surely approaching.

Yüan Hung-tao never realized that poetry was already an exhausted genre or that it was no longer the most expressive genre in Ming literature. Ku Yen-wu (1613–82) stated in his *Jih-chih lu*: 'The literary form of an age, when it has been followed for a long time, no longer allows everyone to say the same things over and over again in it.'[79] Classical poetry in Ming times faced precisely this dilemma. To a certain extent, Yüan Hung-tao and the Masters of the Archaist school committed the same mistake: they all believed that the vitality of classical poetry could be revived without basically and thoroughly changing its form; they were all struggling under the shackles of traditional versification and none of them evolved a new form to set himself free. Not only is time irreversible, but the high point of a literary genre cannot be recaptured. Yüan Hung-tao's failure to realize this crucial point impeded his historical view of literature and limited his poetic achievement.

In his preface to Ts'ai Pu-hsia's poetry ('Ts'ai Pu-hsia shih-hsü'), Yüan Chung-tao wrote: 'Nowadays those who like Chung-lang's poetry forget about its faults, and those who dislike Chung-lang's poetry overlook its merits.'[80] This exactly anticipates the assessment that Yüan Hung-tao received in the Ch'ing dynasty as well as in the early twentieth century. Yüan Hung-tao's poetry was criticized by the Ch'ing critics for being too colloquial in its language and too heedless of the rules of versification. However, these very charges were regarded by the scholars in the 1930s as a distinct and unique quality of his poetry. If Yüan Hung-tao was unfairly condemned in the Ch'ing dynasty, then he was also unfairly applauded in the 1930s. In other words, Yüan Hung-tao was not as radical and destructive as the Ch'ing critics thought, nor was he as unconventional and progressive as the scholars in the 1930s believed him to be. He was, after all, a man of his age, unable to move beyond the conventions of poetry in his early years, despite his professed attempt to do so, and resigned to them, perhaps even convinced of their value, in his late years. What remains appealing and universal in his poetry transcends the immediate problems of versification and theory that he struggled with: it is the clarity of his voice and the genuine quality of his emotions and his reflections on human life.

4
THE PROSE OF YÜAN HUNG-TAO

What is *hsiao-p'in wen?*

From the late sixteenth to the early twentieth centuries Yüan Hung-tao was primarily appreciated as a major poet rather than as an essayist. Criticism throughout the Ch'ing dynasty (1644–1911) mostly concentrated on his poetic style and the influence that he had exerted on the development of late Ming poetry. His prose did not attract scholarly attention until this century when, in the 1930s, Lin Yutang and Chou Tso-jen advocated the writing of *hsiao p'in wen*, a type of short and informal essay. Since Yüan Hung-tao's prose was considered to be the model for *hsiao-p'in wen*, he began to become known as an important prose writer of the Ming period. At this time it was almost forgotten that Yüan Hung-tao had been better known as a poet.

This shift of attention from Yüan's poetry to his prose strongly reflected the interest of scholars in the 1930s. Prose, however, had not been Yüan's own primary interest; his literary theory had dealt mainly with the composition of poetry, not prose. It is ironic that more than three hundred years after his death it was his prose that re-established his literary reputation and came to be recognized by modern literary historians as the major achievement of the Kung-an school.[1] It also came to exert a strong influence on twentieth-century Chinese literature, insofar as it made late Ming prose a subject of importance to students of contemporary Chinese civilization.

Although Yüan Hung-tao's prose has been labeled *hsiao-p'in wen*, the genre has never been clearly defined. The origin of the term *hsiao-p'in* can be traced back to *Shih-shuo hsin-yü*, a collection of anecdotes written in the fifth century AD, where it refers to a condensed version of a Buddhist sutra rather than to a belletristic genre.[2] Only in the late sixteenth century did a great number of writers apply the term to short and personal essays.[3]

As Chou Tso-jen wrote in the postscript of Yü P'ing-po's *Yen-chih ts'ao, hsiao-p'in wen* was 'not merely expositive (*shuo-li*) or narrative (*hsü-shih*), but was primarily lyrical (*shu-ch'ing*).'⁴ By this he meant that *hsiao-p'in wen* had to reflect a writer's emotions or aspects of his personal life; otherwise it would be no different than historical narrative or philosophical discourse. For Chou, *hsiao-p'in wen* was not simply informative or didactic, but rather had to have some lyrical quality drawn from an author's own emotions and feelings. It was the fulfillment of this criterion that made Yüan Hung-tao's prose a typical model for *hsiao-p'in wen*.

Lin Yutang, taking a slightly different approach, considered that the distinction between *hsiao-p'in wen* and *hsüeh-li wen*, which he referred to as 'familiar essay' and 'treatise' respectively, lay in their style rather than in their content. A single subject could be presented in different ways, and a serious, formal and objective treatment of even a trivial subject was nevertheless a treatise; while a personal, familiar and subjective treatment of a solemn subject became a *hsiao-p'in wen*.⁵ As far as subject matter is concerned, *hsiao-p'in wen* provides a writer with total flexibility; anything 'as great as the universe or as tiny as a fly' (*yü-chou chih ta, ts'ang-ying chih wei*), in Lin's phrase, can be treated in this type of prose.⁶ The characteristics of *hsiao-p'in wen*, then, may be summed up by two words: individuality and freedom. The attitude of *hsiao-p'in wen* writers may be characterized as favoring the substitution of aesthetic for utilitarian standards.

Although the term *hsiao-p'in* was not applied to a literary genre until the late sixteenth century, such prose existed before the late Ming. The form that was later to be labeled *hsiao-p'in wen* had in fact reached full maturity in the T'ang and Sung dynasties. Liu Tsung-yüan's landscape essays and the personal correspondence between Su Shih and Huang T'ing-chien (1045–1105) fit the criteria of *hsiao-p'in wen* perfectly.⁷ The differences between these works and late Ming *hsiao-p'in wen*, Chou Tso-jen has pointed out, lie not in their form and content, but rather in their writers' attitude. For T'ang and Sung essayists, writing short and informal essays was considered, at best, no more than a harmless pastime and, at worst, an improper deviation from writing 'classical prose' (*ku-wen*). Their standards for essays were thus dualistic: when writing 'serious' and 'respectable' works, they used classical forms; only trivial or light-hearted subjects were written in the *hsiao-p'in* form. It was not until the late sixteenth century that the distinction between the so called 'proper' (*cheng-ching*) and 'recreational' (*hsiao-ch'ien*) prose style became blurred, and that many essayists adopted a more casual attitude toward literary conventions and became more personal in their expression.⁸

Yüan Hung-tao's prose collection includes a wide-ranging assortment

of essays: prefaces, colophons, biographies, correspondence, reminis-
cences, epitaphs, eulogies, landscape essays, anecdotes, etc. However,
based on the criteria discussed above, a great number of these works
should be excluded from *hsiao-p'in wen*. Among so many types of writing,
personal letters (*ch'ih-tu*) and landscape essays (*yu-chi*), in my opinion,
reflect Yüan Hung-tao's personality and lifestyle most profoundly. They
are the exemplary works of late Ming *hsiao-p'in wen*.

Yüan Hung-tao's personality and his letters

There are six *chüan* of personal correspondence in the forty *chüan* of
Yüan Hung-tao's complete works. These letters cover a wide range of
topics, from political issues to the trivial details of everyday life. The
recipients of these letters included his relatives, teachers, brothers, friends
and followers. These personal letters not only reflect Yüan Hung-tao's
inner personality and idiosyncrasies, but also provide us with firsthand
material on the social and political situation in late Ming times. The
letters are a valuable source for the study of Yüan Hung-tao as well as for
the study of the social and intellectual climate of late Ming China in
general.

As far as Yüan Hung-tao's poetry is concerned, there is a considerable
gap between his literary theories and his practice. His theories were much
more liberal and progressive than was the poetry that he actually composed. This gap virtually disappears in his prose, especially in his correspondence. His defiance of convention and his spirit of revolt appear
much more clearly in his letters than in his poetry. This is not only
because prose is generally a less restrictive genre than poetry, but also
because he addressed a different audience when he wrote prose. Personal
letters were often directed to an individual, while poems were frequently
written for a group of people. An author is much less likely to be concerned about the artistic quality of his writing when he believes his letters
will only be read by a long-acquainted friend, and thus he can express
himself with greater freedom.

Yüan Hung-tao was portrayed in the 1930s by Lin Yutang and Chou
Tso-jen and many of his admirers as a *ming-shih*, a Bohemian with
literary and artistic interests who disregarded conventions and social
norms and who had a deep-seated aversion for politics.

In the forty-two years of Yüan Hung-tao's life he only served for six
years in various government positions.[9] The first office that he held was
that of magistrate of Wu-hsien at the age of twenty-eight. After serving as
a local official for two years, Yüan Hung-tao was totally disillusioned by

the tediousness of his duties and the corruption of the Ming court. He
suffered a great deal, not only mentally but physically as well. He was
afflicted with a severe case of malaria for almost half a year. The *Chin-fan
chi*, a poetry and essay collection written while he was the magistrate of
Wu, is filled with his complaints about his job. In a letter to Ch'iu T'an,
Yüan Hung-tao described his duties as follows:

> The ugliness of being a magistrate is beyond description. In general,
> when I encounter a superior, I am a slave; when entertaining
> visitors, a prostitute; while managing the government treasury, I am
> merely a granary keeper; while governing the people, I am only an
> old maid.[10]

Instead of using abstract description to illustrate the pain of being a
magistrate, Yüan Hung-tao chose to use concrete analogies, such as slave
and prostitute, to dramatize what he had suffered. This technique trans-
formed an intangible feeling into a tangible reality which could be easily
shared with his readers. After living in such unbearable misery, he was of
course overwhelmed with joy when it came time to leave office.

In 1597, just after Yüan had resigned as the magistrate of Wu, he wrote
a letter to Nieh Yün-han in which he expressed his joy at leaving:

> Destroying the iron net, demolishing the bronze shackles, I walked
> out of the mountain of knives and the jungle of swords. I jumped
> into the clean and cool land of Buddha. My happiness is beyond
> description! Beyond description! A few days after I had thrown my
> official hat away, I truly felt the exhilaration of being free from a
> government post. I already have plans to wear a bamboo hat and to
> hold an oxtail, and to become a free man forever.[11]

Yüan Hung-tao does not avoid revealing his contradictory ideas. What
he means by 'wearing a bamboo hat and holding an oxtail' is that he
intends to lead a life of eremitic retirement. This passage illustrates how
happy he was to leave Wu-hsien and to live as a common person. However, after living only a few months in seclusion, in a letter to his friend
Sang Hsüeh-k'uei, Yüan Hung-tao expressed regret over his recent
resignation and pessimistically wrote: 'I am like a leaf after a frost, or like
a piece of ice in the spring time. My lofty ambition is all gone, what is left
is nothing but my skin and bones.'[12] Yüan Hung-tao's life was a struggle
between his conflicting desires to be an official on the one hand and a
recluse on the other. He was miserable while serving as the magistrate of
Wu; however, he was not really happy after he left his post. What is
unusual about Yüan Hung-tao is not his indecisiveness about his career,

but his willingness to reveal openly his deepest feelings. He did not try to find any pretext to justify what he did or how he felt. In a letter to his uncle he confessed his conflicting thoughts without any apologies or embarrassment:

> When I am lonely, I crave excitement; when in an exciting situation, I long for quietness. Human beings are probably all like that. When a monkey is at the foot of a tree, he thinks of the fruit above him, but when he gets up in the tree, he then thinks of food on the ground. Back and forth, back and forth, never ending and, oh, so agonizing.[13]

When comparing himself to the monkey, Yüan Hung-tao admitted his inconsistency and stupidity, but at the same time he indicated that this was simply a part of human nature. There was no need to be ashamed about it.

The turning point in Yüan Hung-tao's political career came in 1600. According to Shen Te-fu's *Wan-li yeh-huo pien,* the Grape Society, the literary organization of the Kung-an school, became extremely popular among the literati in the capital area during 1599 and 1600. This group of intellectuals gradually became disillusioned with the government, their criticism not being welcomed by the grand secretary Shen I-kuan (1531–1615).[14] Yüan Hung-tao witnessed this development and became more cautious, and was reluctant to be involved in these political struggles. In the eighth month of 1600 he was granted a leave of absence for illness and returned to his home town, Kung-an, in Hupeh province. Three months later, his brother, Yüan Tsung-tao, died suddenly at the age of forty-one. Yüan Hung-tao was extremely saddened by this news, which further discouraged him from pursuing his political career. He started a six-year period of secluded life at Liu-lang (Willow Waves), a manor with a huge pond surrounded by thousands of willow trees and man-made hills.[15] In such an environment Yüan Hung-tao intentionally isolated himself from the outside world. His daily activities, according to a letter he wrote to a friend, consisted of nothing more than reading sutras, burning incense and writing poems.[16]

During the period from 1600 to 1606 Yüan Hung-tao enjoyed a peaceful, idyllic life at Liu-lang, and his attitude toward politics underwent a transformation. When he had just left Wu-hsien, he wrote, in a letter to Wu Hua: 'There are three most unpleasant things in the world; however, the fall of a dynasty and the obliteration of family are not included.'[17] He could not have cared less about the well-being of the dynasty or his family, much less about committing himself to government

service. After six years of living in seclusion, Yüan Hung-tao's aversion
for, and caution about, politics diminished, and the loneliness of isolation
became unbearable. In a letter to T'ao Wang-ling he expressed discontent
with his secluded life:

> I have been living in the mountains and have not seen extraordinary
> men for a long time. I constantly think about my old friends. Green
> mountains and white rocks, delicate flowers and beautiful arrow
> bamboo can only appeal to men's eyes; they do not understand
> human language. Snow-white teeth and lovely eyebrows do speak
> human language, but do not comprehend human thought. I have
> not lingered here long, yet already I am bored with the seclusion.[18]

Yüan Hung-tao never denied that he pursued sensual pleasure, but
neither was he ever completely satisfied with beautiful scenery and
women. It was this kind of dissatisfaction that made him keep wavering
between being an official and being an eremite. Yüan Hung-tao's capri-
cious character in the pursuit of his career has been interpreted by many
modern scholars as being indicative of both his strong desire for freedom
and of his carefree attitude toward worldly pursuits. This might be an
overinterpretation of a simple psychological condition. As Yüan Hung-
tao himself explained, what made him bored with seclusion was simply
the lack of variety in pastoral life. It reminded him of one who has eaten
vegetables for too long and desires to eat meat.[19]

The root of his unhappiness, as he himself indicated, lay in his desire
for fame. In a letter to a friend, Yüan Hung-tao wrote:

> Generally speaking, it is easy for people to resign an official post,
> but it is difficult to get rid of the desire for fame. If one is freed from
> an official post but still attached to fame, one's longing for fame is
> no different from one's longing for an official position. To be
> fettered by the desire for fame is the same as to be fettered by an
> official post. How could I be truly happy?[20]

It could not have been easy for him to admit that his unhappiness was
actually caused by his longing for fame. Here we see him offering an
honest assessment of his complex personality. He even confessed that he
was an opportunist and that there was no profound philosophical basis
for his self-contradictory attitude concerning the choice between holding
an official position and seclusion. In a letter to Su Wei-lin, written in
1606, Yüan Hung-tao wrote:

> Am I one who considers those who live in seclusion superior to
> others? An interest in getting some advantage from a pavilion or a

lake [i.e. beautiful scenery] is what makes me good-for-nothing. If I consider a recluse superior to others, then my eyes are no better than a pair of black beans [i.e. extremely shortsighted].[21]

This kind of self-mockery and self-analysis is the true spirit of self-expression. One might laugh at him for his ambivalent opinion about seclusion, but the sincerity behind this capriciousness cannot be doubted.

After six years of living in seclusion Yüan Hung-tao finally realized that if the entire world was in turmoil, a recluse would not be able to enjoy peace alone. A recluse, after all, still lived in this world, and there was no real escape for him.[22] It was this realization that ended Yüan Hung-tao's life of seclusion and made him search for an official post again, in 1606.

The vitality of Yüan Hung-tao's letters comes from his willingness to expose his innermost self and to share his most private experiences with his readers. He had no desire to conceal any part of himself from his friends. What we perceive in his letters, then, is a true-to-life portrait of Yüan Hung-tao, painted with a remarkable psychological and intellectual sensitivity. In a letter to Shen Yen, written in 1605, Yüan Hung-tao limned this self-portrait:

> I am a useless and laughable person, like an old tree root in the mountains, intertwined and bulky. It can neither be made into beams nor be constructed into utensils. It is so ugly that it cannot be treated as a decorative toy. If someone tries to move it, it is ridiculously heavy; only with ten thousand oxen can it be moved. However, there are refined people with extraordinary insights and interests who would appreciate its ancient and plain look and would take it to a mountain retreat and use it as a decoration.[23]

Yüan Hung-tao once grouped people into four categories: 'those who disdain worldly affairs' (*wan-shih*), 'those who transcend worldly affairs' (*ch'u-shih*), 'those who conform to worldly affairs' (*hsieh-shih*) and 'those who are carefree about worldly affairs' (*shih-shih*). He praised 'those who are carefree about worldly affairs' most highly and considered himself a member of this group. In his definition this type of person was neither a Buddhist nor a Confucian. He did not have special skills to make a living and was totally useless in, and harmless to, the world. So the *shih-shih* type of person is always despised by the worthy.[24] Yüan Hung-tao's self-portrait matches this *shih-shih* type perfectly. Yüan never wrote an autobiography or diary, but his letters fully compensate for the lack of such records.

Yüan Hung-tao's philosophy of life was basically hedonistic. Anything

that brought pleasure to life, as far as he was concerned, was morally
sound. His criteria for the quality of life were quite materialistic. He
contended that when a man reached the age of thirty, he should have
'extra money in his pocket, extra food in his granary,' and he should 'live
in a luxurious mansion, drink fine wines and eat meat.' If a man was not
able to afford these luxuries by the age of thirty, Yüan Hung-tao wrote,
'he should feel ashamed.'[25] Given such a philosophical outlook, Yüan
Hung-tao was naturally quite obsessed with the pursuit of sensual
pleasure, and this was fully reflected in his lifestyle. In a letter to his uncle
Kung Chung-ch'ing, written in 1595, he discussed the 'five true happinesses' in life, none of which derived from the fulfillment of responsibilities and hard work. Most were the result of self-indulgence in such
sensual pleasures as food, sex and music:

> One should experience all colors with one's eyes, all sounds with
> one's ears, all delicacies with one's body, and interesting conver-
> sations with one's mouth. This is the first happiness.
>
> In front of the hall, there are cauldrons; in the back, music. All
> the tables are filled with guests, men and women mingling in a room
> filled with the smell of candles. Jewelry is scattered everywhere.
> When the money has run out, one must sell off lands to continue
> this [party]. This is the second happiness.
>
> With ten thousand books in the bookcases, all of them rare, and a
> studio next to the house, a gathering of ten and some really good
> friends is held. In the middle of this group stands a person with
> extraordinary insights like Ssu-ma Ch'ien, Lo Kuan-chung
> [c. 1330–1400] or Kuan Han-ch'ing [d. 1279] acting as a leader. The
> group is divided into several units and each of them will write a
> book, either to criticize the shallowness of pedantic Confucian
> scholars of the T'ang and Sung or to finish a great work of the
> current era. This is the third happiness.
>
> One purchases a boat with a thousand taels of gold. A music
> band, several concubines and idlers come with the boat. Living in
> such a floating house, one does not even realize that one is getting
> old. This is the fourth happiness.
>
> Living so lavishly, within ten years one will exhaust one's re-
> sources and live a miserable life, which will not allow one even to
> plan for the immediate future. So one becomes a beggar, asking for
> food in bars and prostitute houses, sharing dishes with the lonely
> and the old, shamelessly depending on one's relatives. This is the
> fifth happiness. If an intellectual is able to enjoy one of the five

happinesses described above, he will have no regrets while alive and will endure after death.[26]

Apart from the third item, which can be considered an intellectual pursuit, the other four are simply lavish self-indulgences. Although Yüan Hung-tao never went to such extremes, he devoted a great deal of time to such hobbies as traveling and flower arrangement. He believed hobbies (*p'i*) were essential to the cultivation of one's personality. A person without a hobby, in Yüan's opinion, was distasteful and repugnant. This is precisely the philosophical basis behind his 'P'ing-shih' ('Notes on Vase-Flower Arrangement') and 'Shang-cheng' ('Rules of Drinking'), two pamphlets that articulate Yüan Hung-tao's concept of *p'i*. As he defined *p'i*, it was more an obsession than a hobby. In the 'Note on Vase Flower Arrangement,' he gave an example to illustrate what he meant by *p'i*:

> I have observed that all the people in the world who have no taste in repartee and whose countenance is resentful are people without hobbies. If they really had a hobby, they would immerse themselves in it. Their hobbies would be their life. How, then, would they have time for such matters as money, servants, officials and business?
>
> When those among the ancients whose hobby was flowers heard others chatting about some unusual specimens, although the flowers grew in deep valleys or on peaks, in their pursuit of them they would never fear tumbling [down into valleys] or falling [off precipices]. Even in the dead of winter and at the height of summer, when their skins were wrinkled like the scales on fish and their sweat was as dirty as mud, they would be oblivious to all. When the flowers were about to bloom, they would then pack up their pillows and, carrying their quilts, would sleep next to the flowers. They would observe the flower from its first budding to its full bloom, to the time when it falls and dies on the ground. Only then would they leave.
>
> Some of them would grow thousands upon thousands of specimens in order to learn every single aspect of their development; some of them would focus upon several varieties in order to satiate their interest. Some of them, by smelling the leaves, could then know the size of the flower, and some of them, by looking at the stem, could distinguish between the hues of red and white. These people can be called true connoisseurs of flowers; and they are the true hobbyists.[27]

It is clear that what Yüan Hung-tao meant by *p'i* was not simply a hobby or pastime, but actually the focus of one's life. He used the word *chi* (to reside) synonymously with *p'i*. He contended that one must have something to consign oneself to emotionally; only then could one be truly happy. Chess, sex, some special skill, and writing were the four activities that he suggested as hobbies or pastimes. If one could not find anything to concentrate on, in Yüan Hung-tao's opinion, one would be living in a 'hell.'[28] We may conclude then that *p'i* or *chi* was viewed by Yüan Hung-tao as essential to the achievement of human happiness.

What Yüan Hung-tao stated in the 'P'ing-shih' is true. If one had a hobby and was totally obsessed by it, one would have no time and energy to engage in the struggles for fame and power. However, this attitude is really centered on one's own interest. As long as one's desire for this hobby is fulfilled, nothing in the world matters anymore. Such an attitude must result in a lack of commitment to one's responsibilities, to one's family and to society. This attitude is clearly expressed in the following letter:

> I heard that Ts'ao I-hsin died at a young age; how sad! . . . He had no sons, so after his death there was nothing to worry about. This is the happiest thing in the world. However, he had one daughter. This is still a hindrance [to achieving true happiness]. What is good about sons and daughters? They are burdens when one gets old. One cannot even die in peace. Formerly, when I passed Mount Pai, I saw numerous people praying for sons, and I could not help feeling sorry for them. I also followed them and asked a monk to pray for me. What I told him was that I had enough sons and that my only desire was to have a couple of sterile, short-lived concubines.[29]

Yüan Hung-tao's perspective on marriage and the family was neither Confucian nor Buddhist. He enjoyed sex and female companionship, but tried to evade the consequences thereof. What was unique about his personality was not his irresponsibility toward his family, but his frank and unabashed confession of it. Not until he was forty did he refrain from intercourse with women, and this came about owing to his concern for his health. In the last two years of his life, Yüan Hung-tao's health rapidly deteriorated, and he could no longer continue the pursuit of sensual pleasure. As a result he became more content with (or at least resigned to) a simple and routine life.[30]

His sense of humor, a distinctive feature of Yüan Hung-tao's personality, is fully revealed in his correspondence. He not only makes fun of himself, but also of his friends. This letter to Wang Chih-teng is filled with teasing, personal innuendos presented in a light-hearted comic manner:

I heard, Mr Wang, that you now eat even more, and can still make
love to young girls who later bear sons. Though old, I can imagine
how vigorous you are! Not even forty, I am already decrepit; when I
heard of your deeds, I was very envious. Perhaps you have some
secret technique. If not, you must be deceiving me.[31]

With a touch of humor Yüan Hung-tao turned a rather private matter
into a very enjoyable moment for the reader. This short paragraph reveals
the personalities of Yüan and Wang as well as the close relationship
between them. Like an artist's profile, it characterizes a person in a most
economical way.

In a letter to T'ao Wang-ling, Yüan Hung-tao compares himself to
other members of the Grape Society by drawing analogies between their
personalities and the nature of medicines:

I know that members of our society are making great progress. I
think you are all like ginseng and licorice, which are the purest of all
medicines. As for myself, I am croton and rhubarb. When people
feel stuffed full, I can somehow relieve them.[32]

Croton and rhubarb were believed to be the most effective herbs for the
relief of constipation. Yüan Hung-tao's metaphor can also be extended to
explain how his views on literature differed from those of his fellow
society members, for Yüan Hung-tao believed that his theories could
have a cathartic effect on those who were 'stuffed' with archaic
expressions.

Yüan Hung-tao suffered from malaria for almost six months in 1596.
In a letter to a friend, Wu Hua, he joked about his illness:

I have been suffering from malaria, and I do not live like a human
being any more. Once I suddenly felt as if I had been put into a
freezing cellar, and then suddenly I was melting in the extreme heat.
I experienced the southern volcano and the northern ice country in
a single day. There are many ways for Heaven to punish the people
of the earth. Why must it be malaria?[33]

Although Yüan Hung-tao almost died during this severe attack of
malaria, he was still able to write in a lighthearted manner about his
affliction. His sense of humor, on the one hand, makes his suffering vivid
to us; on the other hand, however, it seems to have made the malaria less
disagreeable for him. It was this kind of carefree attitude that enabled him
to make the best out of a disastrous situation and to find some way to
please himself in his misery.

In a letter to Wang Lo, Yüan Hung-tao made some rather amusing observations about self-discipline:

> Recently I have begun to study . . . However, since by nature I have no patience, before finishing one volume, I have already summoned a feeble horse and urged several youngsters to go on an outing with me. Whenever we encountered beautiful mountains and lakes, we would stay there all day. Upon our return I would then feel guilty. Being so stubborn and silly, what could I ever achieve? Therefore I assigned a young maid to keep an eye on me. Whenever I appeared tired in the study, she was authorized to scold me or to tug at my ears, or to knock my head, or to scratch my nose. She had to have a way to awaken me in a hurry. If the maid did not follow my instructions, she was punished.[34]

A sense of humor was a quality unique to late Ming's *hsiao-p'in wen* in general and to Yüan Hung-tao's essays in particular. It was this quality that provided Yüan Hung-tao's correspondence with a magnetic and appealing power.

Although leisure (*hsien-shih*) was one of the major themes in his poetry, his interest in it was never so vividly conveyed as in his letters. The following passage affords a good example of his attitude toward leisure and a carefree lifestyle:

> The recent discussions with my uncles about Zen [Ch'an Buddhism] were especially delightful. If you have a cent (*fen*), enjoy a cent. If you have a dime (*ch'ien*) enjoy a dime. There is no need to plan for your future prosperity. I am living here content with my own lot, and I take great delight in it. If I had the slightest desire to repay my debts, to enrich my family and to buy fine clothes and jewelry, then how could I be so carefree? It is especially unnecessary to buy land and houses. If I am allowed to retire in future years, all that I desire would be to have one *mu* of land and three thatched cottages in Pai-hsia [Nanking]; with these I would be most satisfied. I will leave a few *mu* of land at home to my wife and sons so that they can make a living. I will not bother her and, likewise, she should not bother me. Life is as simple as that. What is the use of worrying?[35]

Yüan Hung-tao's language in this letter is simple and straightforward. There are very few allusions and archaic expressions in his correspondence; the ambiguities possible in classical Chinese rhetoric have been minimized. His letters are powerfully clear, and this results in part from his command of colloquial language. Some sentences in the letter quoted above are almost as colloquial as contemporary vernacular, for example 'If you have a cent, enjoy a cent. If you have a dime, enjoy a dime' (*Yu i-fan, le i-fan; yu i-ch'ien, le i-ch'ien*) and 'I will not bother her and, likewise, she should not bother me' (*Wo pu-kuan ta, ta i chao kuan pu-te wo yeh*). As far as diction is concerned, the informal and conversational style of Yüan Hung-tao's letters faithfully echoes his own theories about writing prose.

In 1597, after he had resigned his post of magistrate of Wu-hsien, Yüan Hung-tao wrote a letter to Huang Lan-fang (*chin-shih*, 1592) describing how happy he was. His language was not only colloquial but vulgar as well:

> This illness [i.e. malaria] almost made me a ghost of Wu-hsien. Fortunately, my request for resignation was granted. Heaven really took pity on me . . . After I had left my post, I felt like a huge fish who had jumped into a great pond . . . Not only did I regret accepting the magistrate's post, but I also wondered why on earth I should go through the toil and trouble of pursuing those bloody *chü-jen* and *chin-shih* degrees (*niao chü-jen chin-shih*), when I could sit peacefully at home.[36]

The word *niao* (literally 'bird,' which here is pronounced *tiao* and means the male genitals) is so vulgar it is almost never found in conventional classical writing.

Chu Tung-jun wrote in his *Chung-kuo wen-hsüeh p'i-p'ing shih ta-kang* (*An Outline History of Chinese Literary Criticism*) that after the mid-sixteenth century, diatribe (*man-ma*) was commonplace and later became a vogue in literary criticism.[37] Yüan Hung-tao's letters clearly reflect this practice. In a letter to Chang Hsien-i, Yüan Hung-tao criticized those writers who did not have their own ideas and who plagiarized ancient works. He wrote:

> [Plagiarizing ancient works] is like chewing dung to find some residual good, like catching a fart in one's open mouth . . . Remembering old and stale stories is called erudition, and those who can use hackneyed expressions are called poets.[38]

It is not unusual to find this sort of vulgarity in Yüan Hung-tao's letters. Yet in a letter to Kuan Chih-ning he contrasted himself with the 'common people,' and made it clear that he was not to be compared with such vulgar people in any way:

> As for the common people, they are shortsighted and blind; their opinions are no better than those who discuss the sun and moon

from inside a vat, or those who comment on the sky from inside a grave . . . If I win them over, it is the same as if I had defeated a cricket. And if I let them take advantage of me, it is like throwing a piece of bone to the ants. How can a dignified man dispute with these people?³⁹

To consider oneself far better than other people is another way to deliver a diatribe. Even though this conceited manner mellowed a great deal in his later years, his adversarial spirit can still be sensed in his letters.

The crude expressions in Yüan Hung-tao's letters not only reflect his personality but also illustrate how deeply he was influenced by contemporary spoken language. He used colloquial expression much more successfully in his prose than in his poetry. However, not all of Yüan Hung-tao's letters were written in this informal style or peppered with so many colloquial expressions. His complete works also contain very refined letters replete with allusions and parallel sentences or phrases. Such letters were often written to his superiors. For example, in a letter responding to Inspector-General Chien Ta,⁴⁰ he almost exclusively used the four–six character parallel form; but this was by no means his typical epistolary style.

In the second preface to Yüan Hung-tao's *Chieh-t'o chi*, Chiang Ying-k'o voiced the following opinion about Yüan's letters:

> As for his letters, every phrase and every word expresses what [Yüan Hung-tao] intended to say. They are written in a casual and straightforward manner . . . Chung-lang's [Hung-tao's] letters vary in length, from scores to hundreds of words. Each flowed from his genuine emotion and reflected a real situation. He exposed his lungs and liver [i.e. his innermost thoughts and feelings] to the people. Thus everyone was moved when reading his letters.⁴¹

Chiang Ying-k'o wrote later in the same preface that Yüan Hung-tao's letters were created by virtue of his courage (*tan*), insight (*shih*) and talent (*ts'ai*), and that anybody who does not possess these three characteristics should not imitate his style. This passage nicely summarizes the characteristics of Yüan Hung-tao's letters, and how his epistolary style related to his personality.

Yüan Hung-tao's letters truly reflect the man. They reflect neither Ch'in and Han, nor T'ang and Sung styles; they reflect the style of the late Ming if anything. They are, in the final analysis, the work of the individual: they could have been written by no one else but Yüan Hung-tao.

Yüan Hung-tao's love of nature and his landscape essays

In China journeying to the 'mountains and streams' (*shan-shui*) has always been regarded as a purgative. Such a journey could, it was held, cleanse someone who had been 'contaminated' through the tedium of bureaucratic life. However, this association of cleansing with traveling was never so strong as it was in the late Ming period. Men of letters craved the intellectual purity epitomized in the lifestyle of a mountain recluse (*shan-jen*),[42] a person considered to be pure and of refined taste. Trips to scenic spots provided late Ming writers with opportunities to meet with friends as well as with inspiration for literary creation. Because of these symbolic and practical considerations, journeying to mountains and lakes became for Yüan Hung-tao an irresistible urge.

In his 'records of travels' (*yu-chi*) Yüan Hung-tao reveals his passionate love for nature, to the extent that landscape is viewed in his essays as an animate creature rather than as an inanimate object. He loved nature, but did not revere it. In 'A Record of a Trip to Mount Hui' ('Yu Hui-shan chi') he clearly expresses this sentiment:

> I am by nature a casual and carefree person; I cannot put up with any kind of bondage. Unfortunately, I share a hobby [i.e. the hobby of traveling] with Tung-p'o [Su Shih] and Pan-shan [Wang An-shih] [1021–86]. Whenever I stay indoors for one day, I feel as if I am sitting on a hot stove. Therefore even on frosty, dark nights, when I have numerous things to do, my mind is always with my friends in the hills and lakes.[43]

In a farewell poem to Fang Tzu-kung (?–1609) Yüan expressed his fondness for nature even more emphatically:

> I would rather be a slave of the West Lake
> than the master of the Wu Palace.
> When I die, I should be buried here,
> and my grave will be soaked in fragrance.[44]

This poem was written directly after Yüan Hung-tao had resigned the post of magistrate of Wu, and the phrase 'the master of the Wu Palace' refers to this post. He regarded his passion for nature as an essential trait that distinguished a man of refinement and culture (*ya-jen*) from a common person (*su-jen*). His trips to the mountains reinforced his belief that he himself was indeed a man of refinement and culture.

Even though Yüan Hung-tao had resigned several times from official posts, he in fact had little interest in becoming a real mountain recluse or of separating himself off altogether from human civilization. He wanted rather to derive pleasure from nature, while at the same time enjoying the advantages of living in a civilized society. Trips into the mountains were a solution to this dilemma; and he justified his conflicting desires by saying that 'those who truly know the zither play it without strings, those who truly know [the enjoyment of] hills and water do not have to reside on a cliff and drink from a stream.'[45]

While he was not able to enjoy both nature and civilization at the same time, he nevertheless found a substitute for traveling to hills and lakes in the enjoyment of cut flowers arranged in a vase (*p'ing-hua*). In the preface to his 'P'ing-shih,' a short work about flower arrangement, he listed flowers and bamboo along with hills and streams as four types of pleasure that could be had without becoming involved in the struggle for fame and power. He recalled his intense desire to climb mountains and visit lakes at a time when he was fettered by official duties and unable to do so. In such a situation, he discovered 'vase-flowers' and found in this pastime a way to quench his thirst for natural scenery.[46] If the enjoyment of flowers in a vase could substitute for trips to remote mountains and lakes, then clearly Yüan Hung-tao did not find natural beauty something mysterious or awesome; rather, it was always accessible and could be enjoyed anytime. It was a simple source of pleasure and happiness. This was basically a sensualist's attitude, and it informs Yüan Hung-tao's landscape essays.[47] This attitude is perhaps most clearly seen when Hung-tao compares a natural scene to a woman. 'Hu-ch'iu [Tiger Hill],' he wrote in an essay entitled 'Shang-fang,' 'is like a seductive woman with heavy make-up.'[48] This kind of simile appears frequently in Yüan's landscape essays, and it suggests that he was seduced rather than awed by natural beauty.

Yüan Hung-tao's love of nature was limited to what might be called 'refined wilderness.' His favorite scenes were either natural sites with human touches (e.g. the West Lake in Hangchow[49] and mountains with Buddhist temples),[50] or delicate scenes (e.g. 'Hu-ch'iu,' a small mountain near Soochow,[51] and 'Man-ching,' a scenic spot near Peking).[52] He had little love for real wilderness; among all his travel diaries, there is not a single essay describing a deserted precipitous mountain, a torrential river, or a pathless forest. This, of course, is because Yüan Hung-tao spent most of his life south of the Yangtze, where there was in the sixteenth century little 'wild' terrain. However, in 1609, when he had to administer a local examination in Shensi province, he made several trips to Mounts Sung and Hua. Nevertheless, hardly any of the trips made during his stay in this plateau province can be considered 'adventurous' or 'dangerous.'

Yüan Hung-tao never intended to conquer nature, but rather to achieve a harmonious relationship with it. Needless to say, this was an attitude toward nature shared by many Chinese literati. However, in Yüan Hung-tao's travel diaries, this attitude is especially tinged with personal and sensual color.

Although Yüan Hung-tao was not attracted by the wilderness, he was not particularly fond of pastoral scenes either. His landscape essays never included such scenes as a field with ripened rice, or a pond with an old fisherman, or a young boy riding on a water buffalo. He appreciated 'beautiful but useless,' scenes of little practical value in human life.

Yüan Hung-tao's aesthetic and sensual appreciation of nature is further evidenced by his fondness for gardens. In his travel diaries there are several essays in which he expresses delight at the exquisite arrangement of pavilions, man-made ponds and artificial hills.[53] These gardens, though beautiful, were hardly natural creations.

In 1600 he resigned from his official post in Peking and returned to his home town Kung-an. He built a huge garden on three hundred *mu* of land and planted thousands of willows. He called the place 'Waves of Willows' (Liu-lang)[54] and spent six years of the most contented period of his life in this artificial 'natural' environment, though eventually the seclusion came to bore him.

Since the pursuit of sensual pleasure was Yüan Hung-tao's principal concern in the travel diaries, his landscape essays sometimes read more like records of exquisitely pleasurable moments than descriptions of natural scenery. In one of his most frequently quoted and translated essays, 'Hu-ch'iu' ('Tiger Hill'), Yüan pays very little attention to the actual location, nor does he describe in detail the geographic features of the place. Instead he focused on a mid-autumn festival held in Soochow, describing in minute detail the singing and other events of the festival.[55] Such urban activities rarely appear in landscape essays written prior to Yüan Hung-tao. He extended the artistic subject matter of travel diaries or records, so that the genre was no longer exclusively devoted to descriptions of landscape.

Many of Yüan Hung-tao's travel diaries are more like expository essays in which the description of scenery is clearly not the focus of his writings. He used these travel diaries to express his ideas on various subjects. For example, his essay 'Ku-shan,' or 'Mount Ku,' does not contain a single reference to the location or appearance of this mountain. The entire essay concerns itself with Yüan Hung-tao's bias against marriage:

The recluse of Mount Ku treated plum trees as his wives and cranes as his sons. He was the most privileged person in the world. By having wives and sons, we simply entangle ourselves in numerous trivial matters. We cannot desert them, and yet we are tired of being close to them. It is like wearing a ragged cotton coat and walking through a field of thorn thickets that catch you with each step.[56]

Later in the same essay Yüan Hung-tao referred to a certain Yü Seng-ju, who behaved like the recluse of Mount Ku. Yüan expressed his great admiration for these two people and concluded the essay by saying that 'each age has extraordinary men.'[57]

In Yüan's landscape essays a geographical name is often used as a vehicle for making comments on historical figures or events associated with the particular place. In 'A Record of Tiao-t'ai,' he again provided no geographical information and discussed only the deeds and personality of Yen Kuang, a recluse of the Han dynasty.[58] In the essay entitled 'Ling-yen' (a hill which reputedly was the site of Hsi-shih's palace), Yüan Hung-tao discussed this renowned beauty of antiquity and argued that the decline of a dynasty had nothing to do with the ruler's fondness for women, and therefore Hsi-shih should not have been accused of causing the fall of the kingdom of Wu.[59] To present such a conclusion in a landscape essay might seem somewhat out of place, but such digressions were both original and typical in Yüan Hung-tao's travel essays.

A disproportionate amount of detail is given to descriptions of special local products in Yüan's landscape essays. In his essay on a trip to Lung-ching (Dragon's Well), a place famous for its tea and its spring, he talked about nothing but four kinds of tea, comparing their flavors, smells and colors.[60] In an essay entitled 'Hsiang-hu' ('Lake Hsiang'), he completely ignored the scenery and concentrated on how to grow and cook water shield (*bracenia porpurea*; *ch'un-ts'ai*), an edible water plant.[61] A great interest in food recurs in Yüan's landscape essays and comprises one aspect of his sensualism.

Random deviations from the set topic and a lack of objective descriptions combine to create an introspective and subjective tone in Yüan Hung-tao's landscape essays. He makes it very clear that it is 'I' viewing scenery, and it is 'I' describing whatever 'I' sees and 'I' thinks. Sometimes, the 'I' becomes so conspicuous and strong that his opinions overshadow the actual scene being perceived. In an essay entitled 'Ch'i-yün,' he spent more than half of the essay criticizing the practice of writing graffiti and inscriptions on rocks and trees in beautiful natural settings:

> The T'ien-men of Ch'i-yün is astonishingly beautiful. The only thing that vexed me was that inscribed stone tablets filled the area below

the cliff. The Hui [An-hui] people love to make inscriptions, and it
is a bad habit. Local officials helped this practice develop into a
vogue. Every piece of white rock was filled with red characters,
which made me gasp in fury. I say there are standard punishments
in the law for those who appropriate the resources of mountains
and dig mines illegally. Why is there no law prohibiting vulgar
scholars from contaminating the spirit of the mountains? Buddha
says that all evil deeds will be recompensed with evil. And this
[making inscriptions on the mountains] is just as evil as murder and
robbery and yet Buddha did not mention it. This is a flaw in the
sutras. What kind of guilt do green mountains and white rocks
have? To disfigure their faces and cut up their skin for no reason at
all. Alas! it is ever so cruel indeed![62]

In this passage Ch'i-yün is never once described – only Yüan Hung-tao's
pique is. His self-awareness makes the distinction between the observer
and the observed very clear. This, on the one hand, makes his landscape
essays very personal and sometimes lyrical; however, on the other hand,
his subjective perspective disinclined him from seeking a state of mind in
which nature and the self merge. Yüan Hung-tao's strong sense of self-
identity made it impossible for him to be absorbed into nature. He was
always the self-conscious observer of nature and never within it.

Although he commonly digressed from the topic of landscape in these
essays, they are nonetheless coherent statements. He was particularly
skilled at representing in detail a particular scene or incident. No matter
how broad or general the title of the essay might be, an intimate portrayal
of some kind appears in the text. The importance of such intimate scenes
usually eclipses the panorama of nature. In a short essay entitled 'A
Record of First Arriving at Shuang-ch'ing Hamlet in Mount T'ien-mu'
('Ch'u-chih T'ien-mu Shuang-ch'ing chuang chi'), he focused on the sound
of a stream:

It had rained for several days, making us extremely miserable. By
the time we arrived at Shuang-ch'ing hamlet, it had cleared up a
little. The hamlet is located at the foot of the mountain. The monks
there invited us to stay in the temple, where their rooms were very
refined. The stream rolling against the rocks made a sound that
could be heard throughout the night as I lay in bed. In his dream
[T'ao] Shih-k'uei thought that it was the sound of rain. He became
so disturbed that [having awakened] he could not fall asleep again.
Next morning the monks served tea and rice porridge and called
Shih-k'uei to rise. Shih-k'uei said: 'It has been raining so heavily,
how can we go back? [The only thing we can do] is to imagine our

journey while lying in bed.' A monk said: 'It has already cleared. The roar you heard was the sound of the stream, not the sound of rain.' Shih-k'uei laughed loudly and hurriedly rose and dressed. After we had drunk several cups of tea, we left together.[63]

Even though Yüan Hung-tao sometimes digresses from the ostensible subject of his landscape essay, it is because he chose to use this genre to expound his own ideas and opinions (*chieh-t'i fa-hui*). In the above example he built the essay around one detail – the sound of the stream – but gave it a general title (*ta-t'i hsiao-tso*). In both cases the title is only tangentially connected to the essay. This disparity between titles and content suggests that some titles were added later. Many of Yüan Hung-tao's landscape essays may have first been written in the form of rough notes as he traveled, something like a literary diary. Indeed, some of his landscape essays still retain their original diary form and read like hasty notes written down to aid his memory rather than as complete records of his trips. The following short essay demonstrates this characteristic:

Shih-ch'iao cliff is somewhat like the area around the T'ien-men, but its pass is a little wider. It is about twenty-five *li* away from Ch'i-yün. Because the day that we roamed Shih-ch'iao cliff was very cloudy and dark, we all brought rain gear with us. However, until the time we returned, to our surprise it did not rain. Those who went with us but turned back halfway all regretted [not having finished the entire trip].[64]

This passage seems to be a brief note prepared for future incorporation in a longer essay, but which was somehow included as a complete piece, first in the *Chieh-t'o* collection and later in his complete works. This hypothesis can be further evidenced by the style of writing in two other selections grouped within Yüan Hung-tao's travel diary. One is entitled 'Ch'ang-wu hou-chi,'[65] and the other 'Mo-hsi.'[66] These two are brief passages beginning with a date and followed by a short description of scenery or activities. These sections should be viewed as examples of Yüan Hung-tao's draft notes for his travel diaries rather than as complete essays. The existence of such a format also explains why some of his landscape essays are so short and unrelated to their titles.

Yüan Hung-tao frequently uses dialogue in his travel diaries. It is not unusual for him to write a landscape essay as conversation, examples being 'A Record of Wen-i Hall' ('Wen-i t'ang chi')[67] and 'A Record of the Three-Religion Temple in the Town of Liang' ('Liang-hsiang san-chiao ssu chi').[68] With the exception of a few narrative lines, these two essays are written as conversations between the author and another person. This kind of conversational style was Yüan Hung-tao's original approach to writing travel diaries. However, such essays suffer from a lack of overall structure. Frequent use of dialogue creates a casual and familiar tone in the essays, but at the same time flaws them.

The travelogues written in Yüan Hung-tao's early years describe the region south of the Yangtze river. This area comprises the provinces of Kiangsu, Chekiang, Hunan and Hupeh. In 1609, the year before his death, he was appointed chief examiner of Shensi province. The travelogues of this trip are included in *Hua-Sung yu-ts'ao* (*Draft Essays on a Trip to Mounts Hua and Sung*). Geographical differences between the northern region and the Yangtze area, and the maturity of Yüan Hung-tao's views on literature, led him to change his travel diaries from casual and brief notes into more ornate and descriptive essays. His attention to geographical features increased and digressions from the subject of the essay decreased.

The most obvious change in his landscape essays during his later years was the increased use of parallelism and four-character phrases, formal features which had been rather rare in his earlier works. The following passage, from 'Another Record of a Trip to Mount Hua' ('Hua-shan pieh-chi'), illustrates his increasingly refined style:

> On that day there were no clouds at all. Green cliffs and crimson trees, the setting sun and the elegant moon were all trying their utmost to please the travelers. I went to bed late at night; the moonlight that danced in through the cracks was like snow.[69]

There are eight phrases in the original Chinese version, six of which are constructed with four characters. His deliberate efforts to write a neat and parallel description are apparent.

Unlike earlier travel essays Yüan Hung-tao's works contain no didactic message. For example, two famous Sung landscape essays, 'A Record of a Trip to Mount Pao-ch'an' ('Yu Pao-ch'an shan chi') by Wang An-shih[70] and 'A Record of Mount Stone Bell' ('Shih-chung shan chi') by Su Shih[71] both instruct the reader with a moral message. Wang An-shih's essay tells the reader that only those who are able to take the risk and bear the pain of mountain-climbing can see the extraordinary beauty of a landscape from on high. Wang An-shih used this as a metaphor to conclude that in order to accomplish a great deed one must have persistence and resolution. Su Shih warns not to believe anything too readily without first personally verifying it. The attitude of both authors is clearly condescending; they are consciously preaching rather than depicting a scenic vista. We find more 'reasoning' (*li*) than passion (*ch'ing*) in these essays. In contrast, Yüan Hung-tao includes no didactic messages in his travel essays. Occasionally he may reflect on the import of ancient remains or of historical sites, but his reflections are always personal and introspective, never preceptive. The reader of these essays is struck by his passion toward nature and is not overwhelmed by intellectualized conclusions derived from observing nature.

Chiang Ying-k'o, one of Yüan Hung-tao's best friends, offered the following praise of his travel essays:

> There are thousands of landscape essays written by contemporary men of letters. In general, they are no more than descriptions of mountains, rivers, clouds, lakes, pavilions, grass, trees and ancient remains. These essays read like gazetteers. Chung-lang's [i.e. Yüan Hung-tao's] accounts of beautiful mountains and lakes describe their joy and anger, their motion and stillness in lifelike detail. It is as if, when sketching portraits, others only try to depict the superficial likeness [of a person], whereas Chung-lang describes subtle expression.[72]

In reading this comment, one is reminded of Hsü Hung-tsu (1586–1641), better known as Hsü Hsia-k'o, the great traveler and writer, who was for his first twenty-four years a contemporary of Yüan Hung-tao. Hsü Hsia-k'o's travel diaries are renowned for their minute and accurate descriptions of geography and topography. Modern geographers have testified to the accuracy of Hsü Hsia-k'o's observations.[73] Such writing is in sharp contrast to Yüan's essays. Hsü's essays are 'objective–descriptive,' while Yüan's are 'subjective–personal.' Hsü's travel, as Li Ch'i has noted, 'was more in quest of knowledge than of pleasure.'[74] In other words, his motivation was more utilitarian than sensual or aesthetic. For Yüan Hung-tao, however, each journey was not a pursuit of knowledge, but was an alternative route to self-expression. The style that Yüan developed in his landscape essays is characterized by a total amalgamation of description and reflection. From reading his travel diaries, one learns not only about the landscape he describes, but, more important, what kind of person Yüan Hung-tao was.

EPILOGUE: THE LEGACY OF THE KUNG-AN SCHOOL

The active period of the Kung-an school lasted no more than fifteen years, from 1595 to 1610. In this short period, the expressive literary trend of the late Ming enjoyed a great vogue, and a writer's ability to express his innate sensibility (*hsing-ling*) was accorded the highest literary praise. However, this vogue did not last; Yüan Hung-tao's death in 1610 was a great setback for the expressive movement. After 1610 the opinions of the Kung-an school for the most part consisted of Yüan Chung-tao's compromised opinions and his somewhat reluctant criticism of his late brother, Hung-tao. Nevertheless, the influence of the Kung-an school not only outlived the death of Yüan Hung-tao, but also survived the decline of the Ming dynasty.

After 1610 the influence of the Kung-an school can be most immediately seen in the rise of the Ching-ling school (*Ching-ling p'ai*). The Ching-ling school has often been presented as the successor to the Kung-an school. Chung Hsing (1574–1624) and T'an Yüan-ch'un (c. 1585–1637), the founders of the Ching-ling school,[1] have been regarded as followers of the three Yüan brothers. This connection can be deduced from the fact that the biographies of Chung Hsing and T'an Yüan-chun were appended to Yüan Hung-tao's biography in the *Official History of the Ming* (*Ming-shih*), instead of being entered as separate biographies.[2] The Ching-ling school did in fact rise to prominence after the decline of the Kung-an school. This does not necessarily imply that Chung and T'an inherited or continued to expound on the ideas of the Yüan brothers.

If we examine the remarks on literature found in the writings of the two founders of the Ching-ling school, and pay especially close attention to their comments on, and criticisms of, the Kung-an school, we find that their stance toward the three Yüan brothers in general, and Yüan Hung-tao in particular, was critical rather than supportive. Chung Hsing and T'an Yüan-ch'un never intended to become the heirs of the Kung-an school; on the contrary, they too were not at all satisfied with the Kung-an school's theory of literature. In the preface to his own collection, *Yin-hsiu hsüan chi*, for example, Chung Hsing remarked: 'I have heard that some gentlemen of recent times taught people to oppose antiquity and that others laughed at those who stuck to ancient ways. These gentlemen have not been honest with themselves. They have abandoned scholarship and followed the prevailing vogue.'[3] Even though Chung Hsing did not mention Yüan Hung-tao by name, his criticism was clearly aimed at the members of the Kung-an school. In a letter to Wang Chih-kung, Chung Hsing compares the influence of the Kung-an school with that of the Latter Seven Masters. He writes: 'What is the difference between learning from Yüan [Hung-tao] and Chiang [Ying-k'o] and learning from Chi-nan [Li P'an-lung] and his followers? I am afraid that the defects of learning from Yüan and Chiang are probably even more serious than those of learning from Chi-nan.'[4] His strongest language was reserved for the impact of the Kung-an school on late Ming literature: 'Today the world is filled with poetic absurdities and vulgar doggerel.'[5] His repugnance against the influence of the Kung-an school is readily apparent.

In Chung Hsing's comparison of the Archaist Masters and the Yüan brothers we find very little sympathy for the Kung-an school. He made this clear in a letter to Ts'ai Fu-i, another important member of the Ching-ling school:

> I often get angry with the famous writers of the Chia [-ching]
> [1523–66] and the Lung [-ch'ing] [1567–72] eras [i.e. the Latter
> Seven Masters]; they adopted what was most shallow, most narrow
> and most stereotyped [of the ancient works], and tried to make
> everything easy for their hands and mouths. They thought [in this
> way] they had obtained the true spirit of the ancients.[6]

In the same letter, he continued to criticize the Yüan brothers: 'Recently there have been some clever people who tried to correct the mistakes [of the Archaist Masters], saying "why must we learn from antiquity? We should write in our own way." '[7] Chung Hsing, commenting on this new approach, said: 'I cannot see any worthy points in their [the Yüan brothers'] arguments; they are merely repetitions of what Yü-ch'uan and Yü-ch'an have already said. How can this convince people?'[8]

Chung Hsing furthermore held that the Kung-an school not only promoted vulgarity in late Ming literature, but also provided unlearned opportunists with an easy shortcut to fame. He particularly disapproved of Yüan Hung-tao's casual manner of writing and never thought that spontaneity had any special merit in literary creation. For Chung Hsing, writing was a much more cautious and less spontaneous activity. He repeatedly told his followers to contemplate before writing, and recommended that they be selective about what they wrote. Learning from the poetry of the ancients became essential in his theory. In a letter to T'an Yüan-ch'un he gave his friend this very thoughtful advice: 'It is better to study thoroughly the poetry of the ancients than to criticize recklessly the poetry of contemporaries. If one reads the works of the ancients carefully, then one would have no time to criticize contemporaries.'[9] In fact, this was not just advice for T'an Yüan-ch'un, but also an attack on Yüan Hung-tao's criticism.

One of the most important works produced by Chung Hsing and T'an Yüan-ch'un was their co-edited collection, *The Source of Poetry* (*Shih-kuei*), in which they selected poems from the period of the legendary Yellow Emperor (Huang-ti) to the T'ang dynasty.[10] They commented on each poem and tried to indicate where the key words in the poem were and what its true meaning was. They believed that their comments could serve as a guide to students of poetry. In the preface to the *Shih-kuei*, Chung Hsing characterized his attitude toward the works of the past thus:

> I selected poetry of the ancients and entitled [the collection] *The Source of Poetry*. This is not to say that what I have selected is the source of ancient poetry; it seems rather that the ancients determined the source of my selection.[11]

Although Chung Hsing did not say what in fact determined his selection of poetry, he believed that the criterion that he adopted was an ancient one.[12] Such a frame of mind was quite the opposite of Yüan Hung-tao's. Yüan championed the concept that contemporary literature was not necessarily inferior to literature of the past, and that contemporary writers should have the confidence to use their own yardsticks in judging the quality of literary works. This kind of independent spirit is not evident in the *Shih-kuei*. The *Shih-kuei* has thirty-six *chüan* of T'ang poetry, but only fifteen *chüan* of poetry prior to the T'ang. It is quite obvious that T'ang poetry comprises the bulk of *Shih-kuei*, and that Chung Hsing and T'an Yüan-ch'un considered it as the source as well as the model for Ming poets. They totally ignored poetry of the Sung and Yüan dynasties.

By editing and publishing the *Shih-kuei*, Chung and T'an were attempting to redirect the expressive trends of the late Ming from colloquialism back to classicism. T'an Yüan-ch'un once pointed out that the decline of Ming poetry was caused by poets' excessive reading of contemporary works and lack of devotion to the writing of poetry in the 'ancient style' (*ku-t'i*).[13] Even though he did not explain what he meant by 'ancient style,' his dissatisfaction with the current trend initiated by the Kung-an school is quite apparent.

As was mentioned in Chapter 2, *ch'ü* was for Yüan Hung-tao one of the most important criteria in judging the quality of literature. Since *ch'ü* is such a subtle and intangible term, it was very easy for writers to use this label to justify the merit of thier own trivial and ephemeral works. In the preface to a collection of Su Shih's selected prose, Chung Hsing pointed out that the significance of *ch'ü* was overemphasized and abused by the Kung-an school:

> Recently there have been many people who selected Su Tung-p'o's prose; however, they did not concern themselves with what is basic and what is secondary. They heedlessly founded their criticism on one word, that is *ch'ü* . . . Even a person with Li Wen-ling's [Li Chih's] insight could not avoid committing this mistake, not to mention those who are less [insightful] than Li Wen-ling.[14]

Since Li Chih and Yüan Hung-tao had edited and commented on Su Shih's works, 'those who are less [insightful] than Li Wen-ling' obviously refers to Yüan Hung-tao.[15]

Chung Hsing witnessed the decline of the Archaist and Kung-an schools, and saw the theoretical defects of both schools. He intended to establish a new theoretical basis for literary criticism which would neither result in plagiarism nor end up in praising vulgarity and shallowness. Therefore, on the one hand, he stressed the importance of individual 'innate sensibility,' and, on the other hand, he did not ignore the significance of 'profundity' (*hou*). In a letter to Kao Hai-chih, Chung Hsing explains the relationship between these two essential elements in poetry: 'Poetry that reaches profundity achieves perfection. However, since antiquity, there has never been anyone lacking a sensitive mind who has been able to write poetry. Profundity derives from sensibility, but sensibility is not necessarily profundity.'[16] The Kung-an school, Chung Hsing believed, had sensibility without profundity.

According to Chung Hsing's literary theory, to achieve a poetic balance between sensibility and profundity was the ultimate poetic accomplishment. However, he never achieved such a balance in his own works. Chung Hsing so feared being criticized as shallow and unlearned that he avoided using any colloquial expressions in his poetry; at the same time, he was aware that simply adopting archaic expressions would not add profundity to his works. Faced with this dilemma, he tried to reach his own literary ideal by using rare words and unusual sentence structures. He once wrote in a poem that 'It is better to be awkward and strange than familiar and hackneyed.'[17] This comment best illustrates his attitude toward writing in general. However, the result of this practice was that his poetry and prose were extremely unnatural and awkward. He failed to achieve either sensibility or profundity. As Ch'ien Ch'ien-i noted in his *Lieh-ch'ao shih-chi hsiao-chuan*, Chung Hsing's and T'an Yüan-ch'un's poetry was a combination of obscurity and vulgarity and their efforts in correcting the errors of the Archaist and Kung-an schools only exacerbated the deterioration of Ming poetry.[18] Ch'ien's criticism of the Ching-ling school was much more severe than his criticism of the Kung-an school, and this resulted in a very different treatment of the two schools.

In his biography of Yüan Hung-tao, Ch'ien Ch'ien-i recorded some of the dialogues he had had with Chung-tao. These not only reveal Ch'ien's different attitudes towards the Kung-an and Ching-ling schools, but also make clear how Yüan Chung-tao felt about Chung and T'an. The conversation starts with Chung-tao's criticism of Chung's and T'an's selection and editing of T'ang poetry. Chung-tao said to Ch'ien Ch'ien-i:

> Tu Fu's 'Ch'iu-hsing,' Po Chü-i's 'Ch'ang-hen ko,' and Yüan Chen's 'Lien-ch'ang kung tz'u' are incomparable masterpieces of ancient times and [part of the] vital essence of literature. What do people from Ch'u [Hupeh] know about this? They audaciously edited and commented on [these works]. You and I should openly criticize this, and point out a right path which will prevent young people from falling into clouds and mist.[19]

The 'people from Ch'u,' in this passage, refers to Chung and T'an, and Chung-tao's criticism focuses on their compilation, the *T'ang-shih kuei*.

Ch'ien Ch'ien-i concluded Chung-tao's biography with contemptuous remarks about the Ching-ling school: 'Critics of today downgrade the Kung-an [school] to the same level as that of the Ching-ling [school]; what a mistake that is!'[20] Evidently, in Ch'ien Ch'ien-i's mind, the Kung-an and Ching-ling schools were two markedly different schools, and the former had a far better claim to recognition than the latter. Moreover, Yüan Chung-tao, the last survivor of the Kung-an school, was not at all pleased with Chung's and T'an's criticism, and was reluctant to recognize the Ching-ling school as the successor of the Kung-an school.

During the formative stage of the Ching-ling school, Chung and T'an actually did consider themselves similar to the three Yüan brothers, and the personal relationship between Yüan Chung-tao and Chung Hsing seems to have been congenial.[21] However, as the Ching-ling school's influence grew stronger, Chung and T'an had less interest in fostering this kinship with the Kung-an school, and the gap between the two schools widened.

Although Ch'ien Ch'ien-i criticized Yüan Hung-tao for initiating a vulgar and shallow style in Ming poetry, Ch'ien credited him for his independent mind and praised his achievement in curbing the influence of the prevailing imitative approach to poetry.[22] As for Chung Hsing and T'an Yüan-ch'un, Ch'ien did not praise them in any respect. Ch'ien even called Chung and T'an 'poetic devils' (*shih-yao*), and said that their poetry was filled with a 'ghostly flavor' (*kuei-ch'ü*) and a 'martial atmosphere' (*ping-hsiang*).[23] As Kuo Shao-yü has pointed, Ch'ien's criticism might not be very fair because he discredited Chung's and T'an's theoretical achievements on the basis of defects in the authors' literary works.[24] Chung's and T'an's literary criticism was indeed superior to their actual works. However, as far as literary development is concerned, the rise of the Ching-ling school was a great setback to the further advancement of the expressive trends in the late Ming. The spirit of freedom and spontaneity was totally absent from Chung's and Tan's literary criticism and works. In trying so hard to find the 'true spirit' in the poetry of the ancients, they forgot that it was more important to embody the poet's own spirit in poetry. One of Yüan Hung-tao's major contributions to literary theory was to stress the poet's emotions as the principal element in literary writing. The criticism of Chung and T'an no longer gave priority to the poet's emotions. On the basis of what has been discussed above, the emergence of the Ching-ling school might better be viewed as a reaction to the excesses of the Kung-an school than as a continuation of the expressive trend in late Ming poetry.

During the Ch'ing dynasty, there was a great revival of classicism in literature, to the extent that the expressive trend of the late Ming was completely obscured. In addition, the Ch'ing government deliberately tried to minimize the influence of the Kung-an school: the works of the three Yüan brothers were included in the *Index Expurgatorius of the Ch'ing Dynasty* (*Ch'ing-tai chin-hui shu-mu ssu-chung*),[25] and the achievements of the Kung-an school were negatively evaluated in the *Ssu-k'u ch'üan-shu tsung-mu t'i-yao*.[26] Thus it is clear that during the Ch'ing dynasty a number of factors joined to forestall or obviate any further development of the trend of self-expression. The names of the three Yüan brothers were hardly even mentioned in the works of Ch'ing writers. Although such writers as Chin Sheng-t'an (1608–61)[27] and Yüan Mei (1716–98)[28] shared Kung-an ideas to a large extent, not one of them identified himself with the three Yüan brothers. Furthermore, during the Ch'ing dynasty, expressive theories of literature were expounded only by isolated individuals and such ideas never developed into influential schools of thought or into literary trends.

It appears at first glance that Kung-an theory was completely over-shadowed by classicism in the Ch'ing period, and that it almost disappeared for more than two centuries. In reality, however, the influence of the Kung-an tradition never died out. The complete works of Yüan Hung-tao were published twice during the latter half of the Ch'ing dynasty, first in 1829,[29] and then in 1869.[30] As Yüan Chao stated in the preface to *The Collected Anecdotes of Yüan Hung-tao* (*Yüan Shih-kung i-shih lu*), a two-volume appendix to the 1869 edition of Yüan Hung-tao's complete works, Yüan Hung-tao's books were still in great demand in the mid-nineteenth century.[31] However, it was not until the eve of the most momentous change in the history of Chinese literature – the beginning of the vernacular movement – that the Kung-an school began to make its presence felt once again.

A great positive response to the ideas of the Kung-an school came three hundred years after Yüan Hung-tao's death.[32] In fact, Chou Tso-jen believed that the vernacular movement of the early twentieth century was rooted in the Kung-an tradition, and that the literary ideas of Hu Shih (1891–1962), the leader of the vernacular movement, were merely a modern version of Yüan Hung-tao's theory. In the *Origins of the New Chinese Literature*, Chou Tso-jen describes Kung-an theory in the following manner:

> Their [the three Yüan brothers'] opinions on literature are very simple; they are similar to those of Mr Hu Shih. The only difference is that in the sixteenth century, Matteo Ricci [1552–1610] had not yet come to China, and there was an absence of Western thought. If we eliminate the Western influence including science, philosophy, literature, and many other aspects of thought from Mr Hu Shih's ideas, [what remains] are the ideas of the Kung-an school.[33]

Throughout this book, Chou Tso-jen continually reiterates one theme: 'The basic direction of our contemporary literary movement is exactly identical to that of the late Ming movement.'[34] Chou did not, however, further explain what elements in Hu Shih's theory he considered to be the result of Western influence, or what the 'basic direction' of these movements actually was. Therefore his statements can easily mislead one to believe that the literary movement in late Ming times was vernacular in nature, and that Hu Shih's theory was directly inspired by the Kung-an school.

This misconception should be corrected on two counts. First, no matter

how similar the theories of the Yüan brothers and those of Hu Shih might
be, the late Ming literary movement was by no means a vernacular
movement. Even though the Yüan brothers did argue that literary
writings should, to a certain extent, reflect the spoken language, they had
no intention whatsoever of abandoning the classical language altogether.
The Kung-an literary movement was basically a movement concerned
with poetry. The goal of the Yüan brothers was to revitalize classical
poetry, which was being stifled by lackluster imitation of the ancient
works. They believed that this revitalization could be achieved through a
more individualistic and expressive approach, and without a fundamental
change in the form of language. The modern literary movement also
concentrated on the poetic reforms at the formative stage, but Hu Shih
never intended to prolong the life of classical poetry. Hu repeatedly
asserted that the classical language was dead and its poetry exhausted,
and that the vernacular language was not only suitable for writing prose,
but was also appropriate for the composition of poetry.[35] In his diary of
1915 Hu Shih proposed that the idea that 'writing poetry was as if [we
were] writing prose' (*tso-shih ju tso-wen*) was the first step in the literary
reform.[36] In Hu Shih's theory, as well as in his works, we see a total
obliteration of the gap between the diction of poetry and prose. Kung-an
theory never went so far in this respect.

Second, the similarities between the theories of the Yüan brothers and
Hu do not allow us to conclude that Hu Shih's ideas were directly inspired by the three Yüan brothers. Yüan Hung-tao's name was mentioned only once in Hu Shih's pre-1935 works – in his diary of 1916,
where he quoted two forged poems attributed to Yüan Hung-tao from
Tseng I's *Chung-kuo wen-hsüeh shih* (*A History of Chinese Literature*) and
expressed his appreciation of these two poems.[37] Nineteen years later, in
1935, Hu Shih confessed in the introduction to his *Chung-kuo hsin wen-
hsüeh ta-hsi* (*Collected Works of Chinese New Literature*) that he had not
read the works of the three Yüan brothers before 1917.[38] There is no
reason to suspect Hu's confession, because at the initial stage of the
literary reform, Hu Shih was very eager to find literary evidence to
support his own arguments. Furthermore, Hu was greatly pleased to
discover previous literary views which were similar to his own.[39] If he had
known of the existence of the Kung-an school's literary theories, it seems
unlikely that he would have concealed this knowledge. It would not be
too far-fetched to surmise that if Hu Shih had indeed been influenced by
the Kung-an school, the influence may have come indirectly through
Yüan Mei, a well-known literary critic of the eighteenth century. Hu Shih
discussed Yüan Mei's literary theories at length in his diary while he was a

student in America.[40] On various other occasions Hu Shih also indicated that, in 1914 and 1915, he was only interested in discussing poetry with his friends. At that time he never dreamed that their discussions would trigger off an unprecedented literary movement in China. Hu Shih used the expression *pi-shang Liang-shan* (literally, 'one is driven to join the Liang-shan rebels', i.e. 'one is forced to go to extremities') to illustrate how incognizant he was of initiating the movement.[41]

On the basis of the evidence that I have found so far, the theoretical similarities between Yüan Hung-tao and Hu Shih can only be regarded as a historical coincidence. They were not the result of deliberate imitation.

The underlying theme shared by both the literary theories of the Kung-an school and of Hu Shih is an emphasis on the gradual evolution of Chinese literature. Their theories insist that literature is a reflection of an era and thus literary forms and styles must change with time. In 1922 Hu Shih summed up his own literary theory in one sentence: 'Hu Shih's attitude toward literature, from the beginning to the end, has always been a historical–evolutionary point of view.'[42] This notion originated from his maxim, 'Do not emulate the ancients,' one of the 'Eight Points' in 'My Tentative Suggestions of Literary Reform,' the manifesto of the verna-cular movement, published in 1917.[43] This idea was later developed into an article entitled 'On the Historical Concept of Literature' ('Li-shih ti wen-hsüeh kuan-nien lun'). There he succinctly states: 'The ancients have created ancient literature and modern people should create modern literature.'[44]

Hu Shih was extremely proud of his 'historical concept of literature' and considered it to be his most effective argument in the debate against the classical orthodox tradition. He used the metaphor of 'a pair of new glasses' to explain this approach: 'This new conception of the develop-ment of Chinese literature,' he writes, 'opens a new literary vista which has not been seen before.'[45] Hu Shih even drew an analogy between the impact of his discovery of the vernacular tradition and Nicolaus Coper-nicus' (1473–1543) discovery of the heliocentric theory which changed 'the positions of heaven and earth.'

In 1935 Hu Shih attributed his conception of literature as an evolving entity to the influence of Darwin's evolutionism.[46] Nevertheless, this concept, as I pointed out in Chapter 2 in the section on Yüan Hung-tao's literary theory, is, historically, quite Chinese.

The true significance of Yüan Hung-tao's literary theory lies precisely in this coincidental similarity to Hu Shih's views, for it is just this kind of historical coincidence that convinces me that the trend of self-expression which originated with the Kung-an school had never ceased to develop during the past four centuries. Like a subterranean current flowing beneath the vast desert of classicism in the Ch'ing dynasty, the trend emerged like a great fountain in the early twentieth century. History has thus proven that the late Ming literary movement led by Yüan Hung-tao to some degree accurately foreshadowed the future direction of Chinese literature.

NOTES

1 The literary scene before the rise of the Kung-an school

1 For an English study on the 'eight-legged essay,' see Ching-i Tu, 'The Chinese Examination Essay: Some Literary Considerations,' *Monumenta Serica*, 31 (1974–5), pp. 393–406. For the civil examination system, see Wolfgang Franke, *The Reform and Abolition of the Traditional Chinese Examination System* (Cambridge, Mass.: Harvard University Press, 1963).

2 Huang Tsung-hsi, 'Ming-wen an hsü,' in *Ming-wen shou-tu* (Tokyo: Kyūko shoin, 1973), p. 2.

3 Wu Ch'iao, 'Ta Wan Chi-yeh shih-wen,' quoted in Liu Ta-chieh, *Chung-kuo wen-hsüeh fa-chan shih* (rpt. Taipei: Chung-hua shu-chü, 1968), p. 847.

4 This point of view is best represented in Liu Ta-chieh's essay, 'Cheng-t'ung wen-hsüeh ti shuai-wei,' in *Chung-kuo wen-hsüeh fa-chan shih*, chapter 24, 'Ming-tai ti wen-hsüeh ssu-hsiang,' pp. 845–8.

5 For example, Ho Liang-chün's *Ch'ü-lun*, Wang Shih-chen's *Ch'ü-tzao* and Shen Te-fu's *Ku-ch'ü tza-yen*. See *Chung-kuo ku-tien hsi-ch'ü lun-chu chi-ch'eng*, vol. 4, ed. Chung-kuo hsi-ch'ü yen-chiu yüan (Peking: Chung-kuo hsi-ch'ü ch'u-pan she, 1959, 10 vols.).

6 For studies on this subject, see Yang T'ien-shih, 'Wan Ming wen-hsüeh li-lun chung ti "ch'ing-chen" shuo,' *Kuang-ming jih-pao* (September 5, 1965); Lu K'an, 'Shih-lun Ming-tai wen-i li-lun chung ti "chu-ch'ing" shuo,' *Wen-hsüeh lun-chi*, 7 (April 1984), pp. 165–80; and Hua-yüan Li Mowry, 'Introduction' to her *Chinese Love Stories from Ch'ing-shih* (Hamden, Connecticut: Shoe String Press, 1983), pp. 1–35.

7 The Archaist movement during the Ming dynasty can be divided into two stages. The first stage was initiated by Li Meng-yang (1473–1529) and Ho Ching-ming (1483–1521) in the late fifteenth century, and Hsü Chen-ch'ing (1479–1511), Pien Kung (1476–1532), K'ang Hai (1475–1541), Wang Chiu-ssu (1468–1551) and Wang T'ing-hsiang (1474–1544) later joined them. These seven men of letters are generally referred to as *Ch'ien ch'i-tzu*, or the 'Former Seven Masters'. The second stage was initiated by Li P'an-lung (1514–70) and Wang Shih-chen (1526–90) supported by Hsieh Chen (1495–1575), Tsung Ch'en (1525–60), Liang Yu-yü (1522–66), Hsü Chung-hsing (1517–78) and Wu Kuo-lun (1524–93). This group is generally referred to as *Hou ch'i-tzu*, or the 'Latter Seven Masters'.

8 The three Yüan brothers are: Yüan Tsung-tao (1560–1600), Yüan Hung-tao, better known as Yüan Chung-lang (1568–1610), and Yüan Chung-tao (1570–1624).

9 This type of criticism appears in the comments by the editors of *Ssu-k'u ch'üan shu tsung-mu t'i-yao*, and in Shen Te-ch'ien's (1673–1769) *Ming-shih pieh-ts'ai*. Their criticisms will be discussed in detail in Chapters 3 and 4.

10 Among these scholars the most eminent ones and their major works are: Chou Tso-jen, *Chung-kuo hsin wen-hsüeh ti'yüan-liu* (Peking: Jen-wen shu-tien, 1934), and many essay collections; Lin Yutang, chief editor of the three popular magazines, *Lun-yü* (1932–7, 1946–9), *Jen-chien shih* (1934–5) and *Yü-chou feng* (1935–47); and Liu Ta-chieh, *Chung-kuo wen-hsüeh fa-chan shih* (Shanghai: Chung-hua shu-chü, 1941).

11 *Chung-kuo hsin wen-hsüeh ti yüan-liu* is also the title of a book published in Peking in 1934. This book consists of several lectures delivered by Chou Tso-jen at Fu-jen University in 1932. For an English study of Chou's literary theory, see David E. Pollard, *A Chinese Look at Literature: The Literary Values of Chou Tso-jen in Relation to the Tradition* (Berkeley, California: University of California Press, 1973).

12 See Li Meng-yang's official biography, in *Ming-shih* (Peking: Chung-hua, 1976), p. 7348.

13 This point of view was strongly argued in Li Meng-yang's 'Po Ho-shih lun-wen shu,' and 'Tsai yü Ho-shih shu,' in *K'ung-t'ung hsien-sheng chi* (1530; rpt. Taipei: Wei-wen, 1976), *ch.* 62, pp. 6a–10a.

14 Wang Shih-chen criticized Li Meng-yang's plagiarism and gave examples of Li's practice; see Wang Shih-chen, *I-yüan chih-yen* (Ting Fu-pao (1874–1952) chiao-k'an pen, n.p., n.d.), *ch.* 4, pp. 11a–b.

15 Li Meng-yang, 'K'o Chu-ko K'ung-ming wen-chi hsü,' in *K'ung-t'ung hsien-sheng chi*, *ch.* 49, p. 4a.

16 This line was quoted by Li Meng-yang in his 'Po Ho-shih lun-wen shu,' *K'ung-t'ung hsien-sheng chi*, *ch.* 61, p. 6a.

17 Ibid., pp. 6a–b.

18 See ibid., p. 6b.

19 Li Meng-yang, 'Chang-sheng shih-hsü,' in *K'ung-t'ung hsien-sheng chi*, *ch.* 50, p. 6b. The term *shih yen-chih* is translated according to James J. Y. Liu, *Chinese Theories of Literature* (Chicago and London: University of Chicago Press, 1975), p. 69.

20 Chou Tso-jen divided Chinese literature into two categories: (1) *shih yen-chih*, and (2) *wen i tsai-tao* (literature is a vehicle for the *Tao*). He considered *shih yen-chih* as the origin of literary expressionism in China. See Chou Tso-jen, 'Chung-kuo wen-hsüeh ti pien-ch'ien,' in *Chung-kuo hsin wen-hsüeh ti yüan-liu*, pp. 25–39. See also Liu, *Chinese Theories of Literature*, pp. 63–87.

21 Li Meng-yang, 'Lin-kung shih-hsü,' in *K'ung-t'ung hsien-sheng chi*, *ch.* 50, p. 5b.

22 This term is found in Li Meng-yang, 'Kuo-kung yao,' in *K'ung-t'ung hsien-sheng chi*, *ch.* 6, p. 3a.

23 Ibid., pp. 2b–3a.

24 Li Meng-yang's *yüeh-fu* poetry is included in *K'ung-t'ung hsien-sheng chi*, *ch.* 6 (38 poems); and *ch.* 7 (34 poems).

25 The line attributed to Confucius appears in *Han-shu* (Peking: Chung-hua, 1973), *ch.* 30, 'I-wen chih,' p. 1746.

26 Li Meng-yang, 'Shih-chi tzu-hsü,' in *K'ung-t'ung hsien-sheng chi*, *ch.* 50, pp. 2b–3a.

27 Ibid., pp. 3b–4a.
28 See Shen Te-fu, 'Shih-shang hsiao-ling,' in *Wan-li yeh-huo pien* (Peking: Chung-hua, 1959), p. 647.
29 Li Meng-yang, 'Fou-yin hsü,' in *K'ung-t'ung hsien-sheng chi, ch.* 51, pp. 4b–5a.
30 See Chu Tung-jun, 'Ho Ching-ming p'i-p'ing lun-shu p'ing,' in *Chung-kuo wen-hsüeh p'i-p'ing chia yü wen-hsüeh p'i-p'ing* (Taipei: Hsüeh-sheng, 1971, 4 vols.), vol. 2, pp. 134–5.
31 F. W. Mote, 'The Arts and the "Theorizing Mode" of the Civilization,' in Christian F. Murck (ed.), *Artists and Traditions* (Princeton: Princeton University Press, 1976), pp. 7–8.
32 See 'K'ung-t'ung chi, 66 chüan' in *Ssu-k'u ch'üan-shu tsung-mu t'i-yao* (Taipei: Shang-wu, 1971), *ch.* 171, 'chi-pu,' 24, 'pieh-chi lei,' 24.
33 See Ch'ien Ch'ien-i, 'Hsieh shan-jan Chen' in *Lieh-ch'ao shih-chi hsiao-chuan* (Shanghai: Ku-chi, 1959, 2 vols.), vol. 2, p. 424.
34 Li Meng-yang discussed these ideas in the two letters he wrote to Ho Ching-ming. See 'Po Ho-shih lun-wen shu' and 'Tsai yü Ho-shih shu,' in *K'ung-t'ung hsien-sheng chi, ch.* 61, pp. 6a–10a.
35 Hsieh Chen, *Ssu-ming shih-hua* (Peking: Jen-min, 1962), pp. 46–7.
36 Ibid., p. 74.
37 See ibid.
38 Ibid., p. 46.
39 Ibid., p. 107.
40 Ibid., p. 47.
41 See ibid., p. 40.
42 Ibid.; pp. 66–7.
43 See Kuo Shao-yü, *Chung-kuo wen-hsüeh p'i-p'ing shih* (rpt. Taipei: Shang-wu, 1969, 3 vols.), vol. 2, pp. 200–6.
44 Wang Shih-chen, 'Wu-yüeh shan-fang wen-kao hsü,' in *Yen-chou shan-jen ssu-pu kao* (Wang-shih shih-ching t'ang k'an-pen, n.p., 1577), *ch.* 67, p. 16a.
45 Wang Shih-chen, *I-yüan chih-yen, ch.* 1, p. 8a.
46 See Ch'ien Ch'ien-i, 'Wang Shang-shu Shih-chen,' in *Lieh-ch'ao shih-chi hsiao-chuan*, pp. 436–7.
47 Wang Shih-chen, *I-yüan chih-yen, ch.* 4, p. 11a.
48 See ibid., *ch.* 5, pp. 1b–2a.
49 Ibid., *ch.* 4, p. 11b.
50 Ibid., *ch.* 7, p. 8a.
51 Wang Shih-chen, 'Ch'en Tzu-chi shih-hsüan hsü,' in *Yen-chou shan-jen hsü-kao*, rpt of Ming Ch'ung-chen edn (Taipei: Wen-hai, 1970, 18 vols.), vol. 5, *ch.* 42, p. 5a.
52 Ibid., *ch.* 4, p. 12b.
53 Wang Shih-chen (ed.), *Su Ch'ang-kung wai-chi* (Yü-chang Chü-shih Yen-shih chai k'an-pen, 1594), pp. 1a–b.
54 Liu Feng, 'Wang Feng-chou hsien-sheng Yen-chou hsü-chi hsü,' in *Yen-chou shan-jen hsü-kao*, vol. 1, p. 33. This anecdote was quoted in Wang Shih-chen's official biography, *Ming-shih* (p. 7381), and it also appeared in Ch'ien Ch'ien-i, *Lieh-ch'ao shih-chi hsiao-chuan*, p. 437.
55 Li Wei-chen, 'Wang Feng-chou hsien-sheng ch'üan-chi hsü,' in ibid., p. 25.

56 Wang Shih-chen, 'Su Ch'ang-kung wai-chi hsü,' in *Yen-chou shan-jen hsü-kao, ch.* 42, p. 14a.

57 See Matsushita Tadashi, 'En Kōdō no seireisetsu no hōga,' *Tōhōgaku,* 19 (November 1959), pp. 98–107.

58 See Li Chih, 'Ch'ien tu yü-shih T'ang-kung,' in *Hsü ts'ang shu* (Peking: Chung-hua shu-chü, 1959), pp. 440–2.

59 See ibid., p. 441.

60 This paraphrase is based on T'ang Shun-chih's 'Tung Chung-feng shih-lang wen-chi hsü,' in *Ching-ch'uan hsien-sheng wen-chi* (Taipei: Shang-wu yin-shu kuan, 1965, *Ssu-pu ts'ung-k'an* edn), *ch.* 10, pp. 207–9.

61 T'ang Shun-chih, 'Ta Mao Lu-men chih-hsien, 2,' in *Ching-ch'uan hsien-sheng wen-chi, ch.* 7, pp. 126–7.

62 Ibid.

63 T'ang Shun-chih, 'Yü Hung Fang-chou shu,' in *Ching-ch'uan hsien-sheng wen-chi, ch.* 7, p. 128.

64 For further discussion on the literary theory of T'ang Shun-chih, see Ching-i Tu, 'Neo-Confucianism and Literary Criticism in Ming China: The Case of T'ang Shun-chih (1507–60),' *Tamkang Review,* 15, nos. 1, 2, 3, 4 (Autumn 1984–Summer 1985), pp. 548–60.

65 Ch'ien Ch'ien-i, 'Hsü chi-shih Wei,' in *Lieh-ch'ao shih-chi hsiao-chuan* (Shanghai: Ku-chi ch'u-pan she, 1959), p. 562.

66 See Hsü Wei, 'Jen-tzu (1552) Wu-chin T'ang Hsien-sheng kuo K'uai-chi, lun-wen chou-chung, fu chieh chu-kung sung-chih K'o-t'ing erh pieh, fu tz'u . . .,' in *Hsü Wei chi* (Peking: Chung-hua shu-chü, 1983, 4 vols.), vol. 1, p. 66.

67 See T'ao Wang-ling, 'Hsü Wen-ch'ang chuan,' in *Hsieh-an chi* (1611 edn; rpt. Taipei: Wei-wen, 1976), *ch.* 12, pp. 62a–b. This biography is also included in *Hsü Wei chi,* vol. 4, pp. 1339–41.

68 See Hsü Wei, 'Chi-p'u,' in *Hsü Wei chi,* vol. 4, p. 1334.

69 See Yü Ch'un-hsi, 'Hsü Wen-ch'ang chi hsü,' in *Hsü Wei chi,* vol. 4, pp. 1353–4.

70 Yüan Hung-tao, 'Hsü Wen-ch'ang chuan,' in *Yüan Chung-lang ch'üan-chi* (Taipei: Shih-chieh shu-chü, 1964; cited hereafter as *Ch'üan-chi*), 'Wen-ch'ao,' p. 1.

71 See Yüan Hung-tao, 'Sun Ssu-li,' in *Ch'üan-chi,* 'Ch'ih-tu,' p. 41.

72 Yüan Hung-tao's 'Hsü Wen-ch'ang chuan' is included in *Ku-wen kuan-chih* (Shanghai: Shang-wu yin-shu kuan, 1946), *ch.* 12, pp. 302–3.

73 See Liang Jung-jo, 'Yüan Hung-tao Hsü Wen-ch'ang chuan cheng-wu,' in *Tso-chia yü tso-p'in* (Taichung: Tunghai University Press, 1971), pp. 116–19. For a more detailed study of Hsü Wei's life and works, see Liang I-ch'eng, 'Hsü Wei (1521–1593): His Life and Literary Works' (Ph.D. dissertation, Ohio State University, 1973); *Hsü Wei ti wen-hsüeh yü i-shu* (Taipei: I-wen, 1977).

74 Yüan Hung-tao, 'Ta T'ao Shih-k'uei,' in *Ch'üan-chi,* 'Ch'ih-tu,' p. 61.

75 See 'Hsü Wen-ch'ang chuan,' in the beginning of *Ch'ing-t'eng shu-wu wen-chi,* p. 6, in the ninth case of *Hai-shan hsien-kuan ts'ung-shu* (Taipei: I-wen yin-shu kuan, 1967). This biography differs slightly from the one included in *Yüan Chung-lang ch'üan-chi.*

76 Yüan Hung-tao, 'Hsü Wen-ch'ang chuan,' in *Ch'ing-t'eng shu-wu wen-chi*, p. 9.
77 Ibid.
78 Ibid., p. 12.
79 *Ssu-k'u ch'üan-shu tsung-mu t'i-yao*, 'Chi'pu', 'Pieh-chi lei', 'Ts'un-mu', no. 5, under the entry of *Hsü Wen-ch'ang chi*.
80 Hsü Wei, 'Hsiao-fu shih-hsü,' in *Hsü Wei chi*, vol. 2, p. 534.
81 These four functions of the *Book of Poetry* were enumerated by Confucius in *Analects*, 17, 9. I borrowed the translation from Liu, *Chinese Theories of Literature*, p. 109. Legge's translation is quite different: 'The *Odes* serve to stimulate the mind. They may be used for purposes of self-contemplation. They teach the art of sociability. They show how to regulate feelings of resentment' (*Chinese Classics, Confucian Analects* (Oxford: 1893; rpt, Taipei: Wen shih che ch'u-pan she, 1971), p. 323).
82 Hsü Wei, 'Ta Hsü K'ou-pei,' in *Hsü Wei chi*, vol. 2, p. 482.
83 Hsü Wei, 'Hsi-hsiang hsü,' in *Hsü Wei chi*, vol. 4, p. 1089.
84 Hsü Wei, 'Yeh Tzu-su shih hsü,' in *Hsü Wei chi*, vol. 2, p. 519.
85 Hsü Wei, 'Nan-tz'u hsü-lu,' in *Li-tai shih-shih ch'ang-pien*, series 2 (Taipei: Ting-wen, 1974), p. 243.
86 Ibid.
87 Hsü Wei wrote and edited several dramas, *Ssu-sheng yüan* being the most famous. See *Hsü Wei chi*, vol. 4, pp. 1175–1230.
88 Jokes, riddles and Buddhist chants are included in *Hsü Wen-ch'ang i-kao*, ch. 24. See *Hsü Wei chi*, vol. 3, pp. 1054–73. For the criticism, see *Ssu-k'u ch'üan-shu tsung-mu t'i-yao*, 'Chi'pu', 'Pieh-chi lei', 'Is'un-mu', no. 5, under the entry of *Hsü Wen-ch'ang i-kao*.
89 This essay is one from a group of seven, in *Hsü Wei chi*, vol. 2, pp. 491–2.
90 This essay is included in *Yüan Chung-lang ch'üan-chi*, 'Wen-ch'ao,' pp. 6–7.
91 See Ku Yen-wu, 'Li Chih,' in *Jih-chih lu* (Taipei: Ming-lun ch'u-pan she, 1970), p. 540.
92 See Wang Fu-chih, 'Hsü-lun no. 3,' 'Tu T'ung-chien lun,' in *Ch'uan-shan ch'üan-chi* (Taipei: Li-hsing shu chü, 1965, 16 vols.), vol. 11, p. 8538.
93 Examples of Yüan Hung-tao's praise and admiration for Li Chih can be found in *Yüan Chung-lang ch'üan-chi*. Yüan often referred to Li as Lao-tzu, one of the greatest philosophers of the pre-Ch'in period. For example, see *Ch'üan-chi*, 'Shih-chi,' p. 211.
94 See T'ang Hsien-tsu, 'Li shih ch'üan-shu tsung-hsü,' in *Li Chih yen-chiu ts'an-k'ao tzu-liao* (Fukien: Jen-min ch'u-pan she, 1975, 3 vols.), vol. 2, pp. 109–10; and 'Ta Kuan Tung-ming,' in *T'ang Hsien-tzu shih-wen chi* (Shanghai: Ku-chi ch'u-pan she, 1979, 2 vols.), vol. 2, p. 1229.
95 Ch'ien Ch'ien-i, 'T'ao Chung-p'u Tun Yüan chi hsü,' in *Ch'ü-hsüeh chi* (Shanghai: Shang-wu, n.d., *Ssu-pu ts'ung-k'an* edn), ch. 31, p. 337.
96 The term *t'ung-hsin* has been translated as 'infant's mind' in K.C. Hsiao, 'Biography of Li Chih,' in Carrington Goodrich and Chaoying Fang (eds.), *Dictionary of Ming Biography (1368–1644)* (New York: Columbia University Press, 1976), p. 811. My translation is borrowed from Liu, *Chinese Theories of Literature*, p. 78.
97 For detailed bibliographies of works on Li Chih, see Theodore de Bary,

'Individualism and Humanitarianism in Late Ming Thought,' note 159, in Theodore de Bary (ed.), *Self and Society in Ming Thought* (New York: Columbia University Press, 1970) pp. 236–8; and Hok-lam Chan (ed.), *Li Chih (1527–1602)* in *Contemporary Chinese Historiography: New Light on His Life and Works* (White Plains, New York: M. E. Sharpe, 1980), pp. 183–207.

98 This paraphrase is based on Li Chih, 'T'ung-hsin shuo,' in *Fen-shu* (Taipei: Ho-lo t'u-shu ch'u-pan she, 1974), pp. 97–9.

99 Ibid., p. 98.

100 Li Chih, 'Tsa-shuo,' in *Fen-shu*, pp. 96–7.

101 Li Chih, 'Ssu-ma T'an, Ssu-ma Ch'ien,' in *Ts'ang-shu* (Peking: Chung-hua, 1959, 4 vols.), vol. 3, *ch.* 40, p. 692.

102 Li Chih, 'Tu-lü fu-shuo,' in *Fen-shu*, p. 133.

103 Li Chih, 'Tsa-shuo,' in *Fen-shu*, p. 96.

104 Ibid.

105 Ibid.

106 Li Chih, 'Shih-wen hou-hsü,' in *Fen-shu*, p. 117.

107 Li Chih, 'T'ung-hsin shuo,' in *Fen-shu*, p. 98.

108 Li Chih, 'Tsa-shou,' in *Fen-shu*, p. 96.

109 Li Chih, 'Pai yüeh,' in *Fen-shu*, p. 196.

110 Li Chih, 'Hung-fo,' in *Fen-shu*, p. 196.

111 Li Chih, 'Ta Teng Ming-fu,' in *Fen-shu*, pp. 36–8.

112 Li Chih, 'Ta Keng Ssu-k'ou,' in *Fen-shu*, pp. 30–1.

113 Ibid.

114 Hu Shih had doubts about the authenticity of Li Chih's commentary and preface to *Shui-hu chuan*. He argued inconclusively that they were forgeries. See Hu Shih, 'Pai erh-shih hui pen Chung-i Shui-hu chuan hsü,' in *Hu Shih wen-ts'un* (Taipei: Yüan-tung t'u-shu kung-ssu, 1968, 4 vols.), vol. 3, p. 421. However, more recent scholarship has proved otherwise. See Wang Li-chi's, 'Shui-hu Li Cho-wu p'ing pen ti chen-wei wen-t'i,' *Wen-hsüeh p'ing-lun ts'ung-k'an*, 2 (Peking, 1979), pp. 365–81. See also Min Tse, 'Kuan-yü Shui-hu chuan ti p'ing-lun ho p'ing-tien,' in his *Chung-kuo wen-hsüeh li-lun p'i-p'ing shih* (Peking: Jen-min wen-hsüeh ch'u-pan she, 1981, 2 vols.), vol. 2, pp. 717–27. For more references on Li Chih's commentary on *Shui-hu chuan*, see Hok-lam Chan, 'Li Chih's Extant Writings,' in Hok-lam Chan (ed.), *Li Chih (1527–1602)* in *Contemporary Chinese Historiography: New Light on His Life and Works*, pp. 180–1.

115 Li Chih, 'Chung-i Shui-hu chuan hsü,' in *Fen-shu*, p. 108.

116 Ibid., p. 109.

117 For a detailed study, see Min Tse, 'Kuan-yü Shui-hu chuan ti p'ing-lun ho p'ing-tien.' See also Ch'en Chin-chao, *Li Chih chih wen-lun* (Taipei: Chia-hsing shui-ni kung-ssu, 1974), pp. 74–102.

2 The literary theories of the three Yüan brothers

1 For a more detailed study of the Grape Society, see Hung Ming-shui, 'Yüan Hung-tao and the Late Ming Literary and Intellectual Movement' (Ph.D. dissertation, University of Wisconsin, 1974), pp. 148–52; and Liang Jung-

jo, 'P'u-t'ao she yü Kung-an p'ai,' *Ch'un wen- hsüeh yüeh-k'an* 6, 1 (1970), pp. 16–24; rpt. in Liang Jung-jo, *Tso-chia yü tso-p'in* (Taichung: Tunghai University Press, 1971), pp. 105–15.

2   For Yüan Tsung-tao's biographical background, see Yüan Chung-tao, 'Shih-p'u hsien-sheng chuan,' in *K'o-hsüeh chai ch'ien-chi* (Hsin-an edn, 1618; rpt. Taipei: Wei-wen, 1976), *ch.* 16, pp. 7a–12b. This biography is also included in *K'o-hsüeh chai chin-chi* (Shanghai: Chung-yang, 1936; rpt. Shanghai: Shang-hai shu-tien, 1982), *ch.* 2, pp. 44–9.

3   Ibid., pp. 7a–b (1618 edn); p. 47 (1936 edn).

4   Yüan Chung-tao, 'Li-pu yen-feng ssu lang-chuang Chung-lang hsien-sheng hsing-chuang,' in *K'o-hsüeh chai ch'ien-chi, ch.* 17, p. 22b.

5   Ch'ien Ch'ien-i, 'Yüan Shu-tzu Tsung-tao,' in *Lieh-ch'ao shih-chi hsiao-chuan*, p. 566.

6   Yüan Tsung-tao, 'Lun-wen,' in *Po Su chai lei-chi* (Ming edn, n. d., with Yao Shih-lin's preface; rpt. Taipei: Wei-wen, 1976), *ch.* 20, pp. 1a–b. The words ascribed to Confucius are to be found in *Analects*, 15, 40. Wing-tsit Chan translates the line: 'In words all that matters is to express the meaning.' See his *A Source Book in Chinese Philosophy* (Princeton: Princeton University Press, 1963), p. 44.

7   See Yüan Tsung-tao, 'Lun-wen,' p. 1b.

8   Ibid., pp. 1b–2a.

9   Ibid.

10   Ibid., pp. 2b–3a.

11   Yüan Hung-tao, 'Tseng P'an Ching-sheng,' in *Ch'üan-chi*, 'Shih-chi,' p. 17.

12   Yüan Hung-tao, 'Hsü Tseng T'ai-shih chi,' in *Ch'üan-chi*, 'Wen-ch'ao,' p. 11.

13   Yüan Hung-tao, 'Hsing-su yüan ts'un-kao yin,' in *Ch'üan-chi*, 'Wen-ch'ao,' p. 16.

14   See Yüan Hung-tao, 'Hsüeh-t'ao ko chi hsü,' in *Ch'üan-chi*, 'Wen-ch'ao,' pp. 6–7.

15   Yüan Tsung-tao, 'Ta T'ao Shih-k'uei,' in *Po Su chai lei-chi, ch.* 16, p. 21b.

16   See Ch'ien Ch'ien-i, *Lieh-ch'ao shih-chi hsiao-chuan*, pp. 567–8; and Shen Te-ch'ien, *Ming-shih pieh-ts'ai* (Shanghai: Shang-wu, 1933), *ch.* 10, p. 68.

17   Cf. Jonathan Chaves, 'The Panoply of Image: A Reconsideration of the Literary Theory of the Kung-an School,' in Susan Bush and Christian Murck (eds.), *Theories of the Arts in China* (Princeton: Princeton University Press, 1983), pp. 341–64.

18   Yüan Tsung-tao, 'Lun-wen,' in *Po Su chai lei-chi, ch.* 20, pp. 2a–b. In making this translation, I have consulted Chaves', 'The Panoply of Image,' p. 343.

19   See Sung P'ei-wei, *Ming wen-hsüeh shih* (Shanghai: Shang-wu, 1934), pp. 157–62; and Liu Ta-chieh, *Chung-kuo wen-hsüeh fa-chan shih*, pp. 857–65.

20   Yüan Tsung-tao used this line as the title of an article in *Po Su chai lei-chi, ch.* 7, pp. 15b–18a.

21   See Yüang Tsung-tao, 'Lun-wen,' part 2, in *Po Su chai lei-chi, ch.* 20, pp. 3a–5a.

22   Ibid., pp. 4b–5a.

23   Ibid.

24 This kind of criticism can be seen in *Ssu-k'u ch'üan-shu tsung-mu t'i-yao, ch.* 179, 'chi-pu,' 32, 'pieh-chi tsung-mu,' 6, under the entry for *Yüan Chung-lang chi* (40 *ch.*), which states: 'The Seven Masters still rooted themselves in scholarship, while the three Yüan [brothers] relied totally on their wits.'
25 See Shen Te-ch'ien, *Ming-shih pieh-ts'ai, ch.* 10, p. 68.
26 For a detailed description of Yüan Tsung-tao's fondness for Po Chü-i and Su Shih, see Yüan Chung-tao, 'Po Su chai chi,' in *K'o-hsüeh chai ch'ien-chi, ch.* 11, pp. 11a–13b.
27 Yüan Tsung-tao, 'Chi san-ti,' in *Po Su chai lei-chi, ch.* 16, pp. 15b–21a.
28 Po Chü-i, 'Yü Yüan chiu shu,' in *Po Chü-i chi* (Peking: Chung-hua shu-chü, 1979, 4 vols.), vol. 3, p. 962. Arthur Waley translates this line as follows: 'The duty of literature is to be of service to the writer's generation; that of poetry to influence public affairs' (*The Life and Times of Po Chü-i* (London: George Allen and Unwin, 1949), p. 110).
29 Po Chü-i, 'Hsin yüeh-fu hsü,' in *Po Chü-i chi*, vol. 1, p. 52.
30 My paraphrase of this legendary story is based on Hu Shih's citation from *Mo-k'o hui-hsi*, in *Pai-hua wen-hsüeh shih* (Taipei: Hu Shih chi-nien kuan, 1969), p. 386.
31 Po Chü-i, 'Hsin yüeh-fu hsü,' in *Po Chü-i chi*, vol. 1, p. 52.
32 The most often cited biographies of Yüan Hung-tao are: (1) Yüan Chung-tao, 'Li-pu yen-feng ssu lang-chung Chung-lang hsien-sheng hsing-chuang,' in *K'o-hsüeh chai ch'ien-chi, ch.* 17, pp. 19a–34a. This is the earliest biography of Yüan Hung-tao; the following two biographies have relied heavily on this one. (2) Yüan Hung-tao's biography in *Ming-shih* (Peking: Chung-hua shu-chü, 1974), pp. 7397–8. (3) Chou Ch'eng-pi, 'The Biography of Yüan Hung-tao,' in Chou Ch'eng-pi (ed.), *Kung-an hsien chih* (first published 1887; rpt. Taipei: Hsüeh-sheng shu-tien, 1969, 3 vols.), vol. 2, *ch.* 6, pp. 19a–23b.
33 Yüan Chung-tao, 'Shu Fang-p'ing ti ts'ang Shen-hsüan chü-shih chüan mo,' in *K'o-hsüeh chai ch'ien-chi, ch.* 20, p. 28b.
34 Yüan Hung-tao, 'Ta Li Yüan-shan,' in *Ch'üan-chi,* 'Ch'ih-tu,' p. 44. For the year of this letter, see Ch'ien Po-ch'eng (ed.), *Yüan Hung-tao chi chien-chiao* (Shanghai: Ku-chi ch'u-pan she, 1981, 3 vols.), vol. 2, p. 764. Cited hereafter as *Chien-chiao.*
35 Yüan Hung-tao, 'Hsüeh-t'ao ko chi hsü,' in *Ch'üan-chi,* 'Wen-ch'ao,' p. 6.
36 Yüan Hung-tao, 'Chiang Chin-chih,' in *Ch'üan-chi,* 'Ch'ih-tu,' p. 37.
37 Ibid.
38 Yüan Hung-tao, 'Hsü Hsiao-hsiu shih,' in *Ch'üan-chi,* 'Wen-ch'ao,' pp. 5–6.
39 Yüan Hung-tao, 'Ta Chang Tung-a,' in *Ch'üan-chi,* 'Ch'ih-tu,' p. 43.
40 This point is well-argued in Chaves' 'The Panoply of Images,' pp. 351–2.
41 Yüan Hung-tao, 'Hsü Chu-lin chi,' in *Ch'üan-chi,* 'Wen-ch'ao,' p. 9.
42 Yüan Hung-tao, 'Ch'iu Ch'ang-ju,' in *Ch'üan-chi,* 'Ch'ih-tu,' pp. 19–20.
43 Ibid., p. 20. 'Tying knots for records' (*chieh sheng*) and observing 'birds tracks' (*niao-chi*) are believed to be the primitive means for recording before the invention of characters. See Hsü Shen (*c.* 58–147), 'Shuo-wen chieh-tzu hsü,' in *Shuo-wen chieh-tzu* (Taipei: I-wen yin-shu kuan, 1965), p. 761.
44 Yüan Hung-tao, 'Chang Yu-yü,' in *Ch'üan-chi,* 'Ch'ih-tu,' p. 34.
45 Yüan Hung-tao, 'Yü Li Lung-hu,' in *Ch'üan-chi,* 'Ch'ih-tu,' p. 42.

46 Yüan Hung-tao, 'Ta Mei K'o-sheng K'ai-fu,' in *Ch'üan-chi*, 'Ch'ih-tu,' pp. 37–8.
47 Yüan Hung-tao, 'Hsüeh-t'ao ko chi hsü,' in *Ch'üan-chi*, 'Wen-ch'ao,' p. 7. For another translation, see Richard John Lynn, 'Tradition and the Individual: Ming and Ch'ing Views of Yüan Poetry,' *Journal of Oriental Studies*, 15, 1 (1977), p. 9.
48 See Chapter 4.
49 Yüan Hung-tao, 'Shih-wen hsü,' in *Ch'üan-chi*, 'Wen-ch'ao,' p. 10.
50 Ch'en Shou-yi commented on the eight-legged essays in his *Chinese Literature: A Historical Introduction* (New York: Ronald Press, 1961): 'The Eight-Legged Essay was destined to fall into ruts with the formalization of the titles and the freezing of rhetorical devices . . . In fact, most histories of Chinese literature had considered it below their dignity even to mention the rise and fall of the Eight-Legged Essay' (p. 508).
51 Yüan Hung-tao, 'Yü Yu-jen lun shih-wen,' in *Ch'üan-chi*, 'Ch'ih-tu,' p. 14.
52 Yüan Hung-tao, 'Hao Kung-yen shih hsü,' in *Ch'üan-chi*, 'Wen-ch'ao,' pp. 11–12.
53 See Ku Yen-wu, 'Sheng-yüan lun,' in *T'ing-lin wen-chi*, which is included in *Ku t'ing-lin i-shu shih-chung* (Taipei: Ku-t'ing shu-chü, 1969), pp. 806–7. See also Huang Tsung-hsi, 'Ch'ü-shih,' *Ming-i tai-fang lu*, p. 9, in *Li-chou i-chu hui-k'an*, vol. 2 (Taipei: Lung-yen ch'u-pan she, 1969).
54 Yüan Hung-tao, 'Hsü Hsiao-hsiu shih,' in *Ch'üan-chi*, 'Wen-ch'ao,' p. 1.
55 Liu Hsieh, 'Yüan Tao,' in Wang Li-ch'i, *Wen-hsin tiao-lung chiao-cheng* (Shanghai: Ku-chi ch'u-pan she, 1980), p. 1. Translated in Liu, *Chinese Theories of Literature*, p. 22.
56 Liu Hsieh, 'Tsung-ching,' in Wang Li-ch'i, *Wen-hsin tiao-lung chiao-cheng*, p. 11. Translated in Vincent Shih, *The Literary Mind and the Carving of Dragons* (New York: Columbia University Press, 1959), p. 17.
57 Liu Hsieh, 'Ch'ing-ts'ai,' in Wang Li-ch'i, *Wen-hsin tiao-lung chiao-cheng* p. 205. Translated in Shih, *The Literary Mind*, p. 174.
58 Chung Jung is also romanized as Chung Hung. The years indicated here follow Liu, *Chinese Theories of Literature*, p. 76. However, Chung Jung's flourished year is indicated as 504 in Ch'en Shou-yi, *Chinese Literature: A Historical Introduction*, p. 191.
59 Chung Jung, *Shih p'in chu* (Taipei: K'ai-ming shu-tien, 1958), p. 1.
60 Ibid., p. 7.
61 Yao Ssu-lien, *Liang-shu, ch.* 49, p. 727 (Peking: Chung-hua shu-chü, 1973). Quoted and translated in Liu, *Chinese Theories of Literature*, p. 77.
62 Kuo Shao-yü, *Ts'ang-lang shih-hua chiao-shih* (Peking: Jen-min wen-hsüeh ch'u-pan she, 1961), p. 26.
63 Shao Yung, 'Kuan-wu wai-p'ien,' in the *Huang-chi ching-shih shu hsü-yen* (*Ssu-pu pei-yao* edn), B, 8B, 16a; translated in Wong Siu-kit, 'Ch'ing in Chinese Literary Criticism' (unpublished doctoral dissertation, Oxford University, 1969), p. 124. Quoted in Lynn, 'Tradition and the Individual: Ming and Ch'ing Views of Yüan Poetry,' p. 3.
64 Yüan Hung-tao, 'Hsü Hsiao-hsiu shih,' in *Ch'üan-chi*, 'Wen-ch'ao,' p. 5.
65 Lin Yutang, 'Hsieh-tso ti i-shu,' in *Yü-t'ang sui-pi* (Taipei: Chih-wen ch'u-pan she, 1966), pp. 78–9.

66   Yüan Hung-tao, 'Liu Yüan-ting shih hsü,' in *Ch'üan-chi*, 'Wen-ch'ao,' p. 12.
67   Yüan Hung-tao, 'Ta Li Yüan-shan,' in *Ch'üan-chi*, 'Ch'ih-tu,' p. 44.
68   Yüan Hung-tao, 'Ch'iu Ch'ang-ju,' in *Ch'üan-chi*, 'Ch'ih-tu,' p. 19.
69   Yüan Hung-tao, 'Hsü Hsiao-hsiu shih,' in *Ch'üan-chi*, 'Wen-ch'ao,' p. 6.
70   This refers to the biography of Mencius and Hsün-tzu in *Shih-chi* ('Meng-tzu Hsün-ch'ing lieh-chuan,' in *Shih-chi* (Taipei: Shih-chieh shu-chü, 1972), *ch.* 74, pp. 2343–50).
71   Yüan Hung-tao, 'Chang Yu-yü,' in *Ch'üan-chi*, 'Ch'ih-tu,' p. 34.
72   Yüan Hung-tao, 'Ta Li Yüan-shan,' in *Ch'üan-chi*, 'Ch'ih-tu,' p. 57.
73   See *Lun-yü*, 6, 16, and 12, 8. For the English translation, see Legge (trans.), *The Chinese Classics*, vol. 1, pp. 155–6, 190.
74   The sentence *wen i tsai Tao* is found in Chou Tun-i (1017–73), *Chou Lien-hsi chi* (*Ts'ung-shu chi-ch'eng ch'u-pien* edn), *ch.* 6, p. 117. Quoted in Kuo Shao-yü, *Chung-kuo wen-hsüeh p'i-p'ing shih*, vol. 1, p. 352.
75   *Lao-tzu*, annotated by Wang Pi (Taipei: Chung-hua shu-chü, 1969), Chapter 81. Translated in D. C. Lau, *Lao Tzu: Tao Te Ching* (Baltimore, Maryland: Penguin, 1963), p. 143.
76   Yüan Hung-tao, 'Hsing-su yüan ts'un-kao yin,' in *Ch'üan'chi*, 'Wen-ch'ao,' p. 16.
77   Ibid.
78   For a study on the subject of *chen shih* (true poetry), see Iriya Yoshitaka, 'Shin shi,' in *Yoshikawa hakushi taikyū kinen chūgoku bungaku ronshū* (Tokyo: Chikuma 1968), pp. 673–81.
79   Yüan Hung-tao, 'T'ao Hsiao-jo Chen-chung i yin,' in *Ch'üan-chi*, 'Wen-ch'ao', p. 14.
80   Yüan Hung-tao, 'Hsü Hsiao-hsiu shih,' in *Chüan-chi*, 'Wen-ch'ao,' p. 6.
81   Ibid.
82   Ibid.
83   Ibid.
84   Ibid.
85   See Li Chih, 'T'ung-hsin shuo,' in *Fen-shu*, pp. 97–9.
86   Yüan Hung-tao, 'Hsing-su yüan ts'un-kao yin,' in *Chüan-chi*, 'Wen-ch'ao,' p. 16.
87   Yüan Hung-tao, 'Shan-hsi hsiang-shih lu hsü,' in *Ch'üan-chi*, 'Wen-ch'ao,' p. 26.
88   Yüan Hung-tao, 'Hsü Ssu-tzu kao,' in *Ch'üan-chi*, 'Wen-ch'ao,' p. 8.
89   Yüan Hung-tao, 'Hsü Kuo-shih chia-sheng chi,' in *Chüan-chi*, 'Wen-ch'ao,' p. 10. Ku K'ai-chih and Wu Tao-tzu are recognized as two of the greatest Chinese artists of all time.
90   Ch'ien Chung-shu, *T'an-i lu* (Shanghai: K'ai-ming shu-tien, 1942), p. 48.
91   Liu Hsieh, 'Ch'ing-ts'ai,' in Wang Li-ch'i, *Wen-hsin tiao-lung chiao-cheng*, p. 205. Translated in Shih, *The Literary Mind and the Carving of Dragons*, p. 174.
92   Lin Yutang, 'On Zest in Life,' in *The Importance of Understanding* (New York: World Publishing, 1960), p. 112.
93   Liu, *Chinese Theories of Literature*, p. 81.
94   Pollard, *A Chinese Look at Literature*, p. 80.

95 These extracts are a translation and paraphrase of Yüan Hung-tao, 'Hsü Ch'en Cheng-fu Hui-hsin chi,' in *Ch'üan-chi*, 'Wen-ch'ao,' p. 5. There are two English translations for this preface: Pollard, *A Chinese Look at Literature*, pp. 79–80; and Lin Yutang, 'On Zest in Life.'

96 Liu, *Chinese Theories of Literature*, p. 81.

97 Yüan Hung-tao, 'Shou Ts'un-chai Chang-kung ch'i-shih hsü,' in *Ch'üan-chi*, 'Wen-ch'ao,' p. 10.

98 This concept of literature was raised by Ssu-k'ung T'u in his letter discussing poetry to a certain Mr Li. Part of this letter is quoted in Kuo Shao-yü, *Chung-kuo wen-hsüeh p'i-p'ing shih*, vol. 1, pp. 295–6, translated in Liu, *Chinese Theories of Literature*, p. 103.

99 Yüan Hung-tao, 'Hsü Kuo-shih chia-sheng chi,' in *Ch'üan-chi*, 'Wen ch'ao,' p. 10.

100 Yüan Hung-tao, 'Chai-chung ou-t'i,' in *Chüan-chi*, 'Shih-chi,' p. 142.

101 See Patrick D. Hanan, 'The Text of the *Chin P'ing Mei*,' *Asia Major*, new series, 9, 1 (April 1962), p. 39; Wei Tzu-yün, 'Yüan Chung-lang yü *Chin P'ing Mei*,' *Shu han jen*, 224 (November 1973), pp. 1–8 (total pp. 1785–92).

102 Yüan Hung-tao, 'Tung Ssu-pai,' in *Ch'üan-chi*, 'Ch'ih-tu,' p. 21. The translation is a modified version of Hanan, 'The Text of the *Chin P'ing Mei*,' p. 40. Hanan translated *yün-hsia man-chih* as 'full of interest.' It is also possible that *yün-hsia* is a misprint for *yün-yü*, which is a euphemism for erotic affairs; see the preface to Sung Yü, 'Kao-t'ang fu,' in *Wen-hsüan* (Sung Ch'un-hsi (1174–89) edn; rpt. Taipei: I-wen, 1967), *ch.* 19, p. 2. Since the *Chin P'ing Mei* is noted for its vivid descriptions of love-making, reading *yün-hsia* as *yün-yü* is not far-fetched.

103 See Liu Ta-chieh, *Chung-kuo wen-hsüeh fa-chan shih*, p. 132.

104 Mei Sheng, 'Ch'i-fa,' in Hsiao T'ung (ed.), *Wen-hsüan*, *ch.* 34, pp. 2–3. Translated in Hans Frankel, *The Flowering Plum and the Palace Lady: Interpretations of Chinese Poetry* (New Haven and London: Yale University Press, 1976), pp. 188–9.

105 Ibid., p. 13. For the English translation, see Frankel, p. 202.

106 This preface was dated 1617 and was included in the *Chin P'ing Mei* (Peking: Wen-hsüeh ku-chi ch'u-pan she, 1957). This edition was designated by Sun K'ai-ti as *Chin P'ing Mei tz'u-hua* in his *Chung-kuo t'ung-su hsiao-shuo shu-mu* (revised edn. Peking: Tso-chia ch'u-pan she, 1957), pp. 116–17.

107 This preface is also included in *Chin P'ing Mei tz'u-hua*.

108 Ibid.

109 Ibid.

110 The poetry of Cheng and Wei in the *Book of Poetry* was considered erotic.

111 This postscript is also included in *Chin P'ing Mei tz'u-hua*.

112 See Hanan, 'The Text of the *Chin P'ing Mei*,' p. 3, note 10.

113 For a study on the didacticism of late Ming novels, see Patrick D. Hanan, 'The Fiction of Moral Duty: The Vernacular Story in the 1640s,' in Robert E. Hegel and Richard C. Hessney (eds.), *Expression of Self in Chinese Literature* (New York: Columbia University Press, 1985), pp. 189–213.

114 For studies of Feng Meng-lung's life, works and ideas, see Jung Chao-tsu, 'Ming Feng Meng-lung ti sheng-p'ing chi ch'i chu-shu,' *Ling-nan hsüeh-pao*, 2, 2 (1931), pp. 61–91; 'Ming Feng Meng-lung ti sheng-p'ing chi ch'i chu-

shu hsü-k'ao,' part 2, *Ling-nan hsüeh-pao*, 2, 3 (1932), pp. 95–124; and Patrick D. Hanan, 'Feng [Meng-lung's] Life and Ideas' and 'Feng's Vernacular Fiction,' in his *The Chinese Vernacular Story* (Cambridge, Mass.: Harvard University Press, 1981), pp. 75–119.

115 Feng Meng-lung (ed.), *Hsing-shih heng-yen* (Peking: Tso-chia ch'u-pan she, 1956), p. 863. This preface was dated 1627 and signed by K'o-i chü-shih from Lung-hsi.

116 The preface to Feng Meng-lung (ed.), *Ching-shih t'ung-yen* (Peking: Jen-min, 1956).

117 Shen Te-fu, *Wan-li yeh-huo pien*, p. 652. Translated in Hanan, 'The Text of the *Chin P'ing Mei*,' p. 47.

118 This expression appears twice in *Jou p'u t'uan* (1705 edn; rpt. Hong Kong: Lien-ho ch'u-pan she, n.d.), *ch.* 1, p. 5b; *ch.* 7, p. 21b. English translation by Richard Martin from the German version by Franz Kuhn (*Jou Pu Tuan* (New York: Grove Press, 1963), p. 376).

119 Yüan Hung-tao, 'Shang-cheng,' in *Ch'üan-chi*, 'Sui-pi,' pp. 22–6.

120 Ibid., p. 25.

121 Ibid.

122 See Liu Ta-chieh, *Chung-kuo wen-hsüeh fa-chan shih*, p. 864.

123 Yüan Hung-tao, 'Shang-cheng,' in *Ch'üan-chi*, 'Sui-pi,' p. 23.

124 Quoted in Yüan Tsung-tao, 'Lun-wen,' part 1, in *Po Su chai lei-chi, ch.* 20, p. 1a.

125 Ibid.

126 Yüan Hung-tao, 'Hsü Hsiao-hsiu shih,' in *Chüan-chi*, 'Wen-ch'ao,' p. 6.

127 Yüan Chung-tao, 'Sung Yüan shih hsü,' in *Hsin-an chi* (Naikaku bunko edn, n.d.), vol. 2, p. 1b.

128 This expression is derived from the 'Yüeh-chi' chapter of *Li-chi* (*Ssu-pu pei-yao* edn), *ch.* 11, p. 8b.

129 Yüan Chung-tao, 'Tan-ch'eng chi hsü,' in *K'o-hsüeh chai ch'ien-chi* (Hsin-an k'an-pen, 1618), *ch.* 10, pp. 40a–b.

130 Kuo Shao-yü, *Ts'ang-lang shih-hua chiao-shih*, p. 24. Translated in Liu, *Chinese Theories of Literature*, p. 39.

131 See Kuo Shao-yü, *Chung-kuo wen-hsüeh p'i-p'ing shih*, vol. 2, pp. 64–83.

132 Richard John Lynn, 'Orthodoxy and Enlightenment: Wang Shih-chen's Theory of Poetry and Its Antecedents,' in de Bary (ed.), *The Unfolding of Neo-Confucianism*, p. 218.

133 Yüan Chung-tao, 'Juan Chi-chih shih hsü,' in *K'o-hsüeh chai ch'ien-chi, ch.* 10, pp. 9b–10a.

134 Yüan Hung-tao, 'Chang Yu-yü,' in *Ch'üan-chi*, 'Ch'ih-tu,' p. 34.

135 Yüan Chung-tao, 'Ts'ai Pu-hsia shih hsü,' in *K'o-hsüeh chai ch'ien-chi, ch.* 10, p. 5a.

136 Yüan Chung-tao, 'Sung Yüan shih hsü,' in *Hsin-an chi*, vol. 2, p. 1a.

137 Yüan Chung-tao, 'Ts'ai Pu-hsia shih hsü,' in *K'o-hsüeh chai ch'ien-chi, ch.* 10, p. 6a.

138 Yüan Chung-tao, 'Ta Ch'iu Ch'ang-ju,' in *K'o-hsüeh chai ch'ien-chi, ch.* 10, p. 6a.

139 Yüan Chung-tao, 'Sung Yüan shih hsü,' in *Hsin-an chi*, vol. 2, p. 2a. Translated in Lynn, 'Tradition and Individual: Ming and Ch'ing Views of Yüan Poetry,' p. 8.

140 Yüan Chung-tao, 'Chieh-t'o chi hsü,' in *K'o-hsüeh chai ch'ien-chi, ch.* 9, pp. 45a–b.
141 Yüan Chung-tao, 'Chung-lang hsien-sheng ch'üan-chi hsü.' This preface is not included in *K'o-hsüeh chai chin-chi*, and *K'o-hsüeh chai ch'ien-chi*. It is found in *K'o-hsüeh chai chi-hsüan* (Wang Ts'ung-chiao k'an-pen, 1622, 24 *ch.*) For a more accessible source, see Ch'ien Po-ch'eng, *Ch'ien chiao*, pp.1711–12.
142 Yüan Chung-tao, 'Ts'ai Pu-hsia shih hsü,' in *K'o-hsüeh chai ch'ien-chi, ch.* 10, p. 5a.
143 See Yüan Chung-tao, *Yüan Hsiao-hsiu jih-chi* (Shanghai: Shang-hai tsa-chih kung-ssu, 1935), pp. 244–5. This diary was originally entitled *Yu-chü shih (fei) lu,* in *K'o-hsüeh chai wai-chi, ch.* 1–12, first published in 1618. For a detailed study on the history of Yüan Chung-tao's diary, see Shen Ch'i-wu, 'K'o-hsüeh chai wai-chi Yu-chü shih-lu,' *Jen chien shih,* 13 (July 1935), pp. 19–25.
144 Ibid.

3   The poetry of Yüan Hung-tao

1 *Ssu-k'u ch'üan-shu tsung-mu t'i-yao, ch.* 179, 'chi-pu,' 32, 'pieh-chi tsung-mu,' 6, under the entry of *Yüan Chung-lang chi* (40 *ch.*).
2 Shen Te-ch'ien, the preface to *Ming-shih pieh-ts'ai,* p. 1.
3 Ibid.
4 This poem is found in *Yüan Chung-lang ch'üan-chi* (Taipei: Shih-chieh shu-chü, 1964), 'Sui-pi', 'K'uang-yen', p. 48. For another translation, see Jonathan Chaves, *Pilgrim of the Clouds* (New York: Weatherhill, 1978), p. 50.
5 This poem is included in *K'uang-yen pieh-chi, ch.* 1, p. 9a. It is not included in *Yüan Chung-lang ch'üan-chi* (Taipei, 1964).
6 Chu I-tsun, *Ming-shih tsung* (Taipei: Shih-chieh shu-chü, 1962), *ch.* 57, p. 19.
7 Tseng-I, *Chung-kuo wen-hsüeh shih* (Shanghai: T'ai-tung t'u-shu kung-ssu, 1915), pp. 273–4.
8 Hsieh Wu-liang, *Chung-kuo ta wen-hsüeh shih* (Shanghai: Chung-hua shu chü, 1918), *ch.* 9, pp. 61–2.
9 Ch'ien Chi-po, *Ming-tai wen-hsüeh* (Shanghai: Shang-wu, 1934), pp. 97–8.
10 Sung P'ei-wei, *Ming wen-hsüeh shih* (Shanghai: Shang-wu, 1934), p. 158.
11 Chaves, *Pilgrim of the Clouds,* p. 50.
12 Ibid., p. 23.
13 Yüan Chung-tao, *Yu-chü shih lu* (*Yüan Hsiao-hsiu jih-chi*), p. 280, entry 1108.
14 See Yüan Chung-tao, *K'o-hsüeh chai chin-chi* (Shanghai: Chung-yang shu-tien, 1936), *ch.* 2, p. 191; *Yu-chü shih lu,* p. 246, entry 984.
15 In writing this paragraph, I consulted Liang Jung-jo, 'Lun i-t'o ti Yüan Hung-tao tso-p'in,' *Kuo-yü jih-pao: shu han jen,* 131 (1970), pp. 6–8 (total pp. 1038–40); rpt. in his *Tso-chia yü tso-p'in,* pp. 120–5.
16 Iriya Yoshitaka, 'Kōan san En chosakuhyō,' *Shinagaku,* 10, 1 (April 1940), pp. 174–5, 179–80.
17 Ch'ien Po-ch'eng, *Chien-chiao,* 'Fan-li,' p. 3.

18 For a detailed study on the biography of Chiang Ying-k'o, see Yüan Chung-tao 'Chiang chin-chih chuan,' in *K'o-hsüeh chai chin-chi, ch.* 3, pp. 65–7.

19 This preface is included in *Yüan Chung-lang ch'üan-chi* (24 *ch.*), (Pei-yüan shu-wu edn, 1829), p. 13.

20 Yüan Chung-tao, 'Wang T'ien-ken wen hsü,' in *K'o-hsüeh chai chin-chi, ch.* 3, pp. 41–2.

21 Yüan Hung-tao, 'Chang Yu-yü,' in *Ch'üan-chi,* 'Ch'ih-tu,' p. 34.

22 This preface is included in *Yüan Chung-lang ch'üan-chi* (1829 edn), p. 8.

23 Yüan Hung-tao, 'Ta Tseng T'ui-ju,' in *Ch'üan-chi,* 'Ch'ih-tu,' p. 76.

24 Yüan Chung-tao, 'Li-pu yen-feng ssu lang-chung Chung-lang hsien-sheng hsing-chuang,' in *K'o-hsüeh chai ch'ien-chi* (Hsin-an k'an-pen, 1618), *ch.* 17, p. 21b. For the year that Yüan Hung-tao first met Li Chih, see Yüan Chung-tao (ed), 'Cha-lin chi-t'an,' in P'an Tseng-hung (ed.), *Li Wen-ling wai-chi* (Ming edn; rpt. Taipei: Wei-wen, 1976), *ch.* 1, p. 12a.

25 Yüan Chung-tao, 'Li-pu yen-feng ssu lang-chung Chung-lang hsien-sheng hsing-chuang,' p. 22b.

26 Ibid., p. 21b.

27 Ibid., p. 21b.

28 Ibid.

29 Ibid. The translation is a modified version of David Pollard's translation in *A Chinese Look at Literature* (pp. 164–5).

30 According to the preface to Yüan Hung-tao's complete works written by Yüan Chung-tao and the record in *Yu-chü shih lu* (p. 246, entry 984), these collections were written in the following years: *Chin-fan chi* (1595–6); *Chieh-t'o chi* (1597); *Kuang-ling chi* (1597); *P'ing-hua chai chi* (1598–1600); *T'ao-yüan yung* (1604); *Hsiao-pi t'ang chi* (1601–6).

31 For a detailed description of this trip, see Yüan Hung-tao, 'Wu Tun-chih,' in *Ch'üan-chi,* 'Ch'ih-tu,' p. 33.

32 Yüan Chung-tao, 'Chung-lang hsien-sheng ch'üan-chi hsü,' in *K'o-hsüeh chai chi-hsüan* (1622 edn), p. 9. For a more accessible source, see Ch'ien Po-ch'eng, *Chien-chiao,* p. 1711.

33 Ibid.

34 Lei Ssu-p'ei, 'Hsiao-pi t'ang chi hsü,' in *Yüan Chung-lang ch'üan-chi* (1829 edn), p. 6. For a more accessible source, see Ch'ien Po-ch'eng, *Chien-chiao,* p. 1695.

35 Ibid.

36 Yüan Hung-tao, 'Ta Li Tzu-jan,' in *Ch'üan-chi,* 'Shih-chi,' p. 40.

37 Yüan Hung-tao, 'Po-hsiu,' in *Ch'üan-chi,* 'Ch'ih-tu,' p. 30.

38 Yüan Hung-tao, 'Feng Cho-an shih,' in *Ch'üan-chi,* 'Ch'ih-tu,' p. 56.

39 Yüan Hung-tao, 'Ta Ch'ien Yün-men i-hou,' in *Ch'üan-chi,* 'Ch'ih-tu,' p. 75.

40 Ma Ku is the name of a legendary beauty. For her biography, see Ko Hung, 'Ma Ku Chuan,' *Shen-hsien chuan, ch.* 7, pp. 1–2, in *Shuo-k'u* (Taipei: Hsin-hsing shu-chü, 1963, 2 vols.), vol. 1, p. 55.

41 'Goddess of the Lo' (Lo shen), a legendary beauty. See Ts'ao Chih, 'Lo shen fu,' in Hsiao T'ung (ed.), *Wen-hsüan, ch.* 19, pp. 11–19.

42 Yüan Hung-tao, 'Ts'ai lien-ko,' in *Ch'üan-chi,* 'Shih-chi,' pp. 8–9. This

poem was originally included in *Pi-ch'ieh chi*, the earliest extant collection of Yüan Hung-tao's poetry, including works composed from 1588 to 1594 (*ch.* 1, p. 8a).

43 Yüan Hung-tao, 'Heng-t'ang tu,' in *Ch'üan-chi*, 'Shih-chi,' pp. 8–9. This poem is found in *Chieh-t'o chi, ch.* 1, p. 2b. This collection was written and published in 1597.

44 See Burton Watson, *Chinese Lyricism: Shih Poetry from the Second to the Twelfth Century* (New York: Columbia University Press, 1971), p. 54.

45 See Hu Shih, *Pai-hua wen-hsüeh shih*, pp. 24–6; and Watson, *Chinese Lyricism*, pp. 52–67.

46 Yüan Hung-tao, 'Ch'ieh po-ming,' in *Ch'üan-chi*, 'Shih-chi,' p. 2. This poem was originally included in *P'ing-hua chai chi, ch.* 1, p. 8b.

47 Yüan Hung-tao, 'Ni ku yüeh-fu,' in *Ch'üan-chi*, 'Shih-chi,' p. 1.

48 Yüan Hung-tao, 'Fang-yen hsiao Yüan-t'i,' in *Ch'üan-chi*, 'Shih-chi,' p. 180. This poem was originally included in *Kuang-ling chi*, p. 19a.

49 Yüan Hung-tao, 'Huai-an chou-chung,' in *Ch'üan-chi*, 'Shih-chi,' p. 85. This poem is one from a set of four, originally included in *P'ing-hua chai chi, ch.* 1, p. 4b. For another translation, see Chaves, *Pilgrim of the Clouds*, p. 41.

50 For more discussion on Sung poetry, see Watson, *Chinese Lyricism*, pp. 197–244; and Burton Watson *Su Tung-p'o* (New York: Columbia University Press, 1965), pp. 3–16.

51 Chou Tzu-chih, *Chu-p'o shih-hua*, p. 24, in Ho Wen-huan (ed.), *Li-tai shih-hua* (Taipei: I-wen, 1971), p. 206. Quoted and translated in Watson, *Chinese Lyricism*, p. 202.

52 Hu Shih (1891–1962) suggested that the diction of Sung poetry was more colloquial than that of T'ang poetry and this, as he believed, was the major difference between the poetry of the T'ang and Sung dynasties. See Hu Shih, 'Pi-shang Liang-shan,' in his *Ssu-shih tzu-shu* (Taipei: Yüan-tung t'u-shu kung-ssu, 1982), p. 107.

53 Yüan Hung-tao, 'Tsui-hsiang t'iao-hsiao yin,' in *Ch'üan-chi*, 'Shih-chi,' p. 5. This poem was originally included in *Chieh-t'o chi, ch* 1, p. 5b.

54 Yüan Hung-tao, 'Tseng Chiang Chin-chih,' in *Ch'üan-chi*, 'Shih-chi,' p. 78.

55 See Yüan Hung-tao, 'Pu-fu yao' and 'Meng-hu hsing,' in *Ch'üan-chi*, 'Shih-chi,' pp. 5, 1.

56 Yüan Hung-tao, 'Hsien-ling kung chi chu-kung i ch'eng shih shan lin wei yün,' in *Ch'üan-chi*, 'Shih-chi,' p. 52. This poem was originally included in *P'ing-hua chai chi, ch.* 4, pp. 1b–2a. For another translation, see Hung Ming-shui, 'Yüan Hung-tao and the Late Ming Literary and Intellectual Movement' (unpublished Ph.D. dissertation, University of Wisconsin–Madison, 1974), pp. 157–8.

57 Yüan Hung-tao, 'Hao ko,' in *Ch'üan-chi*, 'Shih-chi,' p. 9. This poem was originally included in *Pi-ch'ieh chi, ch.* 2, p. 14b.

58 Feng Meng-lung compiled two collections of folk songs: *Shan-ko* (Peking: Chung-hua shu chü, 1962) and *Kua-chih-erh* (Shanghai: Sung-chu shu-tien, 1929). For a study of these folk songs, see Cheng Chen-to, 'Kua-chih-erh,' in his *Chung-kuo wen-hsüeh lun-chi* (Taipei: Ming-lun, n. d.), pp. 469–77.

59 Ch'en T'ien, 'Keng-ch'ien,' in *Ming-shih chi-shih, ch.* 17, p. 2416 (*Kuo-hsüeh chi-pen ts'ung shu* edn).

60 Yüan Hung-tao, 'K'u Chiang Chin-chih,' in *Ch'üan-chi*, 'Shih-chi,' pp. 110–11.
61 Yüan Hung-tao, 'Huang P'ing-ch'ien,' in *Ch'üan-chi*, 'Ch'ih-tu,' p. 71.
62 Yüan Hung-tao, 'Hsüeh-t'ao ko chi hsü,' in *Ch'üan-chi*, 'Wen-ch'ao,' p. 7.
63 Yüan Chung-tao, 'Shu Hsüeh-chao ts'un Chung-lang Hua-yüan shih-ts'ao ts'e hou,' in *K'o-hsüeh chai ch'ien-chi*, ch. 20, pp. 21b–22a.
64 See Yüan Chung-tao, 'Kao Chung-lang hsiung wen,' in *K'o-hsüeh chai chin-chi*, ch. 3, p. 81.
65 Ibid.
66 Yüan Chung-tao, 'Li-pu yen-feng ssu lang-chung Chung-lang hsien-sheng hsing-chuang,' in *K'o-hsüeh chai ch'ien-chi*, ch. 17, p. 30a.
67 Yüan Chung-tao, 'Chung-lang hsien-sheng ch'üan-chi hsü,' in *Chien-chiao*, p. 1711.
68 For a detailed study on Li Ho, see Naotaro Kudo, *The Life and Thoughts of Li Ho* (Tokyo: Waseda University Press, 1972).
69 See Liu Ta-chieh, *Chung-kuo wen-hsüeh fa-chan shih*, pp. 480–5.
70 *Pen-ts'ao* an abbreviation for *Pen-ts'ao kang-mu*, the name of a book listing some 1,000 plants and 1,000 animals of medicinal value, was edited by Li Shih-chen (1518–93) in 1578 and first published in 1590.
71 Yüan Hung-tao, 'Ou-te,' in *Ch'üan-chi*, 'Shih-chi,' p. 159.
72 This poem alludes to a line in the *Confucian Analects*. The Master said: 'A youth is to be regarded with respect. How do you know that his future will not be equal to our present? If he reaches the age of forty or fifty, and has not made himself heard of, then indeed he will not be worth being regarded with respect.' (*Confucian Analects*, 9, 22; translated in Legge, *The Chinese Classics, Confucian Analects*, p. 223).
73 Yüan Hung-tao, 'I-ssu ch'u-tu k'ou-chan,' in *Ch'üan-chi*, 'Shih-chi,' p. 209.
74 Yüan Chung-tao, 'Li-pu yen-fen ssu lang-chung Chung-lang hsien-sheng hsing-chuang,' in *K'o-hsüeh chai ch'ien-chi*, ch. 17, pp. 22a–b.
75 Yüan Hung-tao, 'Pieh Shih-k'ui,' no. 5, in *Ch'üan-chi*, 'Shih-chi,' p. 7.
76 Yüan Hung-tao, 'Te-shan shu-t'an,' in *Ch'üan-chi*, 'Sui-pi,' p. 35. 'Te-shan shu-t'an' was written in 1604.
77 Yüan Hung-tao, 'Lu-ho chou-chung ho Hsiao-hsiu pieh-shih,' no. 4, in *Ch'üan-chi*, 'Shih-chi,' p. 124. This poem was originally included in *P'o-yen chai chi* (written in 1608), ch. 2, p. 8b.
78 Yüan Hung-tao, 'T'u-chung k'ou-chan,' in *Ch'üan-chi*, 'Shih-chi,' p. 189. This poem is one from a set of six.
79 Ku Yen-wu, 'Shih-t'i tai-chiang,' in *Jih-chih lu* (Taipei: Ming-lun ch'u-pan she, 1970), p. 606. Quoted and translated in James J.Y. Liu, *The Art of Chinese Poetry* (Chicago: The University of Chicago Press, 1962), p. 97.
80 Yüan Chung-tao, 'Ts'ai Pu-hsia shih hsü,' in *K'o-hsüeh chai ch'ien-chi*, ch. 10, pp. 5–6. This preface is also included in *K'o-hsüeh chai chin-chi*, ch. 3, pp. 33–4.

4 The prose of Yüan Hung-tao

1 '*Hsiao-p'in wen*,' as Liu Ta-chieh remarked, 'is the only achievement' of the Kung-an literary movement. See *Chung-kuo wen-hsüeh fa-chan shih*, p. 868.

2 Liu I-ch'ing (403–44), *Shih-shuo hsin-yü* (Taipei: Chung-hua shu-chü, 1968), *ch.* 4, 'Wen-hsüeh' (literature), p. 17a:

When Yin Hao was reading the 'Small Version' of the Prajñāpara-mitā-sūtra, he jotted down two hundred notations, all of them intricate subtleties and obscure problems of the age . . . To this day (his annotated copy of) the 'Small Version' still survives.

SSHY Comm.: Of the Buddhist sutras which discuss Emptiness (Śūnyatā, i.e., the prajñāparamitā-sūtras), there is a detailed one, and an abridged one. The detailed one is called 'The Larger Version' (*Ta-p'in*), and the abridged, 'The Smaller Version' (*Hsiao-p'in*). (Translated by B. Mather in his *A New Account of Tales of the World* (Minneapolis: University of Minnesota Press, 1976), p. 114.)

3 Such as Ch'en Chi-ju's (1558–1639) *Wan hsiang-t'ang hsiao-p'in*, Wang Ssu-jen's (1575–1646), *Nüeh-an wen-fan hsiao-p'in* and Chu Kuo-chen's (1557–1632) *Yung-ch'uang hsiao-p'in*. For a study on this subject, see Ch'en Shao-t'ang, *Wan Ming hsiao-p'in lun-hsi* (Taipei: Yüan-liu wen-hua shih-yeh yu-hsien kung-ssu, 1982).

4 Chou Tso-jen, 'Yen-chih ts'ao pa,' in *Yung-jih chi* (Peking: Pei-hsin shu-tien, 1929), p. 179.

5 See Lin Yutang, 'Lun hsiao-p'in wen ti pi-tiao,' *Jen-chien shih*, 6 (June 20, 1934), pp. 10–11; 'Hsiao-p'in wen chih i-hsü,' *Jen-chien shih*, 22 (February 20, 1935), pp. 42–5; 'Hai-shih chiang hsiao-p'in wen chih i-hsü,' *Jen-chien shih*, 24 (March 20, 1935), pp. 35–6.

6 Lin Yutang, 'Lun hsiao-p'in wen pi-tiao,' *Jen-chien shih*, 6, p. 11.

7 For a study of Liu Tsung-yüan's landscape essays, see William H. Nien-hauser Jr. *et al.*, *Liu Tsung-yüan* (New York: Twayne, 1973), pp. 66–79. For the correspondence of Su Shih and Huang T'ing-chien, see Huang Shih (ed.), *Su Tung-p'o Huang Shan-ku ch'ih-tu ho-ts'e* (Taipei: T'ai-shun shu-chü, 1970).

8 See Chou Tso-jen, 'Tsa-pan erh pa,' in *Yung-jih chi*, p. 172. This colophon is partially quoted and translated in Pollard, *A Chinese Look at Literature: The Literary Values of Chou Tso-jen in Relation to the Tradition*, pp. 107–8.

9 Yüan Hung-tao served in the following government positions: (1) Magistrate of Wu-hsien (1595–7); (2) Instructor at Shun-t'ien Prefectural Academy (*Shun-t'ien fu chiao-shou*) (1598); (3) Instructor of the Imperial University (*Kuo-tzu chien chu-chiao*) (1599); (4) Secretary of the Bureau of Ceremonies in the Ministry of Rites (*Li-pu chu-shih*) (1600 and 1606); (5) Vice-Director of the Bureau of Evaluation in the Ministry of Personnel (*Li-pu yen-feng ssu lang-chung*) (1607–8); (6) Chief Examiner of Shensi Provincial Examination (*Shan-hsi chu-shih*) (1609). Yüan Hung-tao often took several months' leave between his transfers to new positions. Thus he was actually in office for less than six years. Translations of the titles according to Charles O. Hucker, 'An Index of Terms and Titles in "Governmental Organization of the Ming Dynasty",' *Harvard Journal of Asiatic Studies*, 23 (1960–1), pp. 127–51; and his *A Dictionary of Official Titles in Imperial China* (Stanford: Stanford University Press, 1985).

10   Yüan Hung-tao, 'Ch'iu Ch'ang-ju,' in *Ch'üan-chi*, 'Ch'ih-tu,' p. 2. This
      letter was written in 1595; see *Chien-chiao*, p. 208.
11   Yüan Hung-tao, 'Nieh Hua-nan,' in *Ch'üan-chi*, 'Ch'ih-tu,' p. 26. For the
      date of this letter, see *Chien-chiao*, p. 311.
12   Yüan Hung-tao, 'Sang Wu-chin,' in *Ch'üan-chi*, 'Ch'ih-tu,' p. 36. This letter
      was also written in 1597; see *Chien-chiao*, p. 513.
13   Yüan Hung-tao, 'Lan-tse, Yün-tse liang shu,' in *Ch'üan-chi*, 'Ch'ih-tu,' p.
      41. This letter was written in 1598; see *Chien-chiao*, p. 747.
14   See Shen Te-fu, 'Tzu-po huo-pen,' in *Wan-li yeh-huo pien*, pp. 690–1.
15   For a detailed description of Liu-lang, see Yüan Chung-tao, 'Liu-lang hu
      chi,' in *K'o-hsüeh chai ch'ien-chi*, ch. 11, pp. 10a–11a.
16   For a description of Yüan Hung-tao's life during this period, see his letter,
      'Kung Wei-hsüeh hsien-sheng,' in *Ch'üan-chi*, 'Ch'ih-tu,' p. 63. This letter
      was written in 1600; see *Chien-chiao*, p. 1234.
17   Yüan Hung-tao, 'Wu Tun-chih,' in *Ch'üan-chi*, 'Ch'ih-tu,' p. 33. This letter
      was written in 1597; see *Chien-chiao*, p. 506.
18   Yüan Hung-tao, 'T'ao Chou-wang Chi-chiu,' *Ch'üan-chi*, 'Ch'ih-tu,'
      p. 75. According to *Chien-chiao*, this letter was written in 1606 (p. 1274).
19   See Yüan Hung-tao, 'P'an Mao-shuo,' in *Ch'üan-chi*, 'Ch'ih-tu,' p. 74. This
      letter was written in 1606; see *Chien-chiao*, p. 1272.
20   Yüan Hung-tao, 'Chu Ssu-li,' in *Ch'üan-chi*, 'Ch'ih-tu,' p. 32. This letter
      was written in 1597; see *Chien-chiao*, p. 509.
21   Yüan Hung-tao, 'Su Ch'ien-fu,' in *Ch'üan-chi*, 'Ch'ih-tu,' p. 75. For the
      date of this letter, see *Chien-chiao*, p. 1273.
22   See Yüan Hung-tao, 'Yü Huang P'ing-ch'ien,' in *Ch'üan-chi*, 'Ch'ih-tu,'
      p. 52. This letter was written in 1607; see *Chien-chiao*, p. 1612.
23   Yüan Hung-tao, 'Ta Shen Ho-shan I-pu,' in *Ch'üan-chi*, 'Ch'ih-tu,' p. 78.
      For the date of this letter, see *Chien-chiao*, p. 1262.
24   See Yüan Hung-tao, 'Hsü Han-ming,' in *Ch'üan-chi*, 'Ch'ih-tu,' p. 4. This
      letter was written in 1595; see *Chien-chiao*, p. 218.
25   Yüan Hung-tao, 'Mao T'ai-ch'u,' in *Ch'üan-chi*, 'Ch'ih-tu,' p. 2. This letter
      was written in 1595 while Yüan Hung-tao was the magistrate of Wu-hsien.
      See *Chien-chiao*, pp. 209–10.
26   Yüan Hung-tao, 'Kung Wei-ch'ang hsien-sheng,' in *Ch'üan-chi*, 'Ch'ih-tu,'
      pp. 1–2. For the date of this letter, see *Chien-chiao*, p. 206.
27   Yüan Hung-tao, 'Hao-shih,' in *Ch'üan-chi*, 'Sui-pi,' p. 21.
28   See Yüan Hung-tao, 'Li Tzu-jan,' in *Ch'üan-chi*, 'Ch'ih-tu,' p. 9.
29   Yüan Hung-tao, 'Wang Po-ku,' in *Ch'üan-chi*, 'Ch'ih-tu,' p. 32.
30   See Yüan Chung-tao, 'Kao Chung-lang hsiung wen,' in *K'o-hsüeh chai chin-
      chi*, ch. 3, pp. 80–2.
31   Yüan Hung-tao, 'Yü Wang Po-ku,' in *Ch'üan-chi*, 'Ch'ih-tu,' p. 74.
32   Yüan Hung-tao, 'T'ao Chou-wang kuan-yü,' in *Ch'üan-chi*, 'Ch'ih-tu,'
      p. 65.
33   Yüan Hung-tao, 'Wu Ch'ü-lo,' in *Ch'üan-chi*, 'Ch'ih-tu,' p. 16.
34   Yüan Hung-tao, 'Wang I-ming,' in *Ch'üan-chi*, 'Ch'ih-tu,' p. 47.
35   Yüan Hung-tao, 'Chia-pao,' in *Ch'üan-chi*, 'Ch'ih-tu,' p. 11.
36   Yüan Hung-tao, 'Huang Ch'i-shih,' in *Ch'üan-chi*, 'Ch'ih-tu,' p. 25.

37 See Chu Tung-jun, *Chung-kuo wen-hsüeh p'i-p'ing shih ta-kang* (Taipei: K'ai-ming shu-tien, 1958), p. 263.

38 Yüan Hung-tao, 'Chang Yu-yü,' in *Ch'üan-chi,* 'Ch'ih-tu,' p. 34.

39 Yüan Hung-tao, 'Kuan Tung-ming,' in *Ch'üan-chi,* 'Ch'ih-tu,' p. 33.

40 See Yüan Hung-tao, 'Ta Chien Tu-fu,' in *Ch'üan-chi,* 'Ch'ih-tu,' pp. 78–9.

41 Chiang Ying-k'o, 'Chieh-t'o chi erh hsü,' in *Hsüeh-t'ao ch'üan chi* (Peking, 1600), pp. 16b–17a. This is one of the two prefaces to *Chieh-t'o chi* written by Chiang Ying-k'o. For a more accessible source, see *Chien-chiao,* p. 1691.

42 For studies of *shan-jen* literature, see A. Ying (Ch'ien Hsing-ts'un), 'Mingmo ti fan shan-jen wen-hsüeh,' in *Yeh-hang chi* (Shanghai: Liang-yu, 1935), pp. 144–9; 'Ming-mo ti fan shan-jen wen-hsüeh pu,' in *Hai-shih chi* (Shanghai: Pei-hsin, 1936), pp. 20–4; and Suzuki Tadashi, 'Mindai sanjin kō,' in *Shimizu hakushi tsuitō kinen Mindai shi ronsō* (Tokyo: Daian, 1962), pp. 357–88.

43 Yüan Hung-tao, 'Yu Hui-shan chi,' in *Ch'üan-chi,* 'Yu-chi,' p. 11.

44 Yüan Hung-tao, 'Hu-shang pieh t'ung Fang Tzu-kung fu,' in *Ch'üan-chi,* 'Shih-chi,' p. 19.

45 Yüan Hung-tao, 'T'i Ch'en shan-jen shan-shui chüan,' in *Ch'üan-chi,* 'Suipi,' pp. 15–16.

46 This paraphrase is based on the preface to 'P'ing-shih' in *Ch'üan-chi,* 'Suipi,' p. 18. For an English translation of this preface, see Lin Yutang, *The Importance of Living* (New York: Reynal and Hitchcock, 1938), p. 310.

47 For this idea I have greatly benefited from the seminar on Chinese landscape essays held by Professor Yu-kung Kao at Princeton University in 1982 and from reading James J. Y. Liu, *Essentials of Chinese Literary Art* (North Scituate, Mass.: Duxbury Press, 1979), pp. 39–44.

48 Yüan Hung-tao, 'Shang-fang,' in *Ch'üan-chi,* 'Yu-chi,' p. 2.

49 The West Lake at Hangchow was one of Yüan Hung-tao's favorite scenes. There are nine essays related to this lake in his 'Yu-chi.'

50 Although Yüan Hung-tao was quite devoted to Buddhism, his visits to temples had little to do with his religious belief. Temples functioned as no more than inns in his travels; they were merely places for lodging and meals.

51 See Yüan Hung-tao, 'Hu-ch'iu,' in *Ch'üan-chi,* 'Yu-chi,' p. 1.

52 Ibid., p. 29. For English translations of 'Man-ching yu-chi,' see Liu, *Essentials,* pp. 42–3; and Ren Fangqiu, 'A Brief Introduction to Yuan Hongdao (Hung-tao),' *Chinese Literature* (February 1981), pp. 122–3.

53 See Yüan Hung-tao, 'Yüan-t'ing chi-lüeh' and 'Pao-weng t'ing chi,' in *Ch'üan-chi,* 'Yu-chi,' pp. 10, 29.

54 'Liu-lang' is listed as one of the eight scenic spots (*pa-ching*) of Kung-an. See Chou Ch'eng-pi (ed.), *Kung-an hsien-chih* (first published 1874; rpt. Taipei: Hsüeh-sheng, 1969, 3 vols.), ch. 1, p. 68.

55 See Yüan Hung-tao, 'Hu-ch'iu,' in *Ch'üan-chi,* 'Yu-chi,' p. 1. There are two English and one French translation of this essay: (1) Chaves, *Pilgrim of the Clouds,* pp. 93–5; (2) Ren Fangqiu, 'A Brief Introduction to Yuan Hongdao,' p. 120–1; (3) Martine Vallette-Hémery, 'La Colline du Tiger,' *Nuages et pierres* (Paris: Publications Orientalistes de France, 1983), pp. 15–16.

56 Yüan Hung-tao, 'Ku shan,' in *Ch'üan-chi*, 'Yu-chi,' p. 13. 'The recluse of
Mount Ku' (*Ku-shan ch'u-shih*) in this essay refers to Lin Pu (T. Chün-fu,
967–1028), a major Sung poet, also known as 'Ho-ching hsien-sheng.' In
making this translation, I have consulted Chaves, *Pilgrim of the Clouds*,
p. 98, adopting several words from his translation.
57 Ibid.
58 See Yüan Hung-tao, 'Tiao-t'ai,' in *Ch'üan-chi*, 'Yu-chi,' p. 27.
59 'Ling-yen,' in ibid., p. 3.
60 'Lung-ching,' in ibid., p. 15.
61 'Hsiang-hu,' in ibid., p. 19.
62 'Ch'i-yün,' in ibid., p. 25. For another English translation, see Chaves,
Pilgrim of the Clouds, pp. 101–2.
63 'Ch'u-chih T'ien-mu Shuang-ch'ing chuang chi,' in ibid., p. 24. Mount
T'ien-mu lies immediately adjacent to Soochow, on the west, between the
city and the northern shores of Lake T'ai (T'ai-hu).
64 'Shih-ch'iao yen,' in ibid., p. 26.
65 'Ch'ang-wu hou-chi' was written in diary form in 1609 and included sixty-
five entries. This short work is included in *Yüan Chung-lang ch'üan-chi*
(Taipei: Shih-chieh, 1964), 'Yu-chi,' pp. 45–50. In Chung Hsing
(1574–1624) (ed.), *Yüan Chung-lang ch'üan-chi* (40 *ch.*) (first published 1629;
rpt. Taipei: Wei-wen, 1976), 'Ch'ang-wu hou-chi' is found in *ch.* 11, directly
after 'Yu-chi' (*ch.* 8–10).
66 'Mo-hsi' is also entitled 'Tsa-chih,' in *Ch'üan-chi* (1964 edn), 'Yu-chi,' pp.
50–4; Chung Hsing (ed.), *Ch'üan-chi, ch.* 11. For more information about
'Mo-hsi,' see Iriya Yoshitaka, 'Kōan san En chosakuhyō,' *Shinagaku*, 10, 1
(April 1940), p. 172.
67 Yüan Hung-tao, 'Wen-i t'ang chi,' in *Ch'üan-chi*, 'Yu-chi,' p. 30.
68 'Liang-hsiang san-chiao ssu chi,' in ibid., p. 31.
69 'Hua-shan pieh-chi,' in ibid., p. 40.
70 Wang An-shih, 'Yu Pao-ch'an shan chi,' in Pei Yüan-ch'en and Yeh Yu-
ming (eds.), *Li-tai yu-chi hsüan* (Hunan: Jen-min, 1980), pp. 36–42.
71 Su Shih, 'Shih-chung shan chi,' in ibid., pp. 43–9.
72 Chiang Ying-k'o, 'Chieh-t'o chi erh hsü, in *Hsüeh-t'ao ch'üan chi, ch.* 8,
pp. 16b–17a; see also *Chien-chiao*, p. 1691.
73 See Li Ch'i, *The Travel Diaries of Hsü Hsia-k'o* (Hong Kong: Chinese
University of Hong Kong Press, 1974), p. 26.
74 Ibid., p. 20.

Epilogue: the legacy of the Kung-an school

1 Both Chung Hsing and T'an Yüan-ch'un were natives of Ching-ling,
Hukuang province (currently T'ien-men, Hupeh province).
2 See *Ming-shih, ch.* 288, 'Lieh-chuan,' 176, 'Wen-yüan,' 4, pp. 7397–9.
3 Chung Hsing, 'Yin-hsiu hsüan chi tzu-hsü,' in *Yin-hsiu hsüan chi* (first
published 1622; rpt. Naikaku bunko, 1976), *Tse-chi*, 'Hsü,' 2, p. 17a.
4 Chung-Hsing, 'Yü Wang Chih-kung hsiung-ti,' in *Yin-hsiu hsüan chi,
Wang-chi*, 'Shu-tu,' 1, pp. 7a–b.

5   Ibid. The original Chinese phrase for 'absurdities' is *niu kuei she shen*, which
    literally means 'demon with the head of an ox and spirits with the body of a
    serpent.'

6   Chung Hsing, 'Tsai pao Ts'ai Ching-fu,' in *Yin-hsiu hsüan chi, Wang-chi*,
    'Shu-tu,' 1, pp. 16b–17a.

7   Ibid.

8   Ibid. The two names in this passage, Yü-ch'üan and Yü-ch'an, have not
    been identified.

9   Chung Hsing, 'Yü T'an Yu-hsia shu,' in *Yin-hsiu hsüan-chi, Wang-chi*,
    'Shu-tu,' 1, p. 5b.

10 *The Source of Poetry* includes two parts: the poems prior to the T'ang
    dynasty were collected under the title of *The Source of Ancient Poetry* (*Ku-
    shih kuei*), and the T'ang poetry under the title *The Source of T'ang Poetry*
    (*T'ang-shih kuei*).

11 Chung Hsing, 'Shih-kuei hsü,' in *Shih-kuei* (Ming edn, preface dated 1617),
    p. 1. This preface is also included in *Chung Po-ching ho-chi* (Shanghai:
    Shang-hai tsa-chih kung-ssu, 1936, 2 vols.), vol. 2, p. 176.

12 Chung Hsing also mentioned a similar idea in a poem to Ts'ai Ching-fu in
    which he again stressed the importance of using the standards of the
    ancients to read poetry. He wrote: 'One must carefully read contemporary
    poetry with the eyes of the ancients' ('Hsüan Ts'ai Ching-fu shih ch'i chi
    shih san lü,' in *Chung Po-ching ho-chi*, vol. 1, p. 92).

13 T'an Yüan-ch'un, 'Hsü Ts'ao-man ts'ao,' in *T'an Yu-hsia ho-chi* (Shanghai:
    Shang-hai tsa-chih kung-ssu, 1935), p. 143.

14 Chung Hsing, 'Tung-p'o wen-hsüan hsü,' in *Yin-hsiu hsüan chi, Tse-chi*,
    'Hsü,' 1, p. 15a.

15 See Yüan Hung-tao, *San-su wen-fan* (Ming, T'ien-ch'i edn, 18 *ch.*); *Tung-p'o
    shih-hsüan* (Ming, T'ien-ch'i edn, 12 *ch.*); and Li Chih, *P'o-hsien chi* (1600,
    16 *ch.*). For the detailed information on the editions of *P'o-hsien chi*, see
    Hok-lam Chan, *Li Chih (1527–1602) in Contemporary Historiography: New
    Light on His Life and Works*, p. 174.

16 Chung Hsing, 'Yü Kao Hai-chih kuan-cha,' in *Yin-hsiu hsüan chi, Wang-
    chi*, 'Shu-tu,' 1, p. 22b.

17 Chung Hsing, 'Pa Lin Ho-ching, Ch'in Huai-hai, Mao Tse shih, Li Jui shu,
    Fan Wen-mu, Chiang Pai-shih, Wang Chi-chih, Shih Ts'an-liao chu tieh,'
    in *Chung Po-ching ho-chi*, vol. 2, p. 400.

18 See Ch'ien Ch'ien-i, 'Chung t'i-hsüeh Hsing,' and 'T'an chieh-yüan Yüan-
    ch'un,' in *Lieh-ch'ao shih-chi hsiao-chuan*, pp. 570–4.

19 Ch'ien Ch'ien-i, 'Yüan i-chih Chung-tao,' in *Lieh-ch'ao shih-chi hsiao-
    chuan*, p. 569.

20 Ibid.

21 The congenial relationship between Yüan Chung-tao and Chung Hsing was
    recorded in Yüan Chung-tao's 'Hua-hsüeh fu yin,' in *K'o-hsüeh chai chin-
    chi, ch.* 3, 'Wen-ch'ao,' pp. 36–7 (1936 edn).

22 See Ch'ien Ch'ien-i, 'Yüan chi-hsün Hung-tao,' in *Lieh-ch'ao shih-chi hsiao-
    chuan*, pp. 567–8.

23 Ibid., pp. 570–4.

24 See Kuo Shao-yü, *Chung-kuo wen hsüeh p'i-p'ing shih*, vol. 2, pp. 283–4.

25   The works of the three Yüan brothers were listed in Yao Chin-yüan (ed.), *Ch'ing-tai chin-hui shu-mu ssu-chung* (Hangchow: Pao ching-t'ang shu-chü, 1931) as follows: Yüan Tsung-tao, *Po Su chai chi*, 5 vols., totally destroyed (*ch'üan-hui*) (*ch.* 1, p. 44); Yüan Hung-tao, *Yüan Chung-lang chi*, 11 vols., totally destroyed (*ch.* 3, p. 11); Yüan Chung-tao, *K'o-hsüeh chai chi*, 12 vols., totally destroyed; *K'o-hsüeh chai chin-chi*, 4 vols., partially destroyed (*ch'ou-hui*) (*ch.* 2, p. 62).

26   See Chapter 3, note 1.

27   For a detailed study on Chin Sheng-t'an, see John Ching-yu Wang, *Chin Sheng-t'an* (New York: Twayne, 1972).

28   For detailed studies on Yüan Mei's literary theory, see Ku Yüan-hsiang, *Sui-yüan shih-shuo ti yen-chiu* (Shanghai: Shang-wu, 1936); and Arthur Waley, *Yüan Mei* (Stanford: Stanford University Press, 1956), pp. 165–204.

29   This edition of Yüan Hung-tao's complete works was published by Yüan Hsien-chien. See Iriya Yoshitaka, 'Kōan san En chosakuhyō,' pp. 173–4.

30   The 1869 edition of Yüan Hung-tao's complete works was published by Yüan Chao. This edition is not included in Iriya Yoshitaka's 'Kōan san En chosakuhyō.'

31   Yüan Chao, 'Yüan Shih-kung i-shih lu hsü,' in *Yüan Shih-kung i-shih lu*, p. 1.

32   Hu Shih's 'Wen-hsüeh kai-liang ch'u-i,' published in 1917, 307 years after the death of Yüan Hung-tao, has been considered the manifesto of the vernacular movement.

33   Chou Tso-jen, *Chung-kuo hsin wen-hsüeh ti yüan-liu*, p. 43.

34   Ibid., pp. 92, 104.

35   These ideas are presented in many of Hu Shih's articles, of which the most important ones are: (1) 'Wen-hsüeh kai-liang ch'u-i'; (2) 'Li-shih ti wen hsüeh kuan-nian lun'; and (3) 'Chien-she ti wen-hsüeh ko-ming lun.' These three articles are included in *Hu Shih wen-ts'un*, vol. 1, pp. 5–17, 33–6, 55–73.

36   Hu Shih, *Hu Shih liu-hsüeh jih-chi* (Shanghai: Shang-wu, 1947, 4 vols.), vol. 3, p. 790.

37   See Hu Shih, *Hu Shih liu-hsüeh jih-chi*, vol. 4, pp. 1024–5. The two quoted poems are 'Hsi-hu' ('West Lake') and 'Ou chien pai-fa' ('Seeing Some White Hair by Chance'). The forgery of these two poems has been discussed in Chapter 3.

38   See Hu Shih, 'Tao-yen,' in *Chung-kuo hsin wen-hsüeh ta-hsi* (Shanghai: Liang-yu t'u-shu kung-ssu, 1935, 10 vols.), vol. 1, *Chien-she li-lun chi*, p. 19.

39   See Hu Shih, 'Chi Yüan Sui-yüan lun wen-hsüeh,' in *Hu Shih liu-hsüeh jih-chi*, vol. 4, pp. 945–51; and diary of July 10, 1922, in 'Hu Shih ti jih-chi hsüan,' *Hsin wen-hsüeh shih-liao*, 5 (November 1979), p. 276.

40   See Hu Shih, 'Chi Yüan Sui-yüan lun wen-hsüeh,' in ibid.

41   'Pi-shang Liang-shan' is the title of an appendix to Hu Shih's auto-biography, *Ssu-shih tzu-shu* (Taipei: Yüan-tung t'u-shu kung-ssu, 1962), pp. 91–123. For more information about Hu Shih's motivation in initiating the vernacular movement, see Hu Shih, 'T'i-ch'ang pai-hua wen ti ch'i-yin,' in *Hu Shih yen-chiang chi* (Taipei: Hu Shih chi-nien kuan, 1970, 3 vols.), vol. 2, pp. 434–43.

42 Hu Shih, 'Wu-shih nien lai Chung-kuo chih wen-hsüeh,' in *Hu Shih wen-ts'un*, vol. 2, p. 247.
43 Hu Shih, 'Wen-hsüeh kai-liang ch'u-i,' in *Hu Shih wen-ts'un*, vol. 1, p. 5.
44 Hu Shih, 'Li-shih ti wen-hsüeh kuan-nien lun,' in *Hu Shih wen-ts'un*, vol. 1, p. 33.
45 Hu Shih, 'Tao-yen,' in *Chung-kuo hsin wen-hsüeh ta-hsi*, vol. 1, p. 21.
46 Ibid., pp. 21–2.

THE MODERN STUDY OF THE THREE YÜAN BROTHERS AND THEIR KUNG-AN SCHOOL: AN INTRODUCTION AND SELECT BIBLIOGRAPHY

The modern study of the Kung-an school and the three Yüan brothers began in 1931. The revival of interest in the Kung-an school has often been attributed to Lin Yutang's and Chou Tso-jen's promotion of late Ming *hsiao-p' in wen* in the 1930s. However, the first scholarly research on Yüan Hung-tao was done by Jen Wei-k'un, a student of Chinese literature at Peking Normal University. Between 1931 and 1933 he wrote three articles on Yüan Hung-tao's biography, friends, thought and literary theory, which were published in *Shih-ta kuo-hsüeh ts'ung-k'an* and *Shih-ta yüeh-k'an*. Although the author was not very sophisticated in presenting his ideas and arranging his materials, these three articles comprise the first attempt to analyze Yüan Hung-tao's works in a systematic fashion.

After 1933 Yüan Hung-tao's name (better known as Yüan Chung-lang) frequently appeared in such popular magazines as *Jen-chien shi* and *Lun-yü*. For about a period of three years, in the early 1930s, Yüan Hung-tao was the most often discussed literary figure. However, the articles published on him are mostly on trivial subjects and are written in a casual style. Almost half of the articles are either anecdotal notes or random reflections on Yüan Hung-tao's works and lifestyle. Among these articles Ch'ien Hsing-ts'un's (A Ying) 'Yüan Hung-tao and Politics' ('Yüan Chung-lang yü cheng-chih'),[1] and Liu Ta-Chieh's 'The Literary Theory of Yüan Hung-tao' ('Yüan Chung-lang ti shih-wen kuan') are the two most substantial studies. Both were published in *Jen-chien shih* in 1934.

1934 is an important year in Yüan Hung-tao's revival as a literary hero in modern times. Not only were his complete works, edited by Lin Yutang and Liu Ta-chieh, published in this year, but the study of Yüan Hung-tao reached a peak with the publication of Chou Tso-jen's *The Origins of Modern Chinese Literature* (*Chung-kuo hsin-wen-hsüeh ti yüan-liu*). In this work the Kung-an school was regarded as one of the major sources for modern Chinese literature, and Yüan Hung-tao as the forerunner of Hu Shih. Such an interpretation gave new inspiration to the admirers of Yüan Hung-tao and brought a new perspective to the Kung-an school.

The interest in Yüan Hung-tao in China subsided after 1936. The more serious scholarly works on this late Ming critic were mostly written by Japanese scholars after 1940. In 1935 Okazaki Fumio published an article, 'The Popularity of Research on Yüan Hung-tao' ('En Chūrō kenkyū no ryūkō'), in *Chinese Literature*

---

[1] The detailed references for the titles of the articles mentioned in this introduction can be found in the bibliography.

Monthly (*Chūgoku bungaku geppo*) in Tokyo. This is the first Japanese article introducing the development of the study of Yüan Hung-tao in China. One of the Japanese scholars who contributed most to the study of Yüan Hung-tao was Iriya Yoshitaka. In 1940 he published a well-researched paper, 'A List of the Works of the Three Yüan Brothers from Kung-an' ('Kōan san En chosakuhyō'). In this essay he presented the works of the three Yüan brothers chronologically and made a thorough textual study of each of the works. In 1954 Iriya Yoshitaka wrote another important article, 'From the Kung-an [School] to the Ching-ling [School] – Focusing on Yüan Chung-tao [Hsiao-hsiu]' ('Kōan kara Kyōryō e: En Shōshū o chūshin to shite'). This is the first modern article that deals with the connection between the Kung-an and Ching-ling schools, and the role that Yüan Chung-tao played in the transition was carefully studied. Iriya Yoshitaka's greatest contribution to Japanese readers was the publication of the selected and annotated poems of Yüan Hung-tao in 1963. The introduction to this book presents a well-summarized picture of Yüan Hung-tao's life and his times.

Matsushita Tadashi was another Japanese scholar who published extensively on Yüan Hung-tao's literary theory. His study sheds much light on the emergence of the Kung-an school and provides a historical perspective on the continuity of late Ming literary criticism from the Archaist Masters to the three Yüan brothers.

After 1949, owing to the change of political ideology in China, Yüan Hung-tao was regarded as a typical representative of the feudalistic bourgeois class. Although study of the Kung-an school was never officially banned, from 1949 to 1979 only several minor articles were published on Yüan Hung-tao in China. The political nature of the studies is clearly reflected in the article entitled 'On the Class Reality of Yüan Hung-tao's Literary Thought' ('Shih-lun Yüan Hung-tao wen-hsüeh ssu-hsiang ti chieh-chi shih-chih'), published in 1979, in which Chen Yü, the pseudonymous author, gave no credit to the three Yüan brothers for their contributions to literary reform and severely criticized Yüan Hung-tao as only 'representing a declining landlord class' in his own time. This article is extremely critical of Yüan Hung-tao; it reads more like a political propaganda tract than a scholarly work. Such political rhetoric gradually disappeared, and scholarly interest toward the Kung-an school slowly revived after 1980.

Since 1980 the most significant event in the study of the Kung-an school was the publication of *The Annotated Complete Works of Yüan Hung-tao* (*Yüan Hung-tao chi chien-chiao*) edited by Ch'ien Po-ch'eng and published in 1981. This is by far the best edition of Yüan's complete works that has been published to date. In this two-volume collection Yüan Hung-tao's works are no longer arranged by such literary genres as poetry, prose and correspondence; rather, they are arranged according to the titles of the several collections originally published by Yüan himself. Under this arrangement the chronological development of Yüan's philosophy and personality can be easily observed. In addition to this change in format, personal and place names have been annotated, and a brief historical background to some events of the late Ming period is provided. What is most valuable about this collection is the editor's meticulous comparison of various available Ming and Ch'ing editions of Yüan Hung-tao's works. The editor has also included the original prefaces to each of Yüan's collections, as well as the comments made by Ming and Ch'ing critics, along with several articles published in the 1930s. This annotated edition not only provides us with the most complete collection of Yüan Hung-tao's works, but also puts this late Ming poet in a historical perspective.

After 1949 the three Yüan brothers and the Kung-an school did not attract much attention from scholars in Taiwan either. For some twenty years Yüan Hung-tao's name fell into oblivion. Except for a few short articles he was not mentioned in any substantial work until 1969.

In 1969 and 1970 Liang Jung-jo wrote four articles on Yüan Hung-tao and the Kung-an school. These marked the emergence in Taiwan of scholarly interest in Yüan Hung-tao, and so he has again enjoyed a little vogue among scholars and graduate students ever since. From 1974 to 1985, Yüan Hung-tao and the Kung-an school were the subject of at least half a dozen M. A. theses and Ph.D. dissertations, some of which have already been published. In 1976 the Ming edition (1629) of Yüan Hung-tao's complete works was reprinted in Taipei.

Yüan Hung-tao was first introduced to the Western world as a nature lover and a connoisseur of flower arrangements rather than as a poet or literary critic. In 1938 Lin Yutang partially translated Yüan's pamphlet 'P'ing-shih' ('Notes on Flower Arrangement') into English; it is included in his book, *The Importance of Living*, published in New York. In 1968 the French scholar André Lévy translated Yüan Tsung-tao's 'On Prose' ('Lun wen') and Yüan Chung-tao's 'A Biography of Yüan Tsung-tao' ('Shih-p'u hsien-sheng chuan'), with an introduction, in *T'oung pao*. This is the first time that the three Yüan brothers were introduced to French readers. In 1982 another French scholar, Martine Vallette-Hémery, wrote a book on Yüan Hung-tao's literary theory and practice. In the same year she also published a French translation of Yüan Hung-tao's prose entitled *Nuages et pierres*. Yüan Hung-tao has gradually won recognition in the Western world as an important Chinese literary figure.

The most comprehensive biography of Yüan Hung-tao in English, written by Hung Ming-shui in 1974, was 'Yüan Hung-tao and the Late Ming Literary and Intellectual Movement,' a Ph.D. dissertation done at the University of Wisconsin (Madison). Jonathan Chaves is another Western scholar who has contributed greatly to the study of the Kung-an school. In 1978 he published *Pilgrim of the Clouds*, a translation of selected works from the three Yüan brothers. In 1983 he wrote a very important article, 'The Reconsideration of the Literary Theory of the Kung-an School,' in which some of the stereotypical criticisms made against the Kung-an school were carefully reassessed and a more balanced interpretation of the most controversial points in Kung-an literary theory put forth.

The following bibliography is a selective list of works that I have cited or consulted in writing this book. The list of the modern studies on the subject is by no means exhaustive; however, it does present a general picture of how the three Yüan brothers and the Kung-an school have been perceived and approached in the past half-century.

Abe Kaneya 阿部兼也. 'Tōshi ki shihyō yōgo shitan – "setsu fushutsu" to "shin"' 唐詩帰詩評用語試探—"説不出"と"深," *Shūkan tōyōgaku* 集刊東洋学, 29 (June 1973), pp. 152–67.
Ai-t'i 艾惕(pseuod.). 'Yüan Hung-tao – Kung-an p'ai ti chu-chiang' 袁宏道— 公安派的主將,*Wu-han wan-pao* 武漢晚報, November 16, 1963.
Aoki Masaru 青木正兒. *Shina bungaku shisō shi* 支那文学思想史. Tokyo: Iwana-

mi shoten 岩波書店, 1943.
——. *Shindai bungaku hyōron shi* 清代文学評論史. Tokyo. Iwanami shoten, 1950.
Araki Kengo. 'Confucianism and Buddhism in the Late Ming.' In Wm. Theodore de Bary (ed.), *The Unfolding of Neo-Confucianism*. New York: Columbia University Press, 1970, pp. 36–66.
Bishop, John L. *The Colloquial Short Story in China*. Cambridge, Mass.: Harvard University Press, 1965.
Chan Hok-lam 陳學霖 (ed.). *Li Chih (1527–1602) in Contemporary Chinese Historiography: New Light on His Life and Works*. New York: M. E. Sharpe 1980.
Chan Wing-tsit 陳榮捷. *A Source Book in Chinese Philosophy*. Princeton: Princeton University Press, 1969.
Chang Ju-chao 張汝釗. 'Yüan Chung-lang ti fo-hsüeh ssu-hsiang' 袁中郎的佛學思想, *Jen-chien shih* 人間世, 20 (January 1935), pp. 14–20.
Chang T'ing-yü 張廷玉 (ed.) *Ming-shih* 明史. Peking: Chung-hua shu-chü 中華書局, 1974.
Chaves, Jonathan, 'The Expression of Self in the Kung-an School: Non-Romantic Individualism.' In Robert E. Hegel and Richard C. Hessney (eds.), *Expression of Self in Chinese Literature*. New York: Columbia University Press, 1985, pp. 123–50.
——. 'The Panoply of Images: A Reconsideration of the Literary Theory of the Kung-an School.' In Susan Bush and Christian Murck (eds.), *Theories of the Arts in China*. Princeton: Princeton University Press, 1983, pp. 341–64.
—— (tr.). *Pilgrim of the Clouds – Poems and Essays by Yüan Hung-tao and his Brothers*, with an introduction. New York: Weatherhill, 1978.
Ch'en Chin-chao 陳錦釗. *Li Chih chih wen-lun* 李贄之文論. Taipei: Chia-hsin shui-ni kung-ssu 嘉新水泥公司, 1974.
Ch'en Min-cheng 陳敏政 (ed.). *Huang-Ming wen-heng* 皇明文衡. First published 1527; Shanghai: Shang-wu yin-shu kuan, n.d.
Ch'en Shao-t'ang 陳少棠. *Wan-Ming hsiao-p'in lun-hsi* 晚明小品論析. Taipei Yüan-liu ch'u-pan she 源流出版社, 1982.
Ch'en Shou-yi. *Chinese Literature: A Historical Introduction*. New York: Ronald Press, 1961.
Ch'en T'ien 陳田 (ed.). *Ming-shih chi-shih* 明詩紀事. First published 1899; Taipei: Shang-wu yin shu-kuan, 1968.
Ch'en Tsung-min 陳宗敏. 'Yüan Chung-lang ti ssu-hsiang yü tso-p'in' 袁中郎的思想與作品, *Kuo-yü jih-pao: Shu han jen* 國語日報：書和人, 352 (December 1978), pp. 1–8 (total pp. 2809–16).
Ch'en Tzu-chan 陳子展. 'Kung-an Ching-ling yü haiao-p'in wen' 公安竟陵與小品文. In Ch'en Wang-tao 陳望道 (ed.), *Hsiao-p'in wen ho man-hua* 小品文和漫畫. Shanghai: Sheng-huo shu-tien 生活書店, 1935, pp. 123–35.
——. 'She-mo chiao-tso Kung-an p'ai ho Ching-ling p'ai? Ta-men ti tso-feng ho ying-hsiang tsen-mo yang?' 什麼叫作公安派和竟陵派？他們的作風和影響怎麼樣? In Fu Tung-hua 傅東華 (ed.), *Wen-hsüeh pai-t'i* 文學百題. First published Shanghai: Sheng-huo shu-tien, 1935; rpt. Hong Kong: Ku-wen shu-chü 古文書局, 1961, pp. 386–95.
Ch'en Wan-i 陳萬益. 'Wan-Ming hsing-ling wen-hsüeh ssu-hsiang yen-chiu' 晚明性靈文學思想研究. Ph. D. dissertation, National Taiwan University, 1978.

Chen Yü 震宇 (pseudo.). 'Shih-lun Yüan Hung-tao wen-hsüeh ssu-hsiang ti chieh-chi shih-chih' 試論袁宏道文學思想的階級實質. In She-hui k'o-hsüeh chan-hsien pien-chi pu 社會科學戰綫編輯部 (ed.), *Wen-i hsüeh yen-chiu lun-ts'ung* 文藝學研究論叢 (August 1979), pp. 375–92.

Cheng Chen-to 鄭振鐸, 'Kua-chih erh' 掛枝兒. In Cheng Chen-to, *Chung-kuo wen-hsüeh lun-chi* 中國文學論集. Taipei: Ming-lun ch'u-pan She 明倫出版社, n. d., pp. 469–77.

Chi Wen-fu 嵇文甫. *Wan-ming ssu-hsiang shih-lüeh* 晚明思想史略. Chungking: Shang-wu yin-shu kuan, 1944.

Chi Yün 紀昀 *et al.* (eds.). *Ssu-k'u ch'üan-shu tsung-mu t'i-yao* 四庫全書總目提要. Completed 1781; Taipei: Shang-wu yin-shu kuan, 1971.

Chiang Pien 江邊. 'Kung-an san yüan' 公安三袁, *Chung-hsüeh yü-wen* 中學語文 (Wu-han shih-yüan 武漢師院), 4 (1979), pp. 57–8.

Chiang Ying-k'o 江盈科. *Hsüeh-t'ao hsiao-shu* 雪濤小書. Shanghai: Chung-yang shu-tien 中央書店, 1948.

——. *Hsüeh-t'ao ko chi* 雪濤閣集. Hsi-ch'u Chiang-shih Pei-ching k'an-pen 西楚江氏北京刊本, 1600.

Ch'ien Chi-po 錢基博. *Ming-tai wen-hsüeh* 明代文學. Shanghai: Shang-wu yin-shu kuan, 1934.

Ch'ien Ch'ien-i 錢謙益. *Lieh-ch'ao shih-chi hsiao-chuan* 列朝詩集小傳. Completed 1643; first published 1698; Shanghai: Chung-hua shu-chü, 1959; Taipei: Shih-chieh shu-chü 世界書局, 1961.

——. *Mu-chai ch'u-hsüeh-chi* 牧齋初學集. First published 1644; rpt. in *Ssu-pu ts'ung-k'an ch'u-pien* 四部叢刊初編. Taipei: Shang-wu yin shu kuan, 1967; Shanghai: Ku-chi ch'u-pan she 古籍出版社, 1985.

——. *Mu-chai yu-hsüeh chi* 牧齋有學集. In *Ssu-pu ts'ung-k'an ch'u-pien*. Taipei: Shang-wu yin-shu kuan, 1967.

Ch'ien Chung-shu 錢鍾書. *T'an-i lu* 談藝錄. Shanghai: K'ai-ming shu-tien 開明書店, 1937; rpt. Hong Kong: Lung-men shu-tien 龍門書店, 1962.

Ch'ien Hsing-ts'un 錢杏村 (A Ying 阿英). *Hai-shih chi* 海市集. Shanghai: Pei-hsin shu-chü, 1936.

——. *Hsiao-shuo hsien-t'an* 小說閒談. Shanghai: Ku-tien wen-hsüeh ch'u-pan she 古典文學出版社, 1958.

——. 'Mo yü ch'ien' 默與謙, *Jen-chien shih*, 1 (April 1934), pp. 36–7.

——. 'Tu T'u Ch'ih-hsui ti hsiao-p'in wen' 讀屠赤水的小品文, *Jen-chien shih*, 3 (May 1934), pp. 31–3.

——. 'Tu Wang Po-ku Mou-yeh chi' 讀王百穀謀野集, *Jen-chieh shih*, 9 (August 1934), pp. 29–33.

——. *Yeh-hang chi* 夜航集. Shanghai: Liang-yu t'u-shu kung-ssu 艮友圖書公司, 1935.

——. 'Yüan Chung-lang yü cheng-chih' 袁中郎與政治, *Jen-chien shih*, 7 (July 1934), pp. 13–17. Rpt. under the title 'Ch'ung-yin Yüan Chung-lang ch'üan-chi hsü' 重印袁中郎全集序. In Ch'ien Hsing-ts'un, *Yeh-hang chi* 夜航集, pp. 131–43.

Ch'ien Po-ch'eng 錢伯城 (Hsin Yü 辛雨). 'Tu Yüan Hung-tao shih-wen chi sui-pi' 讀袁宏道詩文集隨筆. In *Hsüeh-lin man-lu* 學林漫錄, 1 (1980), pp. 48–57. Peking: Chung-hua shu-chü 中華書局; rpt. in Ch'ien Po-ch'eng (ed.), *Yüan Hung-tao chi chien-chiao* 袁宏道集箋校, pp. 1–13.

—— (ed.). *Yüan Hung-tao chi chien-chiao*, 3 vols. Shanghai: Ku-chi ch'u-pan she, 1981.

Ch'iu Han-sheng 邱漢生. 'T'ai chou hsüeh-p'ai ti chieh-ch'u ssu-hsiang chia Li Chih' 泰州學派的傑出思想家李贄, *Li-shih yen-chiu* 歷史研究, 64, 1 (January 1964), pp. 115–32.

Chou Ch'eng-pi 周承弼, (ed.). *Kung-an hsien-chih* 公安縣志. First published 1887; rpt. Taipei: Hsüeh-sheng shu-tien 學生書店, 3 vols., 1969.

Chou Chih-p'ing 周質平. 'Hu Shih wen-hsüeh li-lun t'an-yüan' 胡適文學理論探源, *Hsin-shu yüeh-k'an* 新書月刊, 9 (June 1984), pp. 12–18.

——. 'The Landscape Essays of Yüan Hung-tao,' *Tamkang Review*, 13, 3 (Spring 1983), pp. 297–312.

——. 'P'ing Kung-an p'ai chih shih-lun' 評公安派之詩論, *Chung-wai wen-hsüeh* 中外文學, 12, 10 (March 1984), pp. 70–94.

——. 'The Poetry and Poetic Theory of Yüan Hung-tao (1568–1610),' *Tsing Hua Journal of Chinese Studies*, New Series 15, 1 and 2 (December 1983), pp. 113–42.

——. 'Wan-Ming wen-jen tui hsiao-shuo ti t'ai-tu' 晚明文人對小說的態度, *Chung-wai wen-hsüeh*, 11, 12 (May 1983), pp. 100–9.

——. 'Yüan Hung-tao ti shan-shui p'i chi ch'i yu-chi' 袁宏道的山水癖及其遊記, *Chung-wai wen-hsüeh*, 13, 4 (September 1984), pp. 4–14.

Chou Shao 周邵. 'Tu Chung-lang ou-chih' 讀中郎偶識, *Jen-chien shih*, 5 (June 1934), pp. 32–3.

Chou Shu-jen 周樹人 (Lu Hsün 魯迅). 'Chao-t'ieh chi-ch'e' 招貼即扯 (published under the pseudonym Kung-han 公汗), *T'ai-pai pan-yüeh k'an* 太白半月刊, 1, 11 (February 1935), p. 511; rpt. in Chou Shu-jen, *Ch'ieh-chieh t'ing tsa-wen erh-chi* 且介亭雜文二集. In *Lu Hsün ch'üan-chi* 魯迅全集, 16 vols. Peking: Jen-min ch'u-pan she 人民出版社, 1982, vol. 6, pp. 227–9.

——. *Chung-kuo hsiao-shuo shih-lüeh* 中國小說史略. Shanghai: Pei-hsin shu-tien, 1931; rpt. in *Lu Hsün ch'üan-chi*, vol. 9, pp. 1–340.

Chou Tso-jen 周作人 (Chih-t'ang 知堂). 'Ch'ung-k'an Yüan Chung-lang chi hsü' 重刊袁中郎集序, *Ta-kung pao wen-i fu-k'an* 大公報文藝副刊, 120 (November 17, 1934); rpt. in Chou Tso-jen, *K'u-ch'a an su-pi* 苦茶菴隨筆. Shanghai: Pei-hsin shu-tien 北新書店, 1935, pp. 91–102.

——. *Chung-kuo hsin wen-hsüeh ti yüan-liu* 中國新文學的源流. Peking: Jen-wen shu-tien 人文書店, 1934.

——. *Feng-yü t'an* 風雨談. Shanghai: Pei-hsin shu-tien, 1936.

——. *Yao-t'ang tsa-wen* 藥堂雜文. Shanghai: Pei-hsin shu-tien, 1943.

——. *Yung-jih chi* 永日集. Shanghai: Pei-hsin shu-tien, 1929.

Chou Tzu-chih 周紫芝. *Chu-p'o shih-hua* 竹坡詩話. In Ho Wen-huan 何文煥 (ed.), *Li-tai shih-hua* 歷代詩話. Taipei: I-wen yin-shu kuan 藝文印書館, 1971.

Chu I-tsun 朱彝尊. *Ming shih tsung* 明詩綜. Completed 1705; rpt. Taipei: Shih-chieh shu-chü, 2 vols., 1962.

Chu Ming-han 朱銘漢. 'Yüan Chung-lang chih wen-hsüeh p'i-p'ing kuan' 袁中郎之文學批評觀. M. A. thesis, Tunghai University, Taichung, June 1978.

Chu Tung-jun 朱東潤. *Chung-kuo wen-hsüeh p'i-p'ing shih ta-kang* 中國文學批評史大綱. Shanghai: Ku-tien wen-hsüeh ch'u-pan she 古典文學出版社, 1957; rpt. Taipei: K'ai-ming shu-tien, 1960.

——. 'Ho Ching-ming p'i-p'ing lun shu-p'ing' 何景明批評論述評. In *Chung-kuo wen-hsüeh p'i-p'ing chia yü wen-hsüeh p'i-p'ing* 中國文學批評家與文學批評, 4 vols. Taipei: Hsüeh-sheng shu-chü, 1971, vol. 2, pp. 133–48.

——. 'Shu Ch'ien Mu-chai chih wen-hsüeh p'i-p'ing' 述錢牧齋之文學批評. In *Chung-kuo wen-hsüeh p'i-p'ing chia yü wen-hsüeh p'i-p'ing*, vol. 2, pp. 149–77.

——. 'Yüan Mei wen-hsüeh p'i-p'ing lun shu-p'ing' 袁枚文學批評論述評. In *Chung-kuo wen-hsüeh p'i-p'ing chia yü wen-hsüeh p'i-p'ing*, vol. 3. pp. 67–98.

Chu Wei-chih 朱維之. *Chung-kuo wen-i ssu-ch'ao shih-lüeh* 中國文藝思潮史略. Shanghai: K'ai-ming shu-tien, 1946.

——. *Li Cho-wu lun* 李卓吾論. Fukien: Fu-chien Hsieh-ho ta-hsüeh ch'u-pan pu 福建協和大學出版部, 1935.

Chung Hsing 鍾惺. *Chung Po-ching ho-chi* 鍾伯敬合集, 2 vols. Shanghai: Shanghai tsa-chih-kung-ssu 上海雜誌公司, 1936.

——. *Yin-hsiu hsüan-chi* 隱秀軒集. First published 1622; rpt. Naikaku bunko 內閣文庫, 1976. (Hishi copy of the original in Naikaku bunko, Tokyo, made by Takeo Hiraoka of Kyoto Univeristy.)

Chung Hsing and T'an Yüan-ch'un 譚元春 (eds.). *Ku-shih kui* 古詩歸, 15 *chüan*, and *T'ang-shih kui* 唐詩歸, 36 *chüan*, 1617 edn.

Chung Jung 鍾嶸. *Shih-p'in chu* 詩品注, annotated by Ch'en Yen-chieh 陳延傑. Taipei: K'ai-ming shu-tien, 1958.

Chung-kuo ku-tien hsi-ch'ü lun-chu chi-ch'eng 中國古典戲曲論著集成, 10 vols., ed. Chung-kuo hsi-ch'ü yen-chiu yüan 中國戲曲研究院, vol. 4. Peking: Chung-kuo hsi-ch'ü ch'u-pan she 中國戲曲出版社, 1959.

Chung-shu 中書 (pseudo.). 'Yüan Hung-tao yü Jih-pen ch'a-hua' 袁宏道與日本插花, *Ta-kung pao* 大公報, (February 1, 1966).

de Bary, Wm. Theodore. 'Individualism and Humanitarianism in Late Ming.' In Wm. Theodore de Bary (ed.), *Self and Society in Ming Thought*. New York: Columbia University Press, 1970, pp. 145–247

Fan Yin 樊績. 'Chi fa-hsien Chung-lang mo-chi chih ching-kuo' 記發現中郎墨蹟之經過, *Jen-chien shih*, 17 (December 1934), pp. 22–3.

——. 'Yüan Chung-lang yu Pai-ch'üan' 袁中郎遊百泉, *Lun-yü pan-yüeh k'an* 論語半月刊, 54 (December 1934), pp. 293–5.

Fei Hai-chi 費海磯. 'Ts'ung Yüan Chung-lang shih t'an-tao Ying-kuo shih-jen Ha-tai' 從袁中郎詩談到英國詩人哈代, *Kuo-yü jih-pao: Shu han jen* 國語日報：書和人, 214 (July 1973), pp. 1–7 (total pp. 1705–11).

Feng Meng-lung 馮夢龍. *Ching-shih t'ung-yen* 警世通言. Peking: Jen-min wen-hsüeh ch'u-pan she, 1956.

——. *Hsing-shih heng-yen* 醒世恆言. Peking:Tso-chia ch'u-pan she, 1956.

——. *Shan-ko* 山歌. Peking: Chung-hua shu-chü, 1962.

Franke, Wolfgang. *The Reform and Abolition of the Traditional Chinese Examination System*. Cambridge, Mass.: Harvard University, East Asian Research Center, 1963.

Frankel, Hans H. *The Flowering Plum and the Palace Lady: Interpretations of Chinese Poetry*. New Haven: Yale University Press, 1976.

Goodrich, Carrington and Fang Chaoying (eds.). *Dictionary of Ming Biography, 1386–1644*, 2 vols. New York: Columbia University Press, 1976.

Han Ts'ao 寒操. 'Yüan Chung-lang ho Shui-hu chuan' 袁中郎和水滸傳, *Yang-*

ch'eng wan-pao 羊城晚報 (March 14, 1980).

Hanan, Patrick. D. *The Chinese Short Story: Studies in Dating, Authorship, and Composition*. Cambridge, Mass.: Harvard University Press, 1973.

———. *The Chinese Vernacular Story*. Cambridge, Mass.: Harvard University Press, 1981.

———. 'The Early Chinese Short Story: A Critical Theory in Outline,' *Harvard Journal of Asiatic Studies*, 27 (1967), pp. 168–207.

———. 'The Fiction of Moral Duty: The Vernacular Story in the 1640s.' In Robert E. Hegel and Richard C. Hessney (eds.), *Expression of Self in Chinese Literature*. New York: Columbia University Press, 1985, pp. 189–213.

———. 'Sources of the Chin P'ing Mei,' *Asia Major*, 10 (July 1963), pp. 23–67.

———. 'The Text of the Chin P'ing Mei,' *Asia Major*, 9 (April 1962), pp. 1–57.

Harada Norio 原田憲雄. 'Beika – En Chūrō shiki (2)' 瓶花—袁中郎私記 (2), *Hōkō* 方向, 7 (August 1957), pp. 1–40.

———. 'Heikyo – En Chūrō shiki (3)' 敝筐—袁中郎私記 (3), *Hōkō*, 8 (September 1958), pp. 75–113.

———. 'Tenkyō – En Chūrō shiki (1)' 顚狂—袁中郎私記 (1), *Kyōto joshi daigaku kiyō* 京都女子大学記要, 11 (October 1955), pp. 37–52.

Hashimoto Jun 橋本循. 'Ō Enshū bunshōkan to sono bunshō' 王弇州の文章觀と其文章, *Shinagaku* 支那学, 1, 4 (November 1920), pp. 55–74.

Ho Kuan-piao 何冠彪. 'T'ao Wang-ling, Shih-ling hsiung-ti sheng-tzu k'ao-lüeh' 陶望齡, 奭齡兄弟生卒考略, *Chung-hua wen-shih lun-ts'ung* 中華文史論叢, 33 (1985), pp. 285–91.

Hou Wai-lu 侯外廬. *Chung-kuo tsao-ch'i ch'i-meng ssu-hsiang shih* 中國早期啟蒙思想史. Peking: Jen-min ch'u-pan she, 1956.

———. 'Shih-liu shih-chi Chung-kuo ti chin-pu ti che-hsüeh ssu-ch'ao kai-shu' 十六世紀中國的進步的哲學思潮概述, *Li-shih yen-chiu*, 59, 10 (October 1959), pp. 39–59.

Hsia Chih-ch'ing 夏志淸. *The Classic Chinese Novel*. New York: Columbia University Press, 1968.

Hsiao Kung-ch'üan 蕭公權. 'Li Chih: An Iconoclast of the Sixteenth Century,' *T'ien-hsia Monthly*, 6, 4 (April 1938), pp. 317–41.

Hsiao Teng-fu 蕭登福. 'Kung-an p'ai wen-hsüeh lun' 公安派文學論, *Chung-hua wen-hua fu-hsing yüeh-k'an* 中華文化復興月刊, 12, 4 (April 1979), pp. 55–63.

Hsiao T'ung 蕭統. *Wen-hsüan* 文選. Sung Ch'un-hsi 宋淳熙 (1174–89) edn; rpt. Taipei: I-wen yin-shu kuan, 1967.

Hsieh Chen 謝榛. *Ssu-Ming shih-hua* 四溟詩話. Peking: Jen-min ch'u-pan she, 1962.

Hsieh Wu-liang 謝無量. *Chung-kuo ta wen-hsüeh shih* 中國大文學史. Shanghai: Chung-hua shu-chü, 1918.

Hsü Hung-tzu 徐宏祖. *Hsü Hsia-k'o yu-chi* 徐霞客遊記, 3 vols. Shanghai: Ku-chi ch'u-pan she, 1980.

Hsü Wei 徐渭. *Hsü Wei chi* 徐渭集, 4 vols. Peking: Chung-hua shu-chü, 1983.

———. *Nan-tz'u hsü-lu* 南詞敍錄. In *Li-tai shih-shih ch'ang-pien* 歷代詩史長編, series 2. Taipei: Ting wen shu-chü 鼎文書局 1974, pp. 235–56.

Hu Shih 胡適. *Hu Shih liu-hsüeh jih-chi* 胡適留學日記, 4 vols. Shanghai: Shang wu yin-shu kuan, 1947; rpt. Taipei: Shang-wu yin-shu kuan, 1973.

——. *Hu Shih wen-ts'un* 胡適文存. Shanghai: Ya-tung t'u-shu kuan 亞東圖書館, 1921; rpt. Taipei: Yüan t'ung t'u-shu kung-ssu 遠東圖書公司, 1968.

——. *Hu Shih wen-ts'un, erh-chi* 胡適文存二集. Shanghai: Ya-tung t'u-shu kuan, 1924; rpt. Taipei: Yuan-tung t'u-shu kung-ssu, 1968.

——. *Hu Shih wen-ts'un, san-chi* 胡適文存三集. Shanghai: Ya-tung t'u-shu kuan, 1930; rpt. Taipei: Yüan-tung t'u- shu kung-ssu, 1968.

——. *Pai-hua wen-hsüeh shih* 白話文學史. Shanghai: Hsin-yüeh shu-tien 新月書店, 1928; rpt. Taipei: Hu-shih chi-nien kuan 胡適紀念館, 1969.

——. *Ssu-shih tzu-shu* 四十自述. Shanghai: Ya-tung t'u-shu kuan, 1933; rpt. Taipei: Yüan-tung t'u-shu kung-ssu, 1959.

——. 'Tao-yen' 導言. In Chao Chia-pi 趙家璧 (ed.), *Chung-kuo hsin wen-hsüeh ta-hsi* 中國新文學大系, 10 vols., vol. 1, *Chien-she li-lun chi* 建設理論集. Shanghai: Liang-yu shu-tien 良友書店, 1935, pp. 1–32.

——. *T'i-ch'ang pai-hua wen ti ch'i-yin'* 提倡白話文的起因. In *Hu-shih yen-chiang chi* 胡適演講集, 3 vols. Taipei: Hu Shih Chi-nien kuan, 1970, vol. 2, pp. 434–43.

Huang Tsung-hsi 黃宗羲. *Ming-i tai-fang lu* 明夷待訪錄. In *Li- chou i- chu hui-k'an* 梨州遺著彙刊, vol. 2. Taipei: Lung-yen ch'u-pan she 隆言出版社, 1969.

——. *Ming-wen shou-tu* 明文授讀. Tokyo: Kyūko shoin 汲古書院, 1973.

Hucker, Charles O. *A Dictionary of Official Titles in Imperial China.* Stanford: Stanford University Press, 1985.

——. 'An Index of Terms and Titles in "Governmental Organization of the Ming Dynasty",' *Harvard Journal of Asiatic Studies*, 23 (1960–1), pp. 127–51.

Hui-chih 晦之 (pseudo.). 'San Yüan ho Kung-an p'ai' 三袁和公安派, *Hu-pei jih-pao* 湖北日報 (June 6, 1962).

Hung Ko-i 洪克夷. 'Yüan Hung-tao ho ta ti yu-chi' 袁宏道和他的遊記, *Yü-wen chan-hsien* 語文戰綫, 37 (January 1980), pp. 30–1.

Hung Ming-shui 洪銘水. 'Yüan Hung-tao and the Late Ming Literary and Intellectual Movement.' Ph. D. dissertation, University of Wisconsin – Madison, December 1974.

I-shan 宜珊 (pseudo.). 'Yüan Hung-tao ti shih' 袁宏道的詩, *Chin-jih Chung-kuo* 今日中國, 55 (November 1975), pp. 120–9.

Iriya Yoshitaka 入矢義高. *En Kōdō* 袁宏道. In Yoshikawa Kōjirō 吉川幸次郎 and Ogawa Tamaki 小川環樹 (eds.), *Chūgoku shijin senshū nishū* 中国詩人選集二集. Tokyo: Iwanami 岩波, 1963.

——. 'Kōan kara Kyōryō e: En Shōshū o chūshin to shite' 公安から竟陵へ:袁小修を中心として, *Kyoto daigaku jinmon kagaku kenkyūjo sōritsu 25 shūnen kinen ronbun shū* 京都大学人文科学研究所創立二十五周年論文集, (November 1954), pp. 305–30.

——. 'Kōan san En chosakuhyō' 公安三袁著作表, *Shinagaku* 支那学, 10, 1 (December 1940), pp. 167–86.

——. 'Shiki ni tsuite' 詩帰について, *Tōhō gakuhō* 東方学報, 16 (September 1948), pp. 102–34.

——. 'Shin shi' 真詩. In *Yoshikawa hakushi taikyū kinen chūgoku bungaku ronshū* 吉川博士退休紀念中国文学論集, ed. Yoshikawa kyōju taikan kinen jigyo-kai 吉川教授退官記念事業會. Tokyo: Chikuma 筑摩, 1968, pp. 673–81.

Jen Fang-ch'iu (Ren Fangqiu) 任訪秋. 'A Brief Introduction to Yuan Hongdao

(Hung-tao),' *Chinese Literature* (February 1981), pp. 113–29.

——. 'Kuan-yü Yüan Chung-lang ho t'a so ch'ang-tao ti wen-hsüeh ko-hsin yün-tung' 關於袁中郎和他所倡導的文學革新運動, *Wen-hsüeh i-ch'an* 文學遺產, 2 (September 1980), pp. 97–105; rpt. in Jen Fang-ch'iu, *Chung-kuo ku-tien wen-hsüeh lun-wen chi* 中國古典文學論文集. Ho-nan 河南: Jen-min ch'u-pan she 人民出版社, 1981, pp. 127–43.

——. *Yüan Chung-lang yen-chiu* 袁中郎研究. Shanghai: Ku-chi ch'u-pan she, 1983.

Jen Wei-k'un 任維焜. 'Chung-lang shih-yu k'ao' 中郎師友考 (Yüan Chung-lang p'ing-chuan chih i 袁中郎評傳之一), *Shih-ta kuo-hsüeh ts'ung-k'an* 師大國學叢刊, 1, 2 (May 1931), pp. 67–91.

——. 'Yüan Chung-lang p'ing-chuan (1)' 袁中郎評傳 (1), *Shih-ta yüeh-k'an* 師大月刊, 1, 2 (January 1933), pp. 158–200.

——. 'Yüan Chung-lang p'ing-chuan (2)' 袁中郎評傳 (2), *Shih-ta kuo-hsüeh ts'ung-k'an*, 1, 3 (March 1932), pp. 57–101.

Jung Chao-tsu 容肇祖. *Li Cho-wu p'ing-chuan* 李卓吾評傳. Shanghai: Shang-wu yin-shu kuan, 1937; rpt Taipei: Shang-wu yin-shu kuan, 1973.

——. 'Ming Feng Meng-lung ti Sheng-p'ing chi ch'i chu-shu' 明馮夢龍的生平及其著述, *Ling-nan hsüeh-pao* 嶺南學報, 2, 2 (1931), pp. 61–91.

——. 'Ming Feng Meng-lung ti sheng-p'ing chi ch'i chu-shu hsü-k'ao' 明馮夢龍的生平及其著述續考, *Ling-nan hsüeh-pao*, 2, 3 (1932), pp. 95–124.

——. *Ming-tai ssu-hsiang shih* 明代思想史. Shanghai: K'ai-ming shu-tien, 1941; rpt. Taipei: K'ai-ming shu-tien, 1962.

Kao Pa-mei 高八美. 'Yüan Chung-lang chi ch'i hsiao-p'in wen yen-chiu' 袁中郎及其小品文研究. M. A. thesis, Fujen 輔仁 University, 1978.

Kezuka Eigorō 毛塚榮五郎. 'En Chūrō ni okeru mujun' 袁中郎に於ける矛盾, *Nihon Chūgoku gakkaihō* 日本中国学会報, 9 (1957), pp. 118–28.

——. 'En Chūrō to sono jidai' 袁中郎とその時代. In Hakuyama shigakkai 白山史学会 (ed.), *Jinbutsu to jidai* 人物と時代. Tokyo: Teikoku shoin 帝国書院, 1949, pp. 132–59.

K'o-chan 克展 (pseudo.). 'Yüan Chung-lang k'uang-fu k'uang-yen' 袁中郎狂夫狂言, *I-wen chih* 藝文誌, 152 (May 1978), pp. 45–8.

Ku Yen-wu 顧炎武. *Jih chih lu* 日知錄. Taipei: Ming-lun ch'u- pan she 明倫出版社, 1970

——. *T'ing-lin wen-chi* 亭林文集. In *Ku T'ing-lin i-shu shih-chung* 顧亭林遺書十種. Taipei: Ku-t'ing shu-chü 古亭書局, 1969.

Ku Yüan-hsiang 顧遠薌. *Sui Yüan shih-shuo ti yen-chiu* 隨園詩說的研究. Shanghai: Shang-wu yin-shu kuan, 1936.

Kuo Shao-yü 郭紹虞. *Chung-kuo wen-hsüeh p'i-p'ing shih* 中國文學批評史. Shanghai: Shang-wu yin-shu kuan, 1934; rpt. Taipei: Shang-wu yin-shu kuan, 1969; revised edn, Shanghai: Chung-hua shu-chü, 1961.

——. 'Hsing-ling shuo' 性靈說, *Yen-ching hsüeh-pao* 燕京學報, 23 (June 1938), pp. 47–92.

——. 'Shen-yün yü ko-tiao' 神韻與格調, *Yen-ching hsüeh-pao*, 22 (December 1937), pp. 53–117.

Kuwayama Ryūhei 桑山龍平. 'En Chūrō no bungaku to seikatsu' 袁中郎の文学と生活, *Tenri daigaku gakuhō* 天理大学学報, 24 (October 1957), pp. 86–102.

Lau D. C. (tr.). *Lao Tzu: Tao Te Ching*. Baltimore, Maryland: Penguin, 1963.

Legge, James (tr.). *Confucian Analects*. In *Chinese Classics*. Oxford: Clarendon Press, 1893; rpt. Taipei: Wen shih che ch'u-pan she, 1971.

Lévy, André. 'Un document sur la querelle des anciens et des modernes *more sinico*: De la Prose, par Yuan Zongdao [Tsung-tao] (1560–1600) suivi de sa biographie, composée par son frère Yuan Zhongdao [Chung-tao] (1570–1623),' *T'oung Pao*, 54 (1968), pp. 251–74.

Li Chi 李祁. *The Travel Diaries of Hsü Hsia-k'o*. Hong Kong: Chinese University of Hong Kong Press, 1974.

Li Chien-Chang 李健章. 'Kung-an p'ai ti ch'uang tso-lun – "tu-shu hsing-ling, pu-chü ko-t'ao" tsung-shih' 公安派的創作論—"獨抒性靈, 不拘格套"綜釋. In *Ku-tai wen-hsüeh li-lun yen-chiu* 古代文學理論研究. Shanghai: Ku-chi ch'u-pan she 古籍出版社, 1980, pp. 272–88.

Li Chih 李贄. *Fen-shu* 焚書. Taipei: Ho-lo t'u-shu ch'u-pan she 河洛圖書出版社, 1974.

——. *Hsü Ts'ang-shu* 續藏書, 2 vols. Peking: Chung-hua shu-chü, 1959.

——. *Ts'ang-shu* 藏書, 4 vols. Peking: Chung-hua shu-chü, 1959.

Li Chih yen-chiu ts'an-k'ao tzu-liao 李贄研究參考資料, 3 vols. ed. Hsia-men ta-hsüeh li-shih hsi 廈門大學歷史系. Fukien: Jen-min ch'u-pan she, 1975.

Li Hsien-chao 李憲昭. 'Lüeh-t'an Ming-tai Kung-an p'at ti wen-hsüeh chu-chang' 略談明代公安派的文學主張, *Yü-wen hsüeh-hsi* 語文學習, 45 (March 1983), pp. 44–7.

Li Meng-yang 李夢陽. *K'ung-t'ung hsien-sheng chi* 空同先生集, 66 *chüan* (1602 edn); rpt. Taipei: Wei-wen t'u-shu kung-ssu 偉文圖書公司, 4 vols., 1976.

Li P'an-lung 李攀龍. *Ts'ang-ming hsien-sheng chi* 滄溟先生集, 30 *chüan* (1572 edn); rpt. Taipei: Wei-wen t'u-shu kung-ssu, 3 vols., 1976.

Li Wen-chao 李文紹. *Huang-Ming shih-shuo hsin-yü* 皇明世說新語, 8 *chüan*. Yün-chien Li-shih k'an-pen 雲間李氏刊本, 1610.

Li Yü 李漁. *Jou pu-t'uan* 肉蒲團 (1705 edn); rpt. Hong Kong: Lien-ho ch'u-pan she 聯合出版社, n. d.

Liang I-ch'eng 梁一成. 'Hsü Wei (1529–1593): His Life and Literary Works.' Ph.D. dissertation, Ohio State University, 1973.

——. *Hsü Wei ti wen-hsüeh yü i-shu* 徐渭的文學與藝術. Taipei: I-wen yin-shu kuan, 1976.

Liang Jung-jo 梁容若. 'Lun i-t'uo ti Yüan Hung-tao tso-p'in' 論依托的袁宏道作品, *Kuo-yü jih-pao: Shu han jen*, 131 (March 1970), pp. 6–8 (total pp. 1038–40); rpt. in Liang Jung-jo, *Tso-chia yü tso-p'in* 作家與作品. Taichung: Tunghai University Press, 1971. pp. 120–5.

——. 'P'u-t'ao she yü Kung-an p'ai' 葡萄社與公安派, *Ch'un wen-hsüeh yüeh-k'an* 純文學月刊, 6, 1 (January 1970), pp. 16–24; rpt. in Liang Jung-jo, *Tso-chia yü tso-p'in*, pp. 105–15.

——. 'Yüan Hung-tao Hsü Wen-ch'ang chuan cheng-wu' 袁宏道徐文長傳正誤, *Wen-t'an* 文壇, 123 (September 1970), pp. 6–7; rpt. in Liang Jung-jo, *Tso-chia yü tso-p'in*, pp. 116–19.

——. 'Yüan Hung-tao sheng-p'ing ho tso-p'in' 袁宏道生平和作品, *Kuo-yü jih-pao* 國語日報: *Shu han jen* 書和人, 123 (November 1969), pp. 1–8 (total pp. 969–76); rpt. in Liang Jung-jo, *Tso-chia yü tso-p'in*, pp. 87–104.

Lin Chang-hsin 林章新. 'Yüan Chung-lang yü hua-tao' 袁中郎與花道, *Hua-kuo*

華國 (Chinese University of Hong Kong), 6 (July 1971), pp. 106–27.

Lin Yü-t'ang (Lin Yutang) 林語堂. 'Hai-shih chiang hsiao-p'in wen chih i-hsü' 還是講小品文之遺緒, *Jen-chien shih*, 24 (March 1935), pp. 35–6.

——. 'Hsiao-p'in wen chih i-hsü' 小品文之遺緒, *Jen-chien shih*, 22 (February 1935), pp. 42–5.

——. *The Importance of Understanding*. New York: World Publishing, 1960.

——. 'Lun hsiao-p'in wen pi-tiao' 論小品文筆調, *Jen-chien shih*, 6 (June 1934), pp. 10–11.

——. 'Lun wen' 論文, *Lun-yü pan-yüeh k'an* 論語半月刊, 15 (April 1933), pp. 532–6.

——. 'Lun wen' (2), *Lun-yü pan-yüeh k'an*, 28 (November 1933), pp. 170–3.

——.(tr.). 'The "Vase Flowers" of Yüan Chunglang.' In *The Importance of Living*. New York; Reynal and Hitchcock, 1938, pp. 310–16.

——. *Yü-t'ang sui-pi* 語堂隨筆. Taipei: Chih-wen ch'u-pan she 志文出版社, 1966.

Liu Hsieh 劉勰. 'Kuan-yü Kung-an hsiao-p'in wen chih i-hsi hua' 關於公安小品文之一席話, *Jen-chieh shih*, 8 (July 1934), pp. 10–11.

——. 'Kung-an Ching-ling hsiao-p'in tu-hou t'i' 公安竟陵小品讀後題, *Jen-chien shih*, 16 (November 1934), pp. 14–15.

Liu I-ch'ing 劉義慶. *Shih-shuo hsin-yü* 世說新語. Taipei: Chung-hua shu-chü, 1968.

Liu, James J. Y. *Art of Chinese Poetry*. Chicago: University of Chicago Press, 1962.

——. *Chinese Theories of Literature*. Chicago: University of Chicago Press, 1975.

——. *Essentials of Chinese Literary Art*. North Scituate: Duxbury Press, 1979.

Liu Ta-chieh 劉大杰. *Chung-kuo wen-hsüeh fa-chan shih* 中國文學發展史. Shanghai: Chung-hua shu-chü, 1941; rpt. Taipei: Chung-hua shu-chü, 1968.

—— (ed.). *Ts'ang-lang shih-hua chiao-shih* 滄浪詩話校釋. Peking: Jen-min wen-hsüeh ch'u-pan she, 1961.

——. 'Yüan Chung-lang ti shih-wen kuan' 袁中郎的詩文觀, *Jen-chien shih*, 13 (October 1934), pp. 19–24.

Lu K'an 路侃. 'Shih lun Ming-tai wen-i li-lun chung ti "chu-ch'ing" shuo' 試論明代文藝理論中的"主情"說, *Wen-hsüeh lun-chi* 文學論集, 7 (1984), pp. 165–80.

Lynn, Richard John. 'Alternate Routes to Self-Realization in Ming Theories of Poetry.' In Susan Bush and Christian Murck (eds.), *Theories of Arts in China*. Princeton: Princeton University Press, 1983, pp. 317–40.

——. 'Orthodoxy and Enlightenment: Wang Shih-chen's Theory of Poetry and its Antecedents.' In Wm. Theodore de Bary (ed.), *The Unfolding of Neo-Confucianism*. New York: Columbia University Press, 1975, pp. 217–69.

——. 'Tradition and the Individual: Ming and Ch'ing Views of Yüan Poetry,' *Journal of Oriental Studies*, 15, 1 (1977), pp. 1–19.

Maeno Noaki 前野直彬. 'En Chūrō jushū to Gensei shōnin' 袁中郎十集と元政上人. In Nagasawa sensei koki kinen toshogaku ronshū kankōkai 長沢先生古稀記念図書学論集刊行会 (ed.), *Nagasawa sensei koki kinen toshogaku ronshū* 長沢先生古稀記念図書学論集. Tokyo: Sanseidō 三省堂, 1973, pp. 25–43.

——. 'Min Shichishi no sensei – Yō Itei no bungakukan ni tsuite' 明七子の先声―楊維楨の文学観について, *Chūgoku bungaku hō*, 5 (October 1956), pp. 41–69.

Martin Richard (tr. from German version). *Jou Pu Tuan.* New York: Grove Press, 1963.

Mather, B. (tr.). *A New Account of Tales of the World.* Minneapolis: University of Minnesota Press, 1976.

Matsushita Tadashi 松下忠. 'En Chūrō hinan ni taisuru shiken' 袁中郎非難に対する私見, *Wakayama daigaku gakugei gakubu kiyō* 和歌山大学学芸学部紀要, 11 (1959), pp. 25–44 rpt. in Matsushita Tadashi, *Min Shin no sanshisetsu* 明清の三詩説. Tokyo: Meiji shoin 明治書院, 1978, pp. 119–35.

——. 'En Chūrō no seireisetsu' 袁中郎の性霊説, *Chūgoku bungaku hō*, 3, 9 (1958), pp. 85–126; rpt. in *Min Shin no sanshisetsu*, pp. 77–119.

——. 'En Kōdō no seireisetsu no hōga' 袁宏道の性霊説の萌芽, *Tōhōgaku*, 19 (November 1959), pp. 98–107; rpt in *Min Shin no sanshisetsu*, pp. 136–49.

——. Ō Seitei no kobun jisetsu yorino dakka ni tsuite' 王世貞の古文辞説よりの脱化について, *Chūgoku bungaku hō* 中国文学報, 5 (October 1956), pp. 70–85; rpt. in *Min Shin no sanshisetsu*, pp. 62–76.

Min Tse 敏澤. *Chung-kuo wen-hsüeh li-lun p'i-p'ing shih* 中國文學理論批評史, 2 vols. Peking: Jen-min wen-hsüeh ch'u-pan she, 1981.

Mizoguchi Yūzō 溝口雄三. 'Kōanha no michi' 公安派の道. *In Iriya kyōju, Ogawa kyōju taikyū kinen Chūgoku bungaku gogaku ronshū* 入矢教授、小川教授退休記念中国文学、語学論集. Tokyo: Chikuma shobō, 1974, pp. 619–34.

Mote, Frederick W. 'The Arts and the "Theorizing Mode" of the Civilization.' In Christian Murck (ed.), *Artists and Traditions.* Princeton: Princeton University Press, 1976.

——. 'Confucian Eremitism in the Yüan Period.' In Arthur F. Wright (ed.), *Confucian and Chinese Civilization.* Stanford: Stanford University Press, 1960, pp. 202–40.

——. *The Poet Kao Ch'i (1336–1374).* Princeton: Princeton University Press, 1962.

Mowry, Hua-yüan Li. *Chinese Love Stories from Ch'ing-shih.* Hamden Conn.: Shoe String Press, 1983.

Nakamura Yoshihiro 中村嘉弘. 'En Chūrō shōron – Kairaku to jiteki ni tsuite' 袁中郎小論—快楽と自適について. *Walpurgis* (Kokugakuin Daigaku Gaikokugo Kenkyūshitsu 国学院大学外国語研究室), Tokyo, 1979, pp. 1–12.

Nivison, David S. 'The Probem of "Knowledge" and "Action" in Chinese Thought since Wang Yang-ming.' In Arthur F. Wright (ed.), *Studies in Chinese Thought.* Chicago: University of Chicago Press, 1953, pp. 112–45.

——. 'Protest against Conventions and Conventions of Protest.' In Arthur F. Wright (ed.), *The Confucian Persuasion.* Stanford: Stanford University Press, 1960, pp. 177–200.

Okazaki Fumio 岡崎文夫. 'En Chūrō kenkyū no ryūkō' 袁中郎研究の流行, *Chūgoku bungaku geppō* 中国文学月報, 1, 1 (March 1935), pp. 6–7.

Pei Yüan-ch'en 貝遠辰 and Yeh Yu-ming 葉幼明 (eds.). *Li-tai yu-chi hsüan* 歴代遊記選. Hunan: Jen-min ch'u-pan she, 1980.

Peterson, Willard. *Bitter Gourd: Fang I-chih and the Impetus for Intellectual Change.* New Haven: Yale University Press, 1979.

Po Chü-i 白居易. *Po Chü-i chi* 白居易集, 4 vols. Peking: Chung-hua shu-chü, 1979.

Pollard, David E. *A Chinese Look at Literature: The Literature Values of Chou Tso-jen in Relation to the Tradition.* Berkeley: University of California Press, 1973.

Shao Hung 邵紅. 'Ching-ling p'ai wen-hsüeh li-lun ti yen-chiu' 竟陵派文學理論的研究. *Wen shih che hsüeh-pao* 文史哲學報, 24 (October 1975), pp. 195–244.

——. 'Kung-an Ching-ling wen-hsüeh li-lun ti t'an-chiu' 公安竟陵文學理論的探究, *Ssu yü yen* 思與言, 12, 2 (July 1974), pp. 16–23.

——. 'Yüan Chung-lang wen-hsüeh kuan ti p'ou-hsi' 袁中郎文學觀的剖析, *Kuo-li pien-i kuan kuan-k'an* 國立編譯館館刊, 2, 1 (June 1973), pp. 205–13.

Shen Ch'i-wu 沈啓無. 'K'o-hsüeh chai wai-chi Yu-chü shih-lu' 珂雪齋外集遊居柿錄, *Jen-chien shih*, 31 (July 1935), pp. 18–23.

Shen Ssu 沈思. 'Kuan-yü Yüan Chung-lang yü Wang Po-ku' 關於袁中郎與王百穀, *Jen-chieh shih*, 19 (January 1935), pp. 27–8.

Shen Te-ch'ien 沈德潛. *Ming-shih pieh-ts'ai* 明詩別裁. First published 1739; rpt. Shanghai: Shang-wu yin-shu kuan, 1933.

Shen Te-fu 沈德符. *Wan-li yeh-huo pien* 萬曆野獲編. Prefaced 1619; rpt. Peking: Chung-hua shu-chü, 1959.

Shih, Vincent Yu-chung (tr.). *The Literary Mind and the Carving of Dragons.* New York: Columbia University Press, 1974.

Sun K'ai-ti 孫楷第. *Chung-kuo t'ung-su hsiao-shuo shu-mu* 中國通俗小說書目. Peking: Tso-chia ch'u-pan she, 1957.

Sung P'ei-wei 宋佩韋. *Ming wen-hsüeh shih* 明文學史. Shanghai: Shang-wu yin-shu kuan, 1934.

Suzuki Tadashi 鈴木正. 'Mindai sanjin kō' 明代山人考. In Shimizu hakushi tsuitō kinen Mindai shi ronsō hensaniinkai 清水博士追悼記念明代史論叢編纂委員会 (ed.), *Shimizu hakushi tsuitō kinen Mindai shi ronsō* 清水博士追悼記念明代史論叢. Tokyo: Daian 大安, 1962, pp. 357–88.

Takeda Taijun 武田泰淳. 'En Chūrō ron' 袁中郎論, *Chūgoku bungaku geppo*, 3, 28 (July 1937), pp. 73–83.

T'an Yüan-ch'un 譚元春. *T'an Yu-hsia ho-chi* 譚友夏合集. 1633 edn, Ku-wu Chang Tse k'an-pen 古吳張澤刊本; rpt. Taipei: Wei-wen t'u-shu kung-ssu, 1976.

T'ang Hsien-tzu 湯顯祖. *T'ang Hsien-tzu shih-wen chi* 湯顯祖詩文集 (annotated by Hsü Shuo-fang 徐朔方), 2 vols. Shanghai: Ku-chi ch'u-pan she, 1982.

T'ang Shun-chih 唐順之. *Ching-ch'uan wen-chi* 荆川文集, 17 *chüan; Wai-chi* 外集, 3 *chüan.* In *Ssu-pu ts'ung-k'an ch'u-pien* 四部叢刊初編. Taipei: Shang-wu yin-shu kuan, 1965.

T'ao Wang-ling 陶望齡. *Hsieh-an chi* 歇庵集. 1611 edn, Shan-yin Wang Ying-lin chiao-k'an pen 山陰王應麟校刊本; rpt Taipei: Wei-wen t'u-shu kung-ssu, 1976.

T'ien Su-lan 田素蘭. 'Yüan Chung-lang wen-hsüeh li-lun ti hsing-ch'eng' 袁中郎文學理論的形成, *Kuo-wen hsüeh-pao* 國文學報 (Kuo-li Tai-wan Shih-fan ta-hsüeh 國立台灣師範大學), 10 (June 1981), pp. 97–120; rpt. in T'ien Su-lan, *Yüan Chung-lang wen-hsüeh yen-chiu* 袁中郎文學研究. Taipei: Wen shih che ch'u-pan she 文史哲出版社, 1982, pp. 63–104.

Ting Chih-chien 丁志堅. 'Tu-shu hsing-ling ti Kung-an p'ai ling-hsiu Yüan Hung-tao' 獨抒性靈的公安派領袖袁宏道. In Ting Chih-chien, *Chung-kuo shi-ta san-wen chia* 中國十大散文家. Taipei: Shun-feng ch'u-pan she 順風出版社, 1967, pp. 88–93.

Ts'ai I-chung 蔡義忠. 'Shu-hsieh hsing-ling ti Yüan Chung-lang chi ch'i san-wen tsao-i' 抒寫性靈的袁中郎及其散文造詣. In Ts'ai I-chung, *Chung-kuo pa-ta san-wen chia* 中國八大散文家. Taipei. Nan-ching ch'u-pan kung-ssu 南京出版公司, 1977, pp. 183–202.

Ts'ai Li-ying 蔡麗英. 'Yüan Hung-tao p'ing-chuan' 袁宏道評傳, *Wen-hsüeh chi-k'an* 文學集刊 (January 1968), pp. 38–53.

Ts'ao Chü-jen 曹聚仁. 'Ho-pi Yüan Chung-lang' 何必袁中郎, *T'ai-pai pan-yüeh k'an* 太白半月刊, 1, 4 (November 1934), pp. 189–90.

Tseng I 曾毅. *Chung-kuo wen-hsüeh shih* 中國文學史. Shanghai: T'ai-tung t'u-shu kung-ssu 泰東圖書公司, 1915.

Tu Ching-I 涂經詒. 'The Chinese Examination Essay: Some Literary Considerations,' *Monumenta Serica*, 31 (1974–5), pp. 393–406.

——. 'Neo-Confucianism and Literary Criticism in Ming China: The Case of T'ang Shun-chih (1507–1560),' *Tamkang Review*, 15, 1, 2, 3 and 4 (Autumn 1984 to Summer 1985), pp. 547–60.

Tu Hsin-wu 杜新吾. 'Yüan Hung-tao' 袁宏道. In Chang Ch'i-yün 張其昀 (ed.), *Chung-kuo wen-hsüeh shih lun-chi* 中國文學史論集. Taipei: Chung-hua wen-hua 中華文化, 1958, pp. 943–52.

Tu Jo 杜若. 'Yüan shih san hsiung-ti yü Kung-an wen-t'i' 袁氏三兄弟與公安文體, *T'ai-fei yüeh-k'an* 台肥月刊, 18, 9 (September 1977), pp. 29–35.

Vallette-Hémery, Martine. *Nuages et Pierres: Yuan Hong-dao (Hung-tao)*. Paris: Publications Orientalistes de France, 1982.

——. *Yuan Hongdao [Hung-tao] (1568–1610): Théorie et pratique littéraires*. Paris: Collège de France, *Mémoires de l'Institut des Hautes Études Chinoises*, 18 (1982).

Waley, Arthur. *The Life and Times of Po Chü-i*. London: George Allen and Unwin, 1949.

——. *Yüan Mei*. Stanford: Stanford University Press, 1957.

Wang Chung-min 王重民. 'Feng Meng-lung chih sheng-tzu nien' 馮夢龍之生卒年, *Chung-hua wen-shih lun-ts'ung* 中華文史論叢, 33 (1985), pp. 279–80.

Wang Fu-chih 王夫之. *Tu T'ung-chien lun* 讀通鑑論. In *Ch'uan-shan ch'üan-chi* 船山全集, 16 vols. Taipei: Li-hsing shu-chü 力行書局, 1965, vol. 11.

Wang Hsü 王序. 'Yüan Hung-tao' 袁宏道. In Wang Hsü, *Chung-kuo wen-hsüeh tso-chia hsiao-chuan* 中國文學作家小傳. Hong Kong: Yu-lien ch'u-pan she 友聯出版社, 1958, pp. 237–40.

Wang, John Ching-yü. *Chin Sheng-t'an*. New York: Twayne 1972.

Wang, Li-ch'i 王利器. 'Shui-hu Li Cho-wu p'ing-pen ti chen-wei wen-t'i' 水滸李卓吾評本的眞偽問題, *Wen-hsüeh p'ing-lun ts'ung-k'an* 文學評論叢刊, 2 (1979), pp. 365–81.

—— (ed.). *Wen-hsin tiao-lung chiao-cheng* 文心雕龍校証. Shanghai: Ku-chi ch'u-pan she, 1980.

Wang Shih-chen 王世貞. *I-yüan chih-yen* 藝苑卮言. Ting Fu-pao chiao k'an pen 丁福保校刊本, n. p., n. d.

——. *Su Ch'ang-kung wai-chi* 蘇長公外集. Yü-chang Ch'ü-shih Yen-shih chai k'an-pen 豫章璩氏燕石齋刊本, 1594.

——. *Yen-chou shan-jen hsü-kao* 弇州山人續稿, rpt. of Ming Ch'ung-chen 崇禎

edn. Taipei: Wen-hai ch'u-pan she 文海出版社, 1970.

——. *Yen-chou shan-jen ssu-pu kao* 弇州山人四部稿. 1577 edn, Wang-shih shih-ching t'ang k'an-pen 王氏世經堂刊本.

Watson, Burton. *Chinese Lyricism: Shih Poetry from the Second to the Twelfth Century*. New York: Columbia University Press, 1971.

——. *Su Tung-p'o*. New York: Columbia University Press, 1965.

Wei Chung-kung 韋仲公. *Yüan Chung-lang hsüeh-chi* 袁中郎學記. Taipei: Hsin wen-feng ch'u-pan kung-ssu 新文豐出版公司, 1979.

Wei Tzu-yün 魏子雲. 'Lun Yüan Hung-tao kei Hsieh Chao-che ti che feng hsin' 論袁宏道給謝肇淛的這封信. In Wei Tzu-yün, *Chin P'ing Mei shen-t'an* 金瓶梅審探. Taipei: Shang-wu yin-shu kuan, 1982, pp. 53–69.

——. 'Yüan Chung-lang "Shang-cheng" chih tso' 袁中郎"觴政"之作, *Chung-wai wen-hsüeh*, 5, 9 (February 1977), pp. 106–11; rpt. in Wei Tzu-yün, *Chin P'ing Mei t'an-yüan* 金瓶梅探源. Taipei: Chü-liu t'u-shu kung-ssu 巨流圖書公司, 1979, pp. 103–9.

——. 'Yüan Chung-lang yü Chin P'ing Mei' 袁中郎與金瓶梅, *Kuo-yü jih-pao: Shu han jen*, 224 (November 1973), pp. 1–8 (total pp. 1785–92); rpt. in Wei Tzu-yün, *Chin P'ing Mei t'an-yüan*, pp. 51–72.

——. 'Yüan Hsiao-hsiu yü Chin P'ing Mei' 袁小修與金瓶梅. In Wei Tzu-yün, *Chin P'ing Mei t'an-yüan*, pp. 73–82.

Wu Han 吳晗. 'Chin P'ing Mei ti chu-tso shih-tai chi-ch'i she-hui pei-ching' 金瓶梅的著作時代及其社會背景, *Wen-hsüeh chi-k'an* 文學季刊, 1, 1 (January 1934), pp. 172–93.

——. *Chin P'ing Mei yü Wang Shih-chen* 金瓶梅與王世貞. Prefaced 1933; rpt. Hong Kong: Nan-t'ien shu-chü 南天書局, 1967.

Wu, Nelson. 'Tung Ch'i-ch'ang (1555–1636): Apathy in Government and Fervor in Art.' In Arthur F. Wright and Denis C. Twitchett (eds.), *Confucian Personalities*. Stanford: Stanford University Press, 1962, pp. 260–93.

Wu Pen-hsing 吳奔星. 'Yüan Chung-lang chih wen-chang chi wen-hsüeh p'i-p'ing' 袁中郎之文章及文學批評, *Shih-ta yüeh-k'an*, 30 (October 1935), pp. 227–42.

Wu Tiao-kung 吳調公. 'Lun Kung-an san-Yüan mei-hsüeh kuan chih i-t'ung' 論公安三袁美學觀之異同, *Wen-hsüeh p'ing-lun* 文學評論, 1 (1986), pp. 92–101.

Wu Wu-hsiung 吳武雄. 'Kung-an p'ai chi ch'i chu-shu k'ao' 公安派及其著述考. M. A. thesis, Tunghai University, Taichung, 1981.

Yamashita Ryūji 山下龍二. 'En Chūrō ron – Kōanha bungaku to Yōmeigakuha' 袁中郎論—公安派文学と陽明学派, *Tōhōgaku* 東方学, 7 (October 1953), pp. 95–104.

Yang Hsien-wu 楊憲武. 'Kung-an p'ai yü Kung-an hsien-chih' 公安派與公安縣志, *Hu-pei wen-hsien* 湖北文獻, 40 (July 1976), pp. 69–77.

Yang T'ien-shih 楊天石. 'Wan Ming wen-hsüeh li-lun chung ti "ch'ing-chen" shuo' 晚明文學理論中的"情眞"說, *Kuang-ming jih-pao* 光明日報 (September 5, 1965).

Yao Ssu-lien 姚思廉. *Liang-shu* 梁書. Peking: Chung-hua shu-chü, 1973.

Yang Te-pen 楊德本. *Yüan Chung-lang chih wen-hsüeh ssu-hsiang* 袁中郎之文學思想. Taipei: Wen shih che ch'u-pan she 文史哲出版社, 1976.

Yeh Ch'ing-ping 葉慶炳 and Shao Hung 邵紅 (eds.). *Chung-kuo wen-hsüeh p'i-*

p'ing tzu-liao hui-pien (*Ming-tai*) 中國文學批評資料彙編(明代), 2 vols. Taipei: Ch'eng-wen ch'u-pan she 成文出版社, 1979.

Yokota Terutoshi 橫田輝俊. 'Kōanha no bungakuron' 公安派の文学論, *Hiroshima daigaku bungakubu kiyō* 広島大学文学部紀要, 26, 1 (December 1966), pp. 157–97.

——. 'Mindai bungakuron no tenkai' (2) 明代文学論の展開 (2), *Hiroshima daigaku bungakubu kiyō*, 38, 2 (December 1978), pp. 75–135.

Yoshikawa Kōjirō 吉川幸次郎. 'Ch'ien Ch'ien-i as a Literary Critic.' Paper presented at the Conference on Traditional Chinese Literary Criticism, St Croix, Virgin Islands, December 6–10, 1970. Chang Lien-ti 張連第 (tr.). 'Ch'ien Ch'ien-i ti wen-hsüeh p'i-p'ing' 錢謙益的文學批評, *Ku-tien wen-hsüeh lun-ts'ung* 古典文學論叢, 3 (1982), pp. 220–44.

Yü Ta-fu 郁達夫. 'Ch'ung-yin Yüan Chung-lang ch'üan-chi hsü' 重印袁中郎全集序. In Liu Ta-chieh 劉大杰 (ed.), *Yüan Chung-lang ch'üan-chi*. Shanghai: Shih-tai t'u-shu kung-ssu 時代圖書公司, 1934, pp. 1–3.

Yüan Chao 袁照. *Yüan Shih-kung i-shih lu* 袁石公遺事錄, 2 vols. An appendix to 1869 edn of *Yüan Chung-lang ch'üan chi* 袁中郎全集. Chi-shan shu-wu k'an-pen 繼善書屋刊本.

Yüan Chung-tao 袁中道. *Hsin-an chi* 新安集. Naikaku bunko 內閣文庫 collection, n.d.; rpt. Hishi copy, 1976.

——. *K'o-hsüeh chai chi hsüan* 珂雪齋集選, 24 *chüan*. Wang Ts'ung-chiao k'an-pen 汪從教刊本, 1622.

——. *K'o-hsüeh chai ch'ien-chi* 珂雪齋前集, 24 *chüan*. Hsin-an k'an-pen 新安刊本, 1618; rpt. Taipei: Wei-wen t'u-shu kung-ssu, 1976.

——. *K'o-hsüeh chai chin-chi* 珂雪齋近集, 11 *chüan*. Ming Shu-lin T'ang Kuo-ta k'an-pen 明書林唐國達刊本; rpt. Shanghai: Chung-yang shu-tien 中央書店, 1936; Taipei: Wei-wen t'u-shu kung-ssu, 1976.

——. *Yu-chü shih (fei)-lu* 遊居柿(林)錄 (also known as *Yüan Hsiao-hsiu jih-chi* 袁小修日記). Shanghai: Shang-hai tsa-chih kung-ssu 上海雜誌公司, 1935; rpt. Taipei: Tai-pei shu-chü 台北書局, 1953.

Yüan Hung-tao 袁宏道. *Chieh-t'o chi* 解脫集, 4 *chüan*. Prefaced 1603.

——. *Chin-fan chi* 錦帆集, 4 *chüan*. Prefaced 1603; Naikaku bunko collection, Hishi copy, 1976.

——. *Hsiao-pi t'ang chi* 蕭碧堂集, 20 *chüan*. Kou-wu Yüan-shih shu-chung t'ang k'an-pen 勾吳袁氏書種堂刊本, 1608.

——. *Li-yün kuan lei-ting Yüan Chung-lang ch'üan-chi* 梨雲館類定袁中郎全集, 24 *chüan*. First published 1617; rpt. 1829, 1869.

——. *P'ing-hua chai chi* 瓶花齋集, 10 *chüan*. Yüan-shih shu-chung t'ang k'an-pen, 1608; rpt. n. p., 1911.

——. *Yüan Chung-lang ch'üan-chi* 袁中郎全集, 40 *chüan*. First published 1629; rpt. Taipei: Wei-wen t'u-shu kung-ssu, 1976.

——. *Yüan Chung-lang ch'üan-chi*, ed. Liu Ta-chieh and Lin Yutang. Shanghai: Shih-tai shu-chü 時代書局, 1934.

——. *Yüan Chung-lang ch'üan-chi*. Shanghai: Shih-chieh shu-chü 世界書局, 1935; rpt. Taipei: Shih-chieh shu-chü, 1964.

——. *Yüan Chung-lang ch'üan-chi*, ed. Chin-hsia ko chu-jen 襟霞閣主人. Shanghai: Chung-yang shu-tian, 1936.

——. *Yüan Chung-lang shih-chi* 袁中郎十集, ed. Chou Ying-lin 周應麐. 1614.

Yüan Mei 袁枚. *Sui-yüan shih-hua* 隨園詩話. Peking: Jen-min wen-hsüeh ch'u-pan she, 1982.

Yüan Nai-ling 袁乃玲. *Yüan Chung-lang yen-chiu* 袁中郎研究. Taipei: Hsüeh-hai ch'u-pan she 學海出版社, 1981.

Yüan Tsung-tao 袁宗道. *Po Su chai lei-chi* 白蘇齋類集. Ming edn; rpt. Shanghai: Kuo-hsüeh yen-chui she 國學研究社, 1936; Taipei: Wei-wen t'u-shu kung-ssu, 1976.

CHINESE TITLES OF WORKS TRANSLATED IN CHAPTERS 3 AND 4

GLOSSARY INDEX

All Chinese terms that appear in the text are listed in the Glossary Index, but page references are given only for those terms that are discussed.